THE JOURNAL OF THE ASSOCIATION OF MOVING IMAGE ARCHIVISTS

OVINGIMAGETHEMOVINGIMAGETHEMOVINGIMAGETHEMOVIN

SPRING 2006

The Moving Image (ISSN 1532-3978) is published twice a year in spring and fall by the University of Minnesota Press, 111 Third Avenue South, Suite 290, Minneapolis, MN 55401-2520. http://www.upress.umn.edu

Published in cooperation with the Association for Moving Image Archivists (AMIA). Members of AMIA receive the journal as one of the benefits of membership. For further information about membership, contact the Association of Moving Image Archivists, 1313 North Vine Street, Los Angeles, CA 90028 (or e-mail amia@amianet.org or visit us on the Web at http://www.amianet.org).

Postmaster: Send address changes to *Moving Image,* University of Minnesota Press, 111 Third Avenue South, Suite 290, Minneapolis, MN 55401-2520.

Inquiries and information about manuscript submissions should be sent to *The Moving Image,* c/o Association of Moving Image Archivists, 1313 North Vine Street, Los Angeles, CA 90028 (or e-mail amia@amianet.org). **Do not send manuscripts before sending one-page proposal.** All manuscripts should be submitted in triplicate, double-spaced throughout, using 12-point type, with one-inch margins, parenthetical documentation with a list of works cited (using the *Chicago Manual of Style,* 14th edition), and a file on disc in ASCII and Word or WordPerfect. Contact the editorial office at the address above (or phone at 323-463-1500, or fax at 323-463-1506) for further instructions on style.

Manuscripts will be returned if accompanied by a stamped, self-addressed envelope. Please allow a minimum of four months for editorial consideration.

Address subscription orders, changes of address, and business correspondence (including requests for permission and advertising orders) to *The Moving Image,* University of Minnesota Press, 111 Third Avenue South, Suite 290, Minneapolis, MN 55401-2520.

Subscriptions: Regular rates, U.S.A.: individuals, 1 year (2 issues) $30; libraries, 1 year $75. Other countries add $5 for each year's subscription. Checks should be made payable to the University of Minnesota Press. Back issues are $22.50 for individuals and $56.25 for institutions (plus $4 shipping, $1 for each additional copy). *The Moving Image* is a benefit of membership in the Association of Moving Image Archivists.

Founded in 1991, the **ASSOCIATION OF MOVING IMAGE ARCHIVISTS** is the world's largest professional association devoted to film, television, video, and digital image preservation. Dedicated to issues surrounding the safekeeping of visual history, this journal covers topics such as the role of moving image archives and collection in the writing of history, technical and practical articles on research and development in the field, in-depth examinations of specific preservation and restoration projects, and behind-the-scenes looks at the techniques used to preserve and restore our moving image heritage.

Editor's Introduction

JAN-CHRISTOPHER HORAK

I'm the first to admit that DVDs have made my life easier, especially in terms of teaching film and media history courses at university. And in the future we can certainly look forward to digital technology opening up the whole archive to researchers and students. As anyone who has been a faithful reader of *The Moving Image* knows, more and more of the "film" reviews in these pages are dedicated to DVD releases of classic films that have been restored by our colleagues. Digital technologies are rapidly supplanting analogue media of all kinds.

But while DVD technology offers unlimited technical possibilities of information retrieval for the next generation, films made available through DVD technology are at present, with few exceptions, a function of the marketplace. And the truth is that the numbers of films that are commercially available keep shrinking rather than expanding, at least in relation to the sum of all moving images produced. While we were in an analogue world of videotape, it was still economically feasible, given the relative low cost of analogue tape, for major multinational media companies and smaller specialty distributors to place older historical films in the market. And while there were many titles that were not available, both the Hollywood majors and specialty companies mining the public domain field offered a good representative of titles from the silent period as well as from the classic Hollywood era. Now, many of the titles from the back catalogs that a major motion picture company used to offer on VHS have disappeared with no plans in sight to release them in digital form.

The initial cost of digitalization has at present upped the stakes considerably. The result is that fewer films from the first fifty years of the medium are available on DVD than was the case with VHS. Essentially, the latest blockbusters and a few classics are hawked by the Hollywood majors, who of course are more interested in generating substantial profits from titles with wide audience appeal and recognition than gambling on titles perceived to have smaller audiences.

Almost every other type of cinema is forced into the margins of the market or eliminated altogether. What remains is a reified Hollywood canon, which excludes box office failures, silent films, documentaries, independent films, politically hot topics, and so on. For example, of thousands and thousands of films produced worldwide between 1920 and 1929, less than two hundred titles are available presently on DVD (in 2002 approximately one hundred titles were available). If we break down this informal list by year, we see that the year 1927 takes the prize with twenty-six titles, while 1923 offers a mere eight. Of those twenty-six titles from 1927, 57 percent are American, i.e., Hollywood films; the rest a smattering of English, German, Russian, and French. Why are even silent masterpieces such as *The Big Parade* (1925), *Underworld* (1927), *Noah's Ark* (1928), or *Lonesome* (1929), all formerly available on VHS, not being released on DVD, to say nothing of the many titles not at the top of the film canon?

Now, if you think the situation improves in the sound era, you are mistaken. These are the rough figures I came up with, broken out by year of initial film release, for DVDs available commercially in the United States in September 2005 through one of the largest Internet distributors of "specialty films"—in other words, a distributor who actually specializes in historical films: 1931 (22 titles), 1935 (42 titles), 1940 (66), 1945 (64), 1950 (65), 1955 (90), 1960 (112), 1965 (129), 1970 (163). While these figures represent a 66 percent increase over September 2002, the numbers are still paltry, especially if we subtract nonmainstream American and foreign films: for the year 1970, mainstream American media companies have to date released a mere forty titles on DVD, or less than 24 percent of all 1970 titles available.

The transnational corporations who control moving image media distribution worldwide have little interest in distributing silent or black-and-white films for which they still control copyright, because the perceived market of consumers interested in such films is too small, making the amortization of digital technology and production a difficult proposition. Specialty distributors, on the other hand, while willing to release public domain titles, foreign films, documentaries, and other film ephemera, are too few and too small to take on the staggering numbers of titles that are potentially available. In other words, while the digital world promises unlimited access to film history (certainly a technological possibility), the economic reality is that the number of films available in the marketplace through digital technology remains a fraction of the actual number of films that have been produced historically or are still being produced worldwide.

This in turn affects the construction of film courses, since universities increasingly force professors to teach with DVDs. If only a limited canon is available for such classroom use, then only the canon according to your local video-chain outlet will be taught and shown to students. How do you teach a course on Hollywood genre cinema, on silent cinema, on Third World cinema, on American independent documentary, on classic documentaries from the 1930s, on avant-garde films from any period when virtually no one is at present willing to finance the digitalization of such films? Given these restrictions, students are confronted with a fragmented, incomplete, and distorted view of film history, based on what commercial distributors deem to be viable in the marketplace rather than on what academic discourse and the public at large have deemed important.

I'm reminded of the early days of the Internet, when this new medium was considered the great democratic leveler. Free exchange of information, communication, and ideas was promised for this uncontrollable, even anarchistic net of individuals wired together in cyberspace and not beholden to censorship, government intervention, or social control. The reality twenty years later is that the Internet is increasingly controlled by a few major multinational corporations, who filter, censor, and require payment for content. Certainly, anyone can build a Web site, but the portals and search engines are controlled by the likes of various alphabet acronyms, which through Internet blocking allow only sanctioned content. How much film history will be sacrificed to economic imperatives before digital technology will be cheap enough for public institutions to participate in digital film distribution? Thank goodness for organizations like the National Film Preservation

Foundation, which is not only financing the preservation of film materials but also making selections available through DVD packages like the *American Treasures.*

Intimately involved in both the production process, namely the preservation and restoration of film artifacts, and DVD distribution through the production of digital masters, film laboratories are central to our work. However, as **Gabriel M. Paletz** remarks in our first feature, moving image labs have rarely entered into a film historical discourse. Obviously within AMIA there has never been a lack of consciousness about the pivotal role of laboratories, certainly a function of the large numbers of practitioners in our ranks, yet very little has been theorized. Paletz, who contributed a piece to the first issue of *The Moving Image,* begins that process, while analyzing and celebrating the work of several restoration labs.

Moving image cataloging, another activity at the heart of preservation and restoration, as well as access, is the subject of **Andrea Leigh**'s contribution. She argues that the all-but-standardized process of cataloging moving image artifacts at the item level may be counterproductive in the short and medium term and should be rethought in terms of collection level cataloging. Collection level cataloging would in fact increase access by grouping together unidentified material—home movies, outtakes, and other materials without titles—according to provenance, or informational content, allowing researchers to proceed from the general to specific item level searches. Leigh is also a second-time author for *The Moving Image,* having written about Marian Anderson in our third issue.

Most amateur video, were it to be systematically collected by the archival community, would probably benefit from collection level cataloging, but as **Judi Hetrick** demonstrates, amateur video is still under the radar of most moving image archives. Noting that the Library of Congress's Television/Video Preservation Study, authored by Bill Murphy, points the way, Hetrick argues that the time has come for concrete plans of action and that developing methodologies in the amateur-film field should be applied to video and new digital formats produced by amateurs.

Our final feature piece concerns the construction of film history, as have many closing features in the journal, because to my mind moving image archival work is not possible without a firm understanding of the medium's history. **Maree Delofski** is an Australian filmmaker who in *The Trouble with Merle* deconstructs the myths surrounding Hollywood actress Merle Oberon, using found footage, while foregrounding her own quest for historical truth. The elusiveness of that truth is another theme in her cinematic treatise and is highlighted in her piece, which simultaneously gives us an insider's view of the production process.

Our Forum section begins with **Emily Staresina**'s think piece on the feasibility and desirability of not only rigorous educational standards for moving image archivists, as are now being put into place by various academic programs, but also of instituting either accreditation or certification procedures for the field. Ms. Staresina, a recent graduate of UCLA's MIAS Program, looks in particular at the history of the Society of American Archivists' grappling with this topic and to my mind firmly places this issue on AMIA's agenda for the future.

Our second Forum piece, by **Arianna Turci,** presents the results of a survey of seven European film archives that have used digital restoration tools to varying degrees. Her research presents not only a snapshot of the state of digital restoration in Europe's most important national film archives but also the attitudes of its film restorers to digital work.

The usual book, media, and conference reviews close the issue, our eleventh. It is also the final issue for book review editor Dan Streible, who has joined the AMIA board; Michael Baskett joins us as his successor. My thanks go to all the contributors and the editorial team, not only of this issue but of the previous ten numbers. My gratitude also goes to the AMIA board and office, which has consistently and willingly supported this most rewarding project.

THE FINESSE OF THE FILM LAB

GABRIEL M. PALETZ

A Report from a

Week at Haghefilm

For the technicians

Film laboratories are the nurseries of the movies; they represent both the origins of cinema and its ends. In 1893, the earliest Kinetoscope pictures emerged from Thomas Edison's laboratory in New Jersey.[1] A lab is still the last place in postproduction before the distribution of a new release. It is also the first stop in the revival of an archival print, where, through restoration techniques, a movie may be reborn.[2]

Filmmakers commonly mention a lab only to complain of a badly treated negative that ruined their movie shoot. Recent writings by archivists also gloss over labs' significance. Paolo Cherchi Usai states that the solutions to the aesthetic and ethical issues facing film restorers "is dependent upon individual judgment, a choice between a wide array of options" (2000, 64). The options weighed by archivists are tested, refined, and implemented in a film lab. Ray Edmondson urges his archival colleagues "to present material in such a way that, as far as is now possible in practice, the audience is able to perceive and appreciate it in its original form" (42). "In practice" means what a film lab can achieve in present projection and theatrical conditions.

Among film scholars, lab work has traditionally been seen as the province of technical groups such as the Society of Motion Picture and Television Engineers.[3]

Even in academic studies that address the uses of technologies, labs are typically viewed as lacking the creative potential of crafts such as editing and cinematography, particularly since the beginning of the sound studio era.

In *The Classical Hollywood Cinema,* Kristin Thompson has portrayed how the rise of mechanized developing with sound film "effectively eliminated the possibility of collaboration between laboratory and cinematographer" (Bordwell, Staiger, and Thompson, 279). For Thompson and other scholars, the automated developing machines of a modern lab evoke a film factory. But lab work may also be seen as the fulfillment of filmmaking's collaborative labors. Vsevolod Pudovkin wrote that it is only with laboratory work that "the ideas originated by the scenarist and pursued by the director and cameraman" appear in their "pure form" (135). In film restorations, the lab recreates the efforts of the screenwriter, cinematographer, sound recorder, director, and editor in one location.[4]

This essay provides a fresh foundation for appreciating the work of restoration laboratories through a representative company, Haghefilm, by showing the three ways in which restoration labs occupy a unique position in cinema history. First, laboratories make an "archeology of technology" in their recovery of past films (de Oliveira interview).

Second, labs generate innovative techniques through their unique mix of industry, science, and art. Third, as they fuse archeology and innovation, labs encapsulate cinema's "hybrid future" between film and digital technologies (Meyer interview).

Through lab practice, the study of film history not only rediscovers lost options but adds to the forms of future cinema.

Located in Amsterdam, Holland, Haghefilm has one of the highest lab profiles in the archival and scholarly community, having regularly presented its restorations at Le Giornate del Cinema Muto and at other film festivals.[5] The lab sponsors festivals such as Le Giornate in Italy and grants funding for archival projects. The company awards a new graduate from the Selznick School of Film Preservation at George Eastman House (GEH) the opportunity to restore a single film from the GEH archive in Amsterdam every year. Giovanna Fossati, a curator at the Nederlands Filmmuseum, says of Haghefilm that it is "the only European film lab that can handle almost all kinds of restorations on a large quantity with a relatively high quality" (interview). The lab financed my trip to Haghefilm's offices in The Netherlands for a week in June of 2004. This report on the past and current functions of film labs is based on firsthand observation of the company and other labs, research in books, articles, and pamphlets, and interviews with archivists and technicians in both Europe and the United States.

HAGHEFILM AND RESTORATION LAB HISTORY

Haghefilm

Haghefilm's origins date back to 1926–27, when Dutch film pioneer Willy Mullens established the first laboratory whose name derived from his company's base in the city of The Hague. The firm initially worked on new Dutch releases. As the majority of Dutch films were shot in color from the 1960s on, the company changed its name to the Color Film Center in 1977–78. According to Johan Prijs, the business folded in 1984 due to mismanagement and competition with the second-biggest lab in Holland, Cineco/Cinetone Studios. But technicians Prijs, Max Berg, Wim Kerkhof, Livio Ricci, and Juan Vrijs, who had all worked at Haghefilm or the Color Film Center, then became directors of their own enterprise. They acquired the rights to the Haghefilm name and bestowed it on their new lab, which they devoted to work on archival films.[6]

From the 1980s on, the firm filled a niche for film restorations. According to Prijs, "We decided to concentrate on black-and-white process[es] and difficult formats" which the

Offices of Cineco/Haghefilm.
Courtesy Gabriel Paletz.

other labs did not want to handle (e-mail).[7] The new di-
rectors' strategy succeeded. In 1990 the company's success enabled its owners to purchase
two small bankrupt Dutch labs and turn them into subsidiary companies. Haghefilm itself
expanded its divisions into separate Lab, Conservation, Subtitling, and Optical Services.

This version of the company lasted until 1995, when the directors "could see
the end of the film era" (Prijs e-mail). They sold Haghefilm and its subsidiaries to Cineco,

with Peter Limburg becoming president of the new group. Within two years, Haghefilm began consolidating, reducing the number of its developing machines from twenty-one to seven, and dispensing with its service branches. Haghefilm endures as a restoration and preservation lab while Cineco works on current releases (Prijs e-mail, Prijs and Limburg interviews).[8] The current offices of Cineco and Haghefilm lie in an industrial area in the south of Amsterdam, next to the Over-amstel station.

The Growth of Film Restoration Labs

In its evolution, Haghefilm is a representative restoration lab, as it grew out of individual technical expertise and commercial filmmaking demands.[9] John E. Allen, founder of one of the oldest U.S. labs, Cinema Arts, was a film collector who developed his lab techniques from repairing and duplicating his own pictures. He began using printers to duplicate and supply stock footage professionally in the 1950s.[10] As late as the 1960s, labs that supplied archival footage usually took the attitude of "You're lucky if we give you anything" from copying historic images (Allen interview). The care Allen took with his stock material enabled him to move into film preservation and restoration. Synthesizing footage of different ages and qualities provided the training for his future restoration business.

Another, more recent restoration lab, Cineric, has its roots in special-effects work for films of the late 1970s and early 1980s. The company's sales manager, Chip Wilkinson, notes that special effects require both the same technology — such as optical printers — and the same precision as restoring archival films. Compositing two images together for a special effect calls for the same scrupulousness as reconstructing a frame of an old movie (interview). The histories of Haghefilm, Cineric, and Cinema Arts represent the scale of restoration lab work, from combining different pieces of film into a coherent print, to detailed labor on single frames.

Lab Basics

Restoration labs create new prints from historic moving image materials.[11] A restoration typically entails more complications than just preservation, as a restoration involves re-creating specific qualities of a picture. But even for duplication, films must be repaired. Technicians cope with dirt and the degeneration of image or sound track; shrunken, scratched, and torn film stock; perforation or splicing damage; the separation of the emulsion from the base of the film; color fading; and the collapse into tonal contrasts of black and white.[12]

At Haghefilm, each print is first scanned by eye to assess the basic requirements of its duplication. The sprocket holes must be in a condition to allow the film to pass through the printer. The frame lines must be spaced at the same distances between sprocket holes, or printing will produce a copy with lines inside the frame. The laboratory technician identifies what needs to be done for archival material to run through a lab's printer and developing tanks.

In collaboration with archives, lab technicians then engage in the crucial background work of a restoration, "to recognize and identify the characteristics of the original [picture]" (de Oliveira interview).[13] Technicians look at their source materials to determine a picture's historical résumé. The perusal can take weeks. A film's history resides in minutiae such as colored frame edges that indicate a color tinting. A picture's past includes not only the properties intended by the makers of a film, but also the characteristics that the film has acquired through time and from previous duplications (see Cherchi Usai 2000, 14–16, 49).[14] In scrutinizing a movie, technicians often identify what needs to be undone. Old films may have been damaged by excessive handling or printing, by distributors, and by archives in previous restoration attempts. Even a production studio may have lacquered release prints in an attempt to protect them from wear, as was the case for the two negatives of Fox's 1953 3-D picture *Inferno* (Belston interview).[15]

After determining the processes for a restoration, labs collate their positive and negative visual materials, which are often of varying quality, and from different periods and countries. From these sources, labs strike intermediate copies (internegatives and interpositives) until they have produced a preservation negative, from which future positive prints of the film are made and screened.[16] To produce new prints, labs can use digital and/or analogue methods. With digital methods, a scanner copies and converts film materials into digital media files. Technicians correct the files on computer and "write" the images back onto film stock with a laser. Analogue or photochemical methods use filmstrips exclusively as the carrier of archival images. In analogue processes, a film printer produces new copies of a movie.[17]

An Archeology of Technology

The history of cinema production reveals how the printer developed as a tool of film preservation and restoration.

At the start of film, the printer was essential to process a new camera negative and to expose the negative images through an illuminated gate onto positive stock for screening. By 1915, filmmakers were also using printers to create positive work prints, which allowed them to edit their movies while sparing camera negatives from wear and tear

(Thompson, 278). For the archives and labs that perform restorations, past films have the value of current releases. Thus labs have expanded the printer's capacity for duplication, from creating prints and work prints of new films to restoring movies long after their original productions.

Besides printers, restoration labs experiment with a range of technologies in their operations. At Haghefilm, the lab's research and development technician Gerard de Haan used an old animation table, or rostrum, to restore a moving image format from 1923. Charles Urban's Spirographs contain images on glass discs, with one hundred frames per revolution.[18] Setting the Spirograph on the animation table, De Haan had the rostrum combine horizontal and vertical movements (on the *x* and *y* axis) to move from frame to frame. Above the rostrum, a digital camera with a macro lens rotated 3.6 degrees with every pair of movements to photograph each frame in turn. This system integrated an apparently obsolete tool from animation to recover the Spirograph onto film.[19]

In another example, Haghefilm's chemistry expert Bert Hulshof had preserved rolls of intermediate color film stock where the green and blue dyes had faded. This stock proved essential for striking a new print of a color film with complementary fading. (The red layer of the positive had deteriorated and was balanced by the faded blue and green of the intermediate stock.) Hulshof calls the matching of intermediate and old film "a

Frame enlargement from
Spirograph film, *Oregon
Lumber Flume.* Courtesy
George Eastman House.

happy coincidence," one that demonstrates how restoration labs expand aesthetic options by recycling materials discarded in other phases of moviemaking (interview).

Haghefilm's director Peter Limburg states, "Our company can work only as we can offer people possibilities, and possibilities depend on a range of techniques" (interview).

Labs like Haghefilm not only invent new methods of treating movies, but they accumulate and adapt techniques, most of which have been discarded in modern film production.

Recent films as varied as *Nixon* (1995) and *Buffalo 66* (1998) revived forgotten stocks and cameras, while *Naked* (1993) and *Se7en* (1995) used the uncommon bleach-bypass process in developing prints. Yet compared with the filmmaking industry, restoration labs consistently explore a wider range of techniques. A lab's livelihood rests on the manipulation of machinery and processes from all of movie history.[20] Restoration labs regularly put technologies to uses not intended by their inventors, in order to recover the effects of past films. A lab's archeology of technology provides the basis for its combination of industry, science, and art.

INDUSTRY, SCIENCE, AND ART

One might take this heading for granted in a film essay, as every aspect of moviemaking combines industry, science, and art. Yet, as at the origin of cinema, a modern restoration lab integrates the three fields with particular clarity. As businesses, labs need to turn out a consistent volume of prints and to take on projects that earn them exceptional payment or renown. Laboratory technicians resemble scientists, however, dressing in white coats to experiment with gamma curves, printer light numbers, and the phases of developing baths. The same technicians also discuss color and contrast with the refinement of connoisseurs, equal to that of cinematographers, collectors, and archivists.[21]

In their collaborations with archives, restoration labs seek both "the best and most cost-effective way" to restore films (Musumeci interview).[22] Labs negotiate a range of technical options with the availability of film products, and the desire for historical accuracy with the limits of archival budgets.[23] Every restoration presents a variety of demands, to which a number of solutions apply. Tony Munroe of Triage Laboratories notes that "each project could go on forever" (interview).[24] But a commercial company like Haghefilm survives by its ability to create unique techniques while processing a consistent amount of film.

Recapitulating early cinema's creativity in an industrial setting, film restoration has evolved as "elastic work," where a lab's industrial basis conditions its scientific and artistic experiments (Marino interview).

Industry

Haghefilm is a representative restoration company as it combines the capabilities of both a commercial and an archival lab. Typically, commercial labs work on current movies to turn out volumes of identical prints for theatrical release. Geared toward mass production, commercial firms cannot easily adjust their procedures, such as the length of film developing or the brightness of printer lights, for every project.[25] Archivist Giovanna Fossati claims that, even when it works on restoration projects, "A big commercial lab is much less flexible than a small archival lab" (e-mail).

Archival labs are attuned to the lost characteristics of an individual film and have more time to restore a picture's qualities.[26]

An archival lab works on a restoration project for an associated archive, movie studio, or a distributor of historic pictures, to produce a new print or DVD release of a film. However, while an archival lab typically receives government funding, it earns no payment for its work. A small archival lab has the flexibility to work on single pictures but cannot afford the most advanced equipment that a particular restoration might require. Archival labs are also generally restricted to materials in an archive's collection or from an archive's collaborators.

Haghefilm resembles a small archival lab in its experiments on behalf of single films and in its clientele. Haghefilm differs from an archival lab in its commercial existence. The company has to process a greater amount of film than labs associated with archives. Depending on earnings from clients compels Haghefilm to work with a range of international archives, studios, and distribution companies, such as Lobster Films in Paris. According to Johann Prijs, Cineco's work on new releases financially sustains Haghefilm's restorations (interview). Yet Cinceo's need to maintain industrial standards also allows Haghefilm to harness new technologies for its restoration work.

For example, in partnership with the Nederlands Filmmuseum in the late 1980s and early 1990s, Haghefilm employed new technology to revive a cachet of archival pictures. During that period, the Filmmuseum received a new four-year budget with preservation funds, which it applied to a collection of films from the Dutch distributor and theater owner Jean Desmet (1875–1956). Haghefilm had recently purchased a new Debrie TAI immersion step optical printer, which enabled the lab to copy shrunken and otherwise damaged films frame by frame with a wet gate that removed scratches on the film base. The volume of restoration work made the TAI printer a staple of the lab. Senior Curator Mark-Paul Meyer estimates that, at the height of the project, the Filmmuseum had Haghefilm copy "4,000 to 5,000 meters," almost two-and-a half hours of film, per week (Meyer and Prijs interviews).[27] Archival materials and resources, joined with the lab's technical capabilities, resulted in the Filmmuseum winning Le Giornate del Cinema Muto's 1991 Jean Mitry award for contributions to silent film.[28]

The restoration history of the Desmet Collection is, however, rare. Archives have abundant numbers of films to restore but rarely possess the resources to preserve an entire group of movies.[29] Archives can also rarely afford simultaneous, complex restorations.[30] So a commercial lab like Haghefilm constantly negotiates between the requirements of a particular restoration for an archive or distributor and standardized processes that allow the lab to handle a consistent amount of film. Standardized smoothness in developing and printing assures a lab's economic health. And standardization is secured through science.

Science

"One of the secrets of a lab is keeping up its standards," states René Bruinooge, Haghefilm's film grader or timer (interview).

As I witnessed at Haghefilm, the daily maintenance of standards in developing and grading distinguishes lab work among the phases of film production. Both the processes of printer grading (called "timing" in the United States and Canada) and film developing rely on a lab's ability to produce exact values.[31] The LAD, or Laboratory Aim Density system, provides the foundation of grading, while sensitometry is the basis for the development of negatives.

Dominic Case describes how, when a lab develops negatives, "the actual processing results are checked by running sensitometric strips, or scientifically made exposure wedges" (54). The sensitometer exposes a control wedge, from a company such as Kodak or Fuji, in twenty-one steps from pure transparency to complete black (Read and Meyer, 336). The lab develops a film strip placed in the sensitometer. Once developed, the laboratory strip's spectrum of density, represented as the slope of a characteristic curve called gamma, should match those on a strip already processed by the film company.

At Haghefilm, the sensitometer resembles a topless toaster oven, and lies in a room like a closet. But every day, Haghefilm uses its sensitometer to expose filmstrips and its densitometer to measure the strips' contrast. Through these instruments, a lab can discover if it is developing film outside of calculated parameters of density. If a developed sensitometric strip produces density outside of the values prescribed by Kodak or Fuji, then the lab examines every feature of its developing process. The chemicals, their mixture, and the speed and temperature of the film in the developing bath are all checked. As Haghefilm's digital restorer Paulo de Fonseca observes, digital technologies can manipulate contrast with precision and ease. But if you do not understand the science of gamma, "You will not know the values to set for your [digital] machines" (interview). The control of gamma through developing and timing remains fundamental to every new feature and restored film.

Like film developing, the process of grading, or timing, reveals how science supports industry and art. Grading is the assignment of light numbers to shots of a film for printing. Previously assessed by eye, the numbers are now assigned by computer.[32] Haghefilm uses a scale of 1 to 50, with one applied to low-density, or low-contrast, images and fifty for high-density, or high-contrast, pictures. If an archival nitrate film is in good condition, then one light value may apply to the entire picture. But it is not uncommon to give different print light numbers for each shot of a film and a different value for red, green, and blue for each shot of a color movie. The grading of archival film materials tries to restore to faded or high-contrast images the range of tones they once possessed.

Kodak designed the Laboratory Aim Density system to control grading values. The negative filmstrip of the LAD has as essential a place in grading as the sensitometric wedge has in developing. Both the sensitometer and the LAD strip are tested daily in a film lab. In the LAD system, the negative strip is printed onto different positive stocks. When printed onto any positive with the average printer lights (25-25-25, midway between 1 and 50), the LAD should produce a film with color densities prescribed by Kodak, representing the medium densities for every kind of stock. Producing these densities involves adjusting or "trimming" the printer lights for each primary color—red, green, and blue—to achieve each stock's desired color proportions (Read and Meyer, 291).[33] As with sensitometric tests for developing, different reasons necessitate running the LAD through the printer, from a change of film stocks, to the shifting intensity of a printer's lights throughout the day. Both the sensitometer and the LAD system create scientific targets for producing the same results no matter the stock or condition of the machine.

Cinematographer John Alton noted that a film lab should function with the precision of a well-ordered mind. "The brain's processing department is what every film lab in

Film developer with Haghefilm lab technicians: Alfons
Meyer (right), then head of
the developing department
at Haghefilm, and Herman
Laman (left), developing technician. Courtesy Gabriel Paletz.

the world would like to be" (188). Yet a lab's technicians view a film image as both a set of standardized values and as a palette to paint particular effects. Science is both the basis of a laboratory's standards and the background for its experiments in art.

Art

Lab technicians know that film exists not only as numerical values but also in human perception. In 1949, John Alton wrote, "Negatives should be timed [i.e., graded] first for mathematically correct density, second for feeling, mood. Neither one alone is sufficient. It is an ideal combination of both that makes a good print" (169–70). In their 2000 book *Restoration of Motion Picture Film,* Paul Read and Mark-Paul Meyer concur with the cinematographer. They claim quality control "is made more objective if the characteristics of the process can be converted into numbers." But they distinguish quality control from quality checking, where numbers are "almost never . . . [used] . . . because of the subjective nature of vision" (105). Lab technicians work with both the numerical and aesthetic facets of film in fusing science with art.

A restoration lab may employ artistic variations for several reasons, in recreating the past look of old films, accommodating present perceptions, and accounting for the future wear to a picture.[34] In collaboration with George Eastman House, Haghefilm developed an original process for recreating the look of the Kinemacolor film *The Scarlet Letter* (1913). Kinemacolor originally set red and green filters over its films in projection. The lab alternately exposed each frame of a black-and-white negative with red and green printer lights at the Kinemacolor rate of thirty-six frames per second, so modern audiences could "not just see the film but understand the process" of the two-color additive system (Stratmann interview). In working on color films, Haghefilm technicians also take human perception into account. A computer may assign an identical density value to two scenes both tinted red. But if a scene tinted green appears between them, the second shot will not appear the same to an audience, even though it has the same numeric value. Technicians accordingly adjust the second shot's red density so it will appear to match the first scene. Finally, Haghefilm's technicians will flash films with a printer, or pull films in developing, in order to grade a restored print with a lower contrast than the one they believe the film originally possessed. A lab makes a lower contrast copy knowing that the archive will duplicate the restored print, and that contrast increases through duplication. The lab's treatment will help preserve the film's range of tones.

If a lab's artistry helps determine its creative uses of technologies, so an awareness of film history shapes a lab's artistic choices. A lab's collaboration with film archives, its range of machines, and the career experience of its employees endow it with a sense of cinema's past that guides its operations.[35] An awareness of history sets limits on the manipulation of technology in film restoration. Especially in the digital era, labs may create a copy of a film that has a sharper focus or contrast than the first generation of prints, or even recreate parts of a film. In its restoration of *Sherlock Holmes* (1922) for George Eastman House, Haghefilm performed a partial cleaning of the existing titles of a faded 16mm print. The archive and lab chose not to polish the titles as completely as possible or to remake them completely with digital means (Stratmann interview). The choice of what methods to employ makes up the ethics of lab work in the transition between analogue and digital technologies.

ANALOGUE AND DIGITAL

Analogue or Photochemical Methods

The transition from one technology to another has particular poignancy in restoration labs that resurrect old machines. Analogue techniques may be associated with archival films, and digital methods with modern movies, but lab restoration work reveals the undiscovered possibilities of analogue equipment, with the benefits and limits of digital tools.[36]

Analogue restorations such as the Desmet color method rely on the film printer. Named for Noël Desmet who refined the process at the Belgian Cinémathèque Royale, the method uses what he describes as "double-pass printing" to recover tints and tones from the faded colors and nitrate decomposition of archival materials (interview).[37] In remaking tints, a black-and-white internegative is struck from an archival copy. The internegative is printed once to make a positive, and then the positive runs through the printer a second time, to be flashed with colors. Employing a black-and-white internegative, a Desmet restoration costs less money and achieves a wider range of contrast than one using color stock.

In 2003, Haghefilm and the Filmmuseum invited Desmet to Amsterdam for consultation about his color restoration method. Desmet explained to Haghefilm's technicians that in his process, one should not flash the film with more than two colors at a time, in order to preserve brightness and clarity of hue. Desmet claims that his visit led Haghefilm's graders to alter their machines to be able to add color values of zero (interview). Haghefilm learned from Desmet's visit "that there can be exchange of info[rmation] with people from other labs" (Fossati e-mail). Through the exchange, Haghefilm enhanced the potential of the analogue film printer to produce sharper colors for restored films.

Digital Restoration

When trying to change the contrast of a film through analogue methods, technicians experiment with physical variables. They can change print stocks, the temperature of the processing chemicals, the times of developing (pushing or pulling black-and-white film), or even the developing sequence such as in bleach-bypassing (which leaves silver in color film). Yet as Haghefilm's digital restorer Paulo de Fonseca told me, to change the look of color film by analogue means is difficult. With digital, things that are impossible or difficult to control with precision in analogue restoration, including variations in contrast, color levels, saturation, gamma, and gain can all be reset (e-mail).

During my visit in June of 2004, Haghefilm was renovating its top floor, which housed the photochemical and digital departments, into a completely digital workspace. Photochemical techniques are still commonly applied to archival films, but the situation is changing as digital methods become more affordable.[38] Digital technologies have already transformed the pace of lab operations. With analogue methods, technicians must go through processes to gauge the results. In digital restorations, they can diagnose a problem, apply solutions, immediately judge results, and change values and even methods as they proceed. Yet while some actions in digital restoration are as fast and flexible

Haghefilm digital scanner. Courtesy Gabriel Paletz.

as editing text with a word processor, other work can take much longer than analogue methods. Scanning film into media files, rendering them on computer, and writing the files back onto film are all measured in hours, if not days. According to de Fonseca, it takes two to three days to render and stabilize a feature movie (interview).

Digital technologies have altered both the rhythms of restoration work and the roles of lab technicians.[39]

The operator of a computer workstation now sets the parameters for adjusting film contrast, color, registration, and flicker; cleaning dust; and reconstituting images. Digital technologies will make such processes automatic in film restoration, but automation requires knowledgeable supervision.[40] Ronald Bosdam digitally restores soundtracks for Haghefilm. For him the peril of a digital tool is that "it starts to think for itself" (interview). Without adjusting automatic processes, areas of a film image will be identified as dust and removed, and part of a soundtrack erased along with scratches. Digital technologies have unprecedented power to "manipulate all preexisting analogue media and images, thus obliterating their past histories" (Horak, n.p.). Both Bosdam and de Fonseca also warn against the facility of digital machines, which can lead to intensely detailed labor on image pixels but to little onscreen effect. In the digital era, lab technicians will oversee the results of automation, while deciding the technology's most useful range of manipulation.

The technicians of a lab are attuned to the increased ease and novel risks of digitization. They also directly confront the unknown factors of digital methods. How long the images will last, the right resolution for scanning, the effects of compression on film images, and the time needed for digital processes are all being determined in lab trials (FIRST, 47).

As restoration labs find fruitful uses for past technologies, so they are in the advance guard of developing digital solutions to digital uncertainties.

In order to check its work immediately with archival clients, Haghefilm posts its restorations in progress on its server, which archives can access on the World Wide Web. In sending films via the Internet or posting them on the Web, a lab like Haghefilm uses digital technologies to facilitate communication between its company and archivists, technicians, and scholars. Digital's ability to alter moving images necessitates such freedom of exchange in deciding and documenting what occurs in a film lab.[41]

THE FUTURE OF FILM LABS

Digital communications can multiply the collaborations between different labs and archives. Archives still seek to work with labs near them, in order to monitor projects and save money in film shipping. Yet archives will also seek out the lab, however far away, that can provide the most historically accurate and technically advanced restoration. When

Shin Heike Monogatari trailer.
Courtesy National Film
Center, Tokyo.

the National Film Center of Japan was preparing its cen- tennial retrospective of the films of Yasujiro Ozu, it found a film that existed only on 9.5mm, *Wasei Kenka Tomodachi* (1929), a comedy with the English title *Fighting Friends*. Haghefilm scanned the film to digital and did the first automatic cleaning of the picture using Diamant software. It also scanned the corrected digital files back to film. However, the Tokyo lab Imagica did the film's manual cleaning. Splitting the project allowed the National Film Center to have Haghefilm digitize the picture from 9.5mm and then to su-pervise the analogue restoration in Japan with Imagica (Tsuneishi interview).[42]

The spread and cost of digital technologies have also prompted archives to increase competition between labs. In 2004, Haghefilm prepared a restoration test of Mizoguchi's first color film, *Shin Heike Monogatari* (1955) for the National Film Center, in competition with another European lab. Haghefilm won the competition to restore the film. Chad Hunter, former preservation officer of George Eastman House in New York, notes that thirty years ago, under director James Card, the museum used to work with only one laboratory, Cinema Arts.[43] Now it uses not only Cinema Arts but also four other labs, such as Triage and YCM on the West Coast, and Haghefilm in Europe (interview).

3599

Frame enlargement of 28mm Broncho Billy film. Courtesy George Eastman House.

Haghefilm now retains clients in the United States and Europe, while it has earned new ones in Asia.[44] Among its digital restorations, Haghefilm was working on cleaning and correcting the registration of films in the GEH's collection of 28mm prints during my visit.[45] For Lobster Films in France, Haghefilm continues to work on a hand-colored print of one of the most famous titles in silent cinema.[46] The movie lasts no more than fifteen minutes and has a release date of the end of December 2008, at which time the lab will have been working on the project for eight years (Bromberg interview).

Hagefilm's director, Peter Limburg, states, "We treat archives like film producers" (interview).

In satisfying the demands of both archives and moviemakers, labs distill the future of industry, science, and art in cinema.

With archives, labs have a crucial place in cinema history; they determine the ways films will be restored and the forms in which moving pictures endure. As a preservation consultant to the National Film and Television Archive of Great Britain, Brian Pritchard believes that only restoration labs will deal with film in the future, as the medium will vanish from the commercial world (interview). The present offers causes for both optimism and distress. The markets for restored movies have multiplied from 16mm catalogues to outlets including cable and satellite channels, VHS, and DVD.[47] A film's selection for these outlets depends on its commercial appeal, which may include, if not depend on, its material condition and historic value.[48] There is now more commercial viability for the work of film laboratories, higher expectations of lab quality, and greater appreciation of lab achievements.

Still, the number of restorations archives and studio libraries can afford will never equal the number of films they possess. Cinema's protectors will continue to face the prospect of watching movies succumb to time without recourse. Current archivists have expressed either defiance of the impossibility of preserving movies in the digital era or melancholy as restored films become a minor species of moving images. For Paolo Cherchi Usai, cinema has paradoxically become "the art of destroying moving images" (2001, 7). Raymond Borde, the late founder of the Cinémathèque Toulouse, mourns the approaching age when film archives will become mere "stations-service de l'image sur les autoroutes de l'information" [gas stations of images on the information superhighway] (Borde and Buache, 42).

The work of labs illuminates more heartening possibilities, even ones bound by marketing and mechanical constraints. Labs are places of action that bring films back to the public. In their anthology on silent cinema, Lee Grieveson and Peter Krämer call for scholarship that "engage[s] with seemingly strange forms of filmmaking on their own terms, placing them in the contexts in which they were made" (5). Done conscientiously, the work of film restoration compels retracing a picture's history and instills a material grasp of its contingencies. For Pudovkin, the appearance of new positive images in the lab signals the end of "the organic liaison between all the workers on the film production" (136). But the memory of collaborations between moviemakers returns in the labors of a film laboratory. In preserving techniques, resolving the interests of industry, science, and art, and synthesizing analogue with digital potential, a lab's technicians nurture a richer film future.

Thanks to the technicians, archivists, and scholars quoted in this article. Particular thanks to Giovanna Fossati, Doron Galili, Annette Groschke, Tom Gunning, Fumiko Tsuneishi, and to Peter Limburg and the technicians of Haghefilm.

APPENDIX: A LIST OF COMMERCIAL FILM RESTORATION LABS

This is an initial list of commercial restoration labs in Europe, Asia, and the United States. All laboratories can duplicate films and make intermediates. I have included only those whose company profiles highlight their restoration work. Labs sponsored by civic and national archives have been omitted. These labs can be traced through their umbrella institutions, such as the Cineteca del Comune di Bologna for the well-known Italian lab L'Immagine Ritrovata. A listed telephone number is provided when no Web site was available.

Europe and Asia

Alpha Omega. Munich, Germany. http://www.alpha-omega.de.

Atlantik Film. Hamburg, Germany. http://www.atlantik-film.com/.

Augustus Color Sas. Rome, Italy. Tel.: +39-06-4121-7555/6.

Cinéarchiv. Part of Centrimage Laboratories in Paris, France (Cinéarchiv is located outside of the capital). http://www.centrimage.com/.

Digital Film Finland. Helsinki, Finland. http://www.digitalfilmfinland.fi/.

Digital Film Lab. Copenhagen, Denmark. http://www.digitalfilmlab.com/.

Digital Lab (S'mietanka i Syn). Warsaw, Poland. http://www.dlab.pl.

Éclair Studios. Épinay-sur-Seine, France. http://www.eclair.fr/.

FilmTeknik. Stockholm, Sweden. http://www.filmteknik.se/. This company is owned by Nordsik Film AS, which also owns FilmTeknikk Norge in Oslo, Norway, and Nordisk Film Lab in Copenhagen, Denmark. The three sister companies can all be accessed from FilmTeknik's Web site.

Haghefilm (a division of Cineco Laboratories). Amsterdam, Holland. http://www.haghefilm.nl.

Imagica. Tokyo, Japan. http://www.imagica.com.

Prasad EFX. Offices in India, the United Arab Emirates, and Singapore. http://www.efxmagic.com.

Prestech Ltd. London, England. http://www.prestech.biz.

Soho Images. London, England. http://www.sohoimages.com.

Studio Cine. Rome, Italy. Tel.: +39-06-787-343.

Technicolor Europe. Rome, Italy. http://www.technicolor.com/Cultures/En-Us/Locations/Europe/Italy/ItalyRome/.

North America

(Labs are given by U.S. city and state unless otherwise noted.)

Cinema Arts. Newfoundland, PA. Tel.: (570) 676–4145.

Cineric Inc. New York, NY. http://www.cineric.com/.

Cinesite (A Kodak Company). Los Angeles, CA. http://www.cinesite.com/.

Cinetech. Valencia, CA. http://www.cinetech.com/.

Color Lab Inc. Rockville, MD. http://www.colorlab.com/.

Film Technology Company. Los Angeles, CA. http://www.filmtech.com/.

FotoKem. Burbank, CA. http://www.fotokem.com.

MTI Film, LLC. Providence, RI. http://www.mtifilm.com/.

Monaco Film Labs. San Francisco, CA. http://www.monacosf.com/.

The PPS Group. Cincinnati, OH. http://www.triage.to/home.htm.

Pacific Title and Art Studio. Hollywood, CA. http://www.pactitle.com/.

Summit Film Lab and Media Services. Pittsburgh, PA. http://www.
    summitfilmlab.com/.

Technicolor Entertainment Services. North Hollywood, CA. http://
    www.technicolor.com/Cultures/En-Us/Locations/North+America/USA/
    CANorthHollywood/.

Triage Motion Picture Services. Los Angeles, CA. http://www.triage.to/
    home.htm.

Western Cinema Lab. Englewood, CO. http://www.westerncine.com/.

YCM Labs. Burbank, CA. Tel.: (818) 843–5300.

Besides the commercial laboratories, there are the following specialty groups of interest:

Brodsky and Treadway. Rowley, MA (only for reversal film, 16mm, or smaller
    gauge). http://www.littlefilm.com/.

Film Rescue International. Fortuna, ND (also in Canada). http://
www.filmrescue.com/.

Restoration House Film Group. Ontario, Canada. Tel.: (613) 966–4076.

NOTES

This essay was cowinner of the first annual Student Essay Award given by
Domitor, the Society for the Study of Silent Cinema.

1. "Edison's moving picture machines were actually produced by a team of
technicians working at his laboratories in West Orange, New Jersey, supervised
by the Englishman William Kennedy Laurie Dickson" (Pearson, 14).

2. In his book on silent cinema, Paolo Cherchi Usai distinguishes between
duplication, conservation ("the activities necessary to prevent or minimize
the process of physical degradation of the archival artifact"), restoration ("the
set of . . . procedures aimed at compensating for the loss or degradation of the
moving image artifact, thus bringing it back to a state as close as possible to
its original condition"), reconstruction, and recreation (2000, 66–67). To
Cherchi Usai, film preservation comprises all of these activities. I have sim-
plified his distinctions. In this essay, "preservation" refers to the processes
of duplication and conservation that minimize the degradation of film;
"restoration" refers to the procedures of reconstruction and re-creation that
compensate for film degradation.

3. The article by J. I. Crabtree in the Works Cited appears in a compilation of
articles from the *SMPTE Journal.* The Dominic Case book and the Paul Read
and Mark-Paul Meyer edited collection describe lab processes as a part of
film production and restoration, respectively.

4. In 2003, the Dutch Filmmuseum produced a CD-ROM on restoring films.
The CD-ROM compares the laboratory processes used for a new picture with
those used for an archival film. In work on an old film, "the director [of the
new release] is replaced by the film restorer whose aim is not to make a new
film but, instead, to restore an existing film in a way that does justice to its
original appearance." Laboratory technicians who work with the restorer on
a film represent the equivalent of a movie crew.

5. At the 2002 Giornate, Haghefilm presented a restoration of the 22mm
Edison film *A Christmas Carol.* The original movie came on three columns
of moving images, each approximately 5mm, with two sprocket holes on the
side of each middle frame. The projectionist adjusted the gate to show the
first column, adjusted it again to screen the second column from the bottom
up, and adjusted the gate a third time for the last column. In 2003, the lab
presented its restoration of Charles Urban's Spirographs (see below). The
materials for both restorations came from the George Eastman House.

6. Prijs was coordinator of Haghefilm's photochemical conservation department up to 2000, when he left for the Studio Cine laboratory in Rome and
Juan Vrijs took over the role of conservation manager.

7. Like other small labs, such as Triage in the United States, Haghefilm found its niche by taking on challenging films to restore. Triage co-owner Tony Munroe states his company began by inviting its clients to "send us your worst" materials (interview).

8. Business cards present Cineco on one side and Haghefilm Conservation on the other. Both Cineco and Haghefilm are now part of the Meta Media investment group, according to Johan Prijs (e-mail).

9. According to my interviews, restoring films did not become a social concern or viable enterprise until the 1970s. One of the oldest preservation labs, Film Technology Company of Los Angeles, began in the preservation field in the middle of the decade, after its founder, Ralph Sargent, published *Preserving the Moving Image* (1974), which the company's Web site claims as one of the earliest guides to preserving film.

10. According to Janice Allen (née John Allen, the son of the company's founder), her father began his career in the 1920s in Rochester, New York. Besides being a collector, the first Mr. Allen showed films in a tent and was a dealer of Bell and Howell equipment before going into the stock footage business (interview).

11. This summary cannot cover the many details of film restoration. Among other subjects of technical interest during my visit to Haghefilm, I have left out discussions of the different uses of contact and optical printers and the intricacies of wet-gate printing. For detailed discussions of lab techniques, I refer the reader to the anthologies of the Joint Technical Symposia, to the article by Crabtree, and to the books by Read and Case.

12. Anke Wilkening of the Murnau-Stiftung Archive in Germany wrote me: "We are always looking for labs that are specialised on restoration due to the often problematic condition of our film materials" (e-mail).

13. The California lab Cinetech creates Electronic Film Evaluations (EFE) as part of its restoration work. An EFE provides an archive with an electronic document describing the problems and proposed treatment of a film, with links to video or photo files, so the archivist can evaluate the lab's proposals.

14. João de Oliveira would like to develop tests to determine how films have been printed and developed, the contents of their original dyes, and the films in an archive's collection that need immediate preservation (interview).

15. A 3-D picture from the 1950s has two negatives, one for each eye.

16. The making of internegatives and interpositives is common to both new and restored films. John Allen notes that for the mockumentary *A Mighty Wind* (USA, 2003), directed by Christopher Guest and shot in Super-16, his lab made three color interpositives: one for video copies, one for theatrical film releases, and one set aside for preservation. Allen believes it is rare to make three color interpositives from a Super-16 film, and also to prepare a preservation copy at the same time as distribution materials (interview). But Richard Dayton, president of YCM, sees the production of preservation copies with distribution copies as an increasing trend (interview).

17. With archival films, labs usually handle positive prints to strike a new intermediate negative, as positive prints of a film are more likely to have survived. Berlin archivist Annette Groschke states that most of her colleagues would prefer to make two preservation negatives and at least three positive prints. Yet most have the funds for only one preservation negative, one positive answer print for review, and one correction print that an archive approves for projection and public access (interview).

18. Even though the disk's circumference narrows, the one hundred frames per revolution are maintained as the space between frames decreases toward the disk's interior.

19. Following the work with the Spirographs, Haghefilm has collaborated with George Eastman House to use the rostrum to restore other formats whose images will not fit into a film gate: Kammatographs (other images on glass disks), shrunken 28mm film, and images from flip-card Mutoscopes (Stratmann interview).

20. Machines have pride of place in a film lab, reversing the focus of film production, where attention is directed at the actors and set. Walking through a lab resembles passing through a cinema museum without explanations, with each machine as an exhibit meant to be touched.

21. Of all the people who shoot a film, cinematographers have the closest ties to a film lab, as they are most responsible for the onscreen image. Director of photography John Alton noted in his book on cinematography: "One could hardly call himself a professional photographer without having at least a working knowledge of what goes on in the laboratory. Just as a painter has to know how to mix his paints, so the successful cameraman needs to know the chemical process his film must go through before it reaches the screen. Cameramen should start at the lab" (167). Like lab workers, directors of photography tinker with industrial conventions to make technical innovations. Both crafts carry on the spirit of the original film inventors, who developed the medium by improving on one another's ideas.

22. Given the investment in restoring a film, an archive's relationship to a lab resembles a marriage, states Mario Musumeci of the Italian National Archive. An archive may develop strong ties with a particular lab, such as the one between the Nederlands Filmmuseum and Haghefilm described above. But archives also do not want labs to take their patronage for granted (interview).

23. As an example of the limits of archival budgets, Paola Ruggiero, head of the foreign division of the Cinecittà Holding Archive in Rome, states that she receives an annual budget of 150,000 euros (approximately $180,000) from the Italian government. For the 2004 Venice film festival, Cinecittà Holding wanted to restore the first film directed by the noted actor Massimo Troisi for a screening marking the tenth anniversary of his death. Ms. Ruggiero notes that Troisi's first picture, *Ricominciò da Tre* (1981), had problems not only from age but also from its original shoot, such as dialogue obscured by production noise. The project cost 30,000 euros, ($36,000). Performing the extensive work required by the Troisi film, Cinecittà could afford only five film restorations a year (interview).

The National Film Preservation Foundation's *Film Preservation Guide* estimates that it costs between $1,550 and $2,800 to strike a new internegative and viewing print from one thousand feet of 16mm black-and-white film. As a thousand feet of 16mm is around twenty-eight minutes of running time at 24 fps, the lowest estimates to make a basic preservation of a 16mm black-and-white feature film would be around $4,650 ($1,550 multiplied by 3), but only if all source materials were in "relatively good condition" (42).

24. Completing a restoration may take as long as developing a project in Hollywood. However, the actual lab work can be performed as quickly as a film production once a project has received financing. The press kit of Milestone Films' 2001 re-release of *La Grande Strada Azzurra* (*The Wide Blue Road*, Italy, 1957) highlights the restoration of the film done by Johan Prijs working at Studio Cine, and Giovanni Schiano at the Cineteca Nazionale, both in Rome. Noting the "often unglamorous, time-intensive, and highly technical" process of film restoration, the Milestone statement summarizes: "The process of restoring a film is usually extremely laborious and in many cases the lab technicians are the true—and almost always, unsung—heroes of any restoration." The press release offers a chronology that suggests that the restoration took twenty-one years. However, Schiano wrote me in an e-mail that his lab work for Milestone "started in the late summer of 2000 to be completed in early spring of 2001." Perhaps the Milestone press kit includes all lab work on the film since its original release, beyond the requirements for the most recent restoration:

1974 Create a technical report on the negative elements

1975 Repair perforation and/or tears

1976 Synchronization check

1977 Negative picture rejuvenation

1978 Intermediate negative rejuvenation to duplicate sequences

1979 Negative sound track cleaning

1980 Strike check print from negative picture

1981 Strike 35mm color print paper to paper printing from intermediate negative

1982 Manual cleaning negative picture after 'check print' control

1983 Strike intermediate positive paper to paper from intermediate negative of the sequences to substitute

1984 Create intermediate positive print

1985 Edit new sequences into intermediate positive

1986 Create intermediate negative print

1987 Positive sound track two sides (wet printing)

1988 Positive sound track single side (wet printing)

1989 Sound restoration including re-recording to DAT, digital sound restoration, re-recording from restored DAT to optical 35mm negative

1990 Processing restored negative soundtrack

1991 Sync picture and sound

1992 Answer print from intermediate negative and restored soundtrack

1993 Strike projection prints

1994 Newly translate the Italian title list to English subtitles

1995 Laser subtitles struck on new projection prints

25. In printing, even a change of film stock means resetting or trimming a printer's lights to achieve the recommended Laboratory Aim Densities (see above under "Science"). Changing one variable such as the stock entails resetting the lab's machines, ensuring their standardization but decreasing their productivity.

26. The largest European archival labs belong to the Bundesarchiv in Germany, the National Film and Television Archive in England, Cinecittà Studios in Italy, and the Centre National de la Cinématographie in France. In the United States, the Library of Congress has one of the most significant restoration labs for archival films. Among archival labs of smaller countries, both Belgium's Cinémathèque Royale and the Czech Národní Filmový Archiv are distinguished by their processes for remaking the tints and tones of early films. Noël Desmet developed the Desmet color restoration method in Belgium (see below).

27. This calculation is based on the 35mm sound film speed of twenty-four frames per second (fps). Silent film could run at sixteen frames per second or at an even slower rate. At 16 fps, a film of 4,000 meters would run for three hours and forty minutes, or more than half an hour longer than *The Birth of a Nation* (1915).

28. The restoration of the collection has also resulted in an academic study by Ivo Blom, a former archivist at the Filmmuseum: *Jean Desmet and the Early Dutch Film Trade* (Amsterdam: Amsterdam University Press, 2003).

29. If the Desmet Collection lay in the Filmmuseum's vaults following Desmet's death, then it took approximately thirty years before the archive and Haghefilm began comprehensive work on it.

30. Brian Pritchard was co-owner and manager of Henderson's film lab in England and now serves as preservation consultant to the National Film and Television Archive. He believes that archives are entering an era where the preservation of films will take predominance over restoration (interview). Indeed, Henderson's closed in the summer of 2004.

31. The importance of science to a film lab recalls the stress on scientific precision in the developments of series photography preceding motion pictures. At the start of his essay describing his "Chronophotographie," Etienne-Jules Marey stated, "Les sciences progressent en raison de la précision de leurs méthodes et de leurs instruments de mesure" [The sciences progress by the precision of their methods and their measuring instruments] (quoted in Mannoni et al., 288).

32. Technicians such as Haghefilm's Juan Vrijs and René Bruinooge, who have each restored films for more than twenty years, can still grade archival prints by eye.

33. The LAD negative strip has a color balance of .80 red, 1.20 green, and 1.60 blue, densities representing 18 percent gray, or midway between the minimum and maximum contrast values.

34. As a result of the many considerations for a restoration, an archive almost always requires corrections of a lab's first answer print.

35. Schools now exist for students interested in both film production and archiving but not yet for those who wish to be lab technicians. Labs still use the apprenticeship system.

36. As an adjective, *analogue* is a synonym for photochemical methods used to restore films. Analogue contrasts with *digital* techniques, even though the two may be combined on one restoration project. According to Tom Wallis, chief technical officer of Kodak Imaging, creating film images through analogue methods entails photoelectrical transformations on a filmstrip. Microscopic silver halide crystals that are randomly suspended in a three-dimensional pattern in a film's emulsion develop a logarithmic reaction to light during exposure. Both the random arrangement of the crystals and their logarithmic reaction to light echo the order of rods and cones and the reaction to light of the human eye. A latent image develops from silver atoms formed in the crystal structure, an image amplified by the chemicals in the developing or processing bath. In digital restoration, images on film are also generated by a photoelectrical reaction. But the base of the reaction is a fixed two-dimensional grid of pixels, whose electrons react in a linear scale of values to light (n.p.).

37. In the silent era, tinted and toned scenes were cut up and dyed in baths according to the colors desired for the separate shots. Desmet claims his method, developed in the early 1970s, is only meant to replicate the atmosphere, or "l'ambience," of film colors before the era of soundtracks (interview).

38. The costs of digital restoration may be decreasing but remains prohibitively expensive for most archives. Paolo de Fonseca estimates that the 2K scanning, color correction, cleaning of dust and scratches, and creation of a new negative for a feature six-reel film costs around 120,000 euros at Haghefilm (interview). This price approaches Ms. Ruggiero's yearly budget of 150,000 euros at Cinecittà Holding.

39. Transformations in industrial forms require a reassessment of roles. A historian of early cinema has demonstrated how a commercial crisis between 1900 and 1903 led to shifts in the control of film narrative from the exhibitor to the producer (Musser, 297).

40. Already at the Joint Technical Symposium of 1995 in London, Paul Watkins of Kodak's Cinecon Digital Film System emphasized the importance of lab restorers in a coming age of "semi-automation" (Boston, 139).

41. The range of digital tools, and the resulting need for communication between archivists and lab technicians, was demonstrated by a conversation between Paolo Cherchi Usai and Paulo de Fonseca on October 13, 2004, at Le Giornate del Cinema Muto Film Festival in Sacile, Italy. In a special presentation, Fonseca discussed Haghefilm's color digital restoration of Mizoguchi's first color film, *Shin Heike Monogatari* (1955). During the presentation, the following exchange occurred:

> CHERCHI USAI: What are your points of reference [for digital restoration of color films]?
>
> FONSECA: If we don't get a reference from the customer, I don't know... I try to make [the colors] neutral.
>
> CHERCHI USAI: So the best thing that could happen to you would be a reference print [from the archive].
>
> FONSECA: But with a color-faded film, we don't have that... When nobody knows what to do, I try to make everything neutral. But I don't know the minds of the filmmakers.

42. Haghefilm began its association with the National Film Center when Fumiko Tsuneishi, one of the Center's assistant curators, saw the lab's restoration of the 22mm *A Christmas Carol* (1910) at Le Giornate del Cinema Muto in October 2002 (see note 5). Watching this restored small-gauge film reminded her of a movie by the Japanese director Daisuke Ito, *Zanjin Zanbaken* (1929), that existed only on 9.5mm. (The survival of films only on a small-gauge format is not unusual in Japan, even for works by the country's famous filmmakers.) Tsuneishi's travel back from the festival included a layover in Amsterdam, where she visited Haghefilm and observed the capabilities of the lab's Oxberry Cinescan. The equipment was uniquely fitted to restore Ito's film in two ways. The machine can scan small-gauge movies, even ones where the strip has shrunken "like a snake" (Tsuneishi interview). Haghefilm's equipment can also scan films frame by frame, an essential quality when trying to achieve registration with fragile archival pictures.

43. Until the early 1980s, Kodak's nitrate lab was also handling preservation work. However, Ed Stratmann of Eastman House responds that the museum still had a choice (interview).

44. At Le Giornate del Cinema Muto festival in October 2004, Peter Limburg informed me that Haghefilm has just been asked to restore a film for a client in India.

45. Pathé marketed 9.5mm and 28mm "Pathéscope" films as one of the earliest home viewing formats before Kodak's introduction of "Kodascope" home formats of 8 and 16mm circa 1923. The Pathéscope 28mm films had a cellulose diacetate base, and included many actualities, but also features, including ones shot for Pathé in the United States by Native American filmmakers (Hunter interview).

46. Serge Bromberg of Lobster requested that I withhold the title of the film until the restoration has been completed.

47. The conditions for specialty distributors of DVDs, like the conditions for labs, present a horizon of technical possibilities limited by financial concerns. Two interviews on the Web site for Turner Classic Movies in May 2005 clarify the balance between technological experiments and budgets. Joyce Shen, one of the heads of NoShame Films, a distributor of Italian pictures, states that, for their restorations, "We are always trying to test new grounds of technology." In a separate interview, Dennis Doros, cofounder of the acclaimed DVD distributor Milestone Films, notes that there are three ways for his company to distribute archival pictures. Milestone picks up films from archives that have already restored the pictures through labs. Milestone also encourages archives to restore certain films and contributes financially to the work. Finally, Milestone has "acquired original material and worked with the labs to restore films ourselves—that has been enormously costly." Both NoShame's and Milestone's desire to bring out movies on DVD is constrained by the condition of materials they find for a film and the decisions of both archives and labs to assist in the films' restorations. The interview for NoShame Films can be found at http://www.turnerclassicmovies.com/MovieNews/Index/0,,94474,00.html; the one for Milestone is at http://www.turnerclassicmovies.com/MovieNews/Index/0,,95285,00.html.

48. Movie studios prefer the term "asset protection" to "film preservation" when restoring their library titles, to justify those films as future assets that can be sold.

WORKS CITED

Alton, John. *Painting with Light.* 1949; repr., Berkeley and Los Angeles: University of California Press, 1995.

Aubert, Michelle, and Richard Billeaud, *Image and Sound Archiving Access: The Challenges of the Third Millennium. Proceedings of the Fifth Joint Technical Symposium (Paris, January 19–22, 2000).* Colombes, France: Fontenaille Arts Graphiques, 2000.

Borde, Raymond, and Freddy Buache. *La Crise des Cinémathèques...et du Monde.* Lausanne, Switzerland: L'Age d'Homme, 1997.

Bordwell, David, Janet Staiger, and Kristin Thompson. *The Classical Hollywood Cinema: Film Style and Mode of Production to 1960.* New York: Columbia University Press, 1985.

Boston, George, ed. *Technology and Our Audio-Visual Heritage: Technology's Role in Preserving the Memory of the World (Fourth Joint Technical Symposium, January 1995, London).* Downs Barn, Milton Keynes: Stantonbury Parish Print, 1999.

Bowser, Eileen, and John Kuiper, eds. *A Handbook for Film Archivists.* New York: Garland Publishing, 1991.

Brownlow, Kevin. *The Parade's Gone By...* New York: Ballantine Books, 1968.

Case, Dominic. *Film Technology in Post Production.* 2d ed. Woburn, MA: Focal Press, 2001.

Cherchi Usai, Paolo. *Silent Cinema: An Introduction.* London: BFI Publishing, 2000.

———. *The Death of Cinema: History, Cultural Memory, and the Digital Dark Age.* London: BFI Publishing, 2001.

Crabtree, J. I. "The Motion-Picture Laboratory." 1955. Repr. in *A Technological History of Motion Pictures and Television: An Anthology from the Pages of the Journal of the Society of Motion Picture and Television Engineers,* ed. Raymond Fielding, 150–72. Berkeley and Los Angeles: University of California Press, 1983.

Edmondson, Ray. *A Philosophy of Audiovisual Archiving.* Paris: UNESCO, 1998.

The Film Restoration and Conservation Strategies Project (FIRST). *European Film Heritage on the Threshold of the Digital Era: The FIRST Project's Final Report.* Brussels, Belgium: Royal Film Archive (Curator Gabrielle Claes), 2004.

Grieveson, Lee, and Peter Krämer, eds. *The Silent Cinema Reader.* New York: Routledge, 2004.

Horak, Jan-Christopher. "Change and Nothing But Change." Review of *Change Mummified* by Philip Rosen. *Film-Philosophy* 7, no. 40 (November 2003). http://www.film-philosophy.com/vol7-2003/n40horak.

Keil, Charlie, and Shelley Stamp, eds. *American Cinema's Transitional Era: Audiences, Institutions, Practices.* Berkeley and Los Angeles: University of California Press, 2004.

Mannoni, Laurent, Donata Pesenti Campagnoni, and David Robinson, eds. *Light and Movement: Incunabula of the Motion Picture, 1420–1896.* Gemona, Italy: La Cineteca del Friuli/Le Giornate del Cinema Muto, 1995.

McGreevey, Tom, and Joanne L. Yeck. *Our Movie Heritage.* New Brunswick, NJ: Rutgers University Press, 1997.

Musser, Charles. *The Emergence of Cinema: The American Screen to 1907.* New York: Charles Scribner's Sons, 1990.

The National Film Preservation Foundation's Film Preservation Guide. http://www.filmpreservation.org/preservation/fpg.pdf.

Orbanz, Eva, Helen P. Harriso, and Henning Schou, eds. *Archiving the Audio-Visual Heritage: A Joint Technical Symposium, Federation Internationale des Archives de Television, International Association of Sound Archives.* Berlin, Germany: Stiftung Deutsche Kinematek, 1988.

Pearson, Roberta E. "Early Cinema." In *The Oxford History of World Cinema,* ed. Geoffrey Nowell-Smith, 13–23. Oxford: Oxford University Press, 1996.

Pudovkin, Vsevolod. *Film Technique and Film Acting: The Cinema Writings of V. I. Pudovkin.* Trans. Ivor Montagu. Intro. Lewis Jacobs. New York: Lear Publishers, 1949.

Read, Paul, and Mark-Paul Meyer, eds. *Restoration of Motion Picture Film.* Oxford: Butterworth-Heinemann, 2000.

Vachon, Christine, with David Edelstein. *Shooting to Kill: How an Independent Producer Blasts Through the Barriers to Make Movies that Matter.* New York: HarperCollins, 1998.

Wallis, Tom. "The Differences between Film and Digital Video." *In Camera* (July 2001). http://www.kodak.com/country/US/en/motion/news/wallis.shtml.

The Wide Blue Road. Press kit. Milestone Film and Video. http://www.milestonefilms.com/pdf/WideBlueRoadPresskit.pdf.

Zelf films Restaureren (Restore Films Yourself). CD-ROM. Amsterdam, Holland: Nederlands Filmmuseum, 2003.

INTERVIEWS AND CORRESPONDENCE

All the interviews were conducted in English, except the ones in Italy, which were conducted in Italian and for which I have provided the translations. All the correspondence was in English.

Allen, John. Head of Cinema Arts Laboratories. Telephone interview. September 2, 2004.

Belston, Schawn. Executive director of film preservation, Fox Studios. Telephone interview. September 9, 2004.

Bromberg, Serge. Co-owner of Lobster Films, France. Personal interview. July 9, 2004.

Dayton, Richard. President of YCM Laboratories. Telephone interview. September 13, 2004.

Desmet, Noël. Archivist and technician, Cinémathèque Royale of Belgium, and inventor of Desmet Color Restoration System. Personal interview. July 9, 2004.

Fonseca, Paulo de. Head of digital restoration, Haghefilm. E-mail to Gabriel M. Paletz. September 11, 2004.

Fossati, Giovanna. Conservator, Nederlands Filmmuseum. Personal interview. June 30, 2004.

———. E-mail to Gabriel M. Paletz. July 20, 2004.

Groschke, Annette. Scholar-archivist, Film Museum Berlin. Telephone interview. September 16, 2004.

Haghefilm managers and staff. Personal interviews. June 28–July 2, 2004.

Hunter, Chad. Preservation officer, Motion Picture Department, George Eastman House, Rochester, NY. Personal interview. September 5, 2003.

Kalas, Andrea. Senior preservation manager, National Film and Television Archive, England. Personal interview. August 12, 2004.

Lukow, Gregory. Chief of the Motion Picture, Broadcasting, and Recorded Sound Division, Library of Congress, United States. Telephone interview. May 10, 2005.

Marino, Valerio. Former director of the archive of the Luce Institute, Italy. Personal interview. July 20, 2004.

Meyer, Mark-Paul. Senior curator, Nederlands Filmmuseum. Personal interview. July 10, 2004.

Munroe, Tony. Co-owner of Triage Laboratories. Telephone interview. August 26, 2004.

Musumeci, Mario. Head of preservation, Italian National Film Archive. Personal interview. July 20, 2004.

de Oliveira, João Socrates. Former head of research and development, Conservation Centre, National Film and Television Archive. Currently director of Prestech Laboratories Ltd., England. Personal interview. July 27, 2004.

Olivier, Joseph. Head of special projects, Cinetech Labs. Telephone interview. August 30, 2004.

Prijs, Johann A. Film restoration consultant, head of Studio Cine Lab in Rome, and former director of Haghefilm. Personal interview. July 10, 2004.

———. E-mail to Gabriel M. Paletz. September 26, 2004.

Pritchard, Brian. Motion picture and archive consultant, British Film Institute. Personal interview. August 12, 2004.

Ruggiero, Paola. Director of foreign department, Cinecittà Holding. Personal interview. July 20, 2004.

Schiano, Giovanni. Manager, Preservation Unit, Film and Video Archive, Imperial War Museum, Duxford, England. E-mail to Gabriel M. Paletz. August 11, 2005.

Stratmann, Edward. Assistant Curator, George Eastman House. Telephone interview. July 22, 2005.

Tsuneishi, Fumiko. Assistant curator of film, Japanese National Film Center. Personal interview. July 6, 2004.

———. E-mails to Gabriel M. Paletz. August 12 and 19, 2004.

Wilkening, Anke. Archivist, Murnau-Stiftung, Germany. E-mail to Gabriel M. Paletz. July 20, 2004.

Wilkinson, Chip. Sales manager and technical consultant, Cineric Laboratories. Telephone interview. September 10, 2004.

CONTEXT! CONTEXT! CONTEXT!

ANDREA LEIGH

Describing Moving Images

at the Collection Level

INTRODUCTION

Branding resources as collections is not new; librarians and archivists have all considered the items within their custody to form groupings. However, the manner by which collections are most often described differs among the information professions. As Randall C. Jimerson summarizes, it is common for each information profession to develop its own procedures to collect, organize, manage, and make accessible its resource materials, often borrowing techniques from other fields.[1] Moving image archives are no exception. Traditionally, the choice in cataloging moving images has been at the item level, as description favors completed moving image works where titles and credits are transcribed from the film itself. This approach is borrowed from item level descriptive practices common in libraries. With the proliferation of digital content, increased publication and distribution of print and media material, as well as the shift in the way users access information, a reconceptualizing of this strict item level approach, considering the array of emerging standards within a variety of professional communities, is underway.

Chief among these standards is the Functional Requirements for Bibliographic Records (FRBR), a conceptual model spearheaded by the International Federation of Library Associations and Institutions (IFLA). FRBR's entity-relationship model suggests that catalogers relate items (or manifestations) to the expressions (versions) of the work that they represent so that materials that share the same ideational content will be grouped together regardless of physical format.[2]

An adherence to FRBR potentially can alleviate the frustration end users may have when selecting works that have proliferated into multiple versions and formats, an all-too-common occurrence with moving images.

Emerging standards specifically tailored to moving images include MPEG-7 and the ISO International Standard Audiovisual Number (ISAN).[3] The ISAN is a persistent work identifier in numeric form that can be embedded into a single exemplar of a digital moving image work so that its identification can be tracked irrespective of the means of access. MPEG-7 is an emerging standard that describes or expresses "the semantic meaning of the information and therefore enable[s] people to discover what is in a set of audiovisual objects without having to access the information itself."[4] The concept is that information exchange is semantically linked with reference to a single narrative's components, such as background, participants, and objects, that contextually make up a moving image. MPEG-7 describes audiovisual information regardless of its storage, coding display, transmission, medium, or technology, addressing the problem of proliferation of audiovisual and media formats in digital form.

What these and other emerging models and standards have in common is an awareness that works do not exist as islands alone at sea, that, in fact, works inspire new works that exist as distinct entities unto themselves but do not exist isolated from each other.

There is a greater recognition that, in today's rapidly evolving information environment, describing cultural objects based on format alone segregates a vast array of materials from the broader spectrum of the information landscape.

It is important to acknowledge that each cultural heritage community has its own traditions and vocabulary, that there exists no canonical metadata standard, and that each views its resources differently. As will be illustrated in this article, descriptive practices are shifting away from the isolated silo effect and moving toward a stronger preference for grouping together material containing the same provenance, subject matter, or ideational content with a goal of achieving greater interoperability. Two specific case studies will be presented from the UCLA Film & Television Archive's collections.

WHAT IS A COLLECTION?

Before providing methodologies for grouping moving image materials together, it is important to understand the different types of collections that exist. In the broadest sense, a collection is any aggregate of items. A library catalog is a collection of items held by a particular institution. An inventory is a collection in that it brings a grouping of individual items together either by provenance or subject matter.

A description of a collection may include information about the aggregate as a whole, the individual items that make up the collection, or information about some groupings of the items that form a subset of the whole.

To further break down these distinctions, the museum and visual resources community defines an archival *group* as an aggregate of items that share a common provenance, while a *collection* may comprise multiple items that are conceptually or physically arranged together for the purpose of cataloging and retrieval.[5]

Michael Heaney suggests that collection descriptions may be classified as belonging to a small number of types.[6] The principal distinction is between an *analytic* finding aid, consisting of information about the individual items, and a *unitary* finding aid, which describes the collection as a whole. A *hierarchic* finding aid provides information about both the whole and the items, including contextual information about the relationship of the items to the whole. In practice, as Heaney acknowledges, an analytic finding aid may contain structure that dictates that meaning is conveyed by the relationship between the descriptions of individual items.

Collection level descriptions serve both to provide superficial overviews for large bodies of otherwise uncataloged materials, as well as play an important role in reducing the quantity of material returned in an initial search query across multiple services. This design model is important in that users expect online catalogs to become a portal or gateway for the discovery of information. Instead of searching from one stand-alone database to another, users want to search from one location and be guided to a multiplicity of information resources that span across databases.

ARCHIVAL VERSUS BIBLIOGRAPHIC CONTROL

In addition to recognizing the different collection types, it is also important to recognize that both archival control and bibliographic control exploit recorded knowledge and focus on specific items that require organization and identification. The two methods are similar in that both describe physical and intellectual properties and attempt to anticipate user needs by providing a means of access. More to the point, both methods produce written descriptions allowing a user to find, identify, select, and obtain pertinent materials.

There are, however, significant distinguishing characteristics. Bibliographic materials are often publications or other media meant for public consumption, contain a chief source of information (usually a title page), copyright notice, statement of responsibility or statement of production, and are for the most part known items and works. Both fiction and nonfiction works are created to stand alone, to be read or viewed from beginning to end, each with a focus on a particular topic, genre, theme, person, place, or event.

Archival materials and manuscripts traditionally tend to be produced as a result of some activity and relate to functions rather than to a specific intellectual subject and do not arrive at the repository with the equivalent of a title page. Archival description is the process of analyzing, organizing, and recording details about the formal elements of groupings of materials or collection items to facilitate identification, management, and understanding.[7] Archival description is similar to bibliographic description, except that in the absence of a title page to serve as the chief source of information, archival description requires a significant amount of the content description to be supplied from the context of the materials being described. In essence, archival description is an iterative process, updated as materials are acquired and preservation treatments recorded.

Moving image archives collect known items and works both in the form of commercially distributed motion pictures and television programs as well as materials that come into a repository with little identification or organization, such as home movies, outtakes, trims, and the like.

Standards (if used at all) have been adapted chiefly from those used in libraries where commonalities exist between commercially published textual materials; that is, each physical format encapsulates a known work that contains a title screen, copyright notice, and statement of responsibility in the form of credits.

Since moving image archives have a historic precedent of collecting primarily completed works, when a known moving image work does enter into the archive with related noncommercial components—such as unedited production elements—the tendency may be to describe each component at the item level. With a myriad of acquisition types coming into a moving image archive, simply using one set of descriptive principles will ultimately limit access to types of material, so it is important to consider alternative methods for access. Besides the standard item level approach, an archival perspective incorporating the fundamental principles of provenance (origin of the source) should determine the organizational method when moving image materials are a result of an activity or function, since the relationships that exist between items convey meaning in addition to the content of the items themselves. Certain types of materials, such as home movies from an individual, outtakes derived from a major feature film, or a series of commercials are best described at the collection level, as researchers can better study individual items when each is examined as emerging from the larger context of the whole.[8]

Collection level description does not preclude item level cataloging at a later date. As Margaret F. Nichols suggests, a collection level description can stand in temporarily for item level records until an archive has the resources to create them, but even after those records have been created, it can continue to be a useful overview to them.[9] Collection level treatment is best employed to address situations where individual items tend to fall into lower priorities for access. This might include collections consisting of a large number of moving image materials that come from a single donor and were never distributed commercially. Describing this type of collection through provenance based description would free up the cataloger, who is often hindered by a lack of information to adequately describe these materials. By adopting a collection level approach, access may actually be increased, since the contextual information of the grouped items would not be lost, thereby increasing the collection's integrity, authenticity, and evidential value.[10]

IMPORTANCE OF THE WORK ENTITY

The UCLA Film & Television Archive began looking into the feasibility of describing a number of their acquisitions at the collection level when a significant source of motion picture marketing material entered the archive in 2002. These trailers and electronic press kits for major motion picture releases initially were described at the item level, but as the number of items increased into the thousands, it became apparent that continuing in this direction would prevent more frequently requested materials — most notably the archive's preserved titles — from entering the catalog in a timely fashion. In addition, the sheer volume of material meant the staff could not realistically view each instantiation, which meant that variations or differences in extent would be difficult to ascertain.[11]

Since available resources dictated that all that could be done with the electronic press kits and trailers was to create brief minimal level records consisting of title, date, and physical description taken from the can labels and video boxes, serious thought went into providing an overview of the collection materials that users could use to discover the collection first, then allow them to browse through a listing of available titles that would be linked to the record. Proceeding in this manner meant that a single search in the catalog by title would not be feasible.[12] However, this loss would be minimized through the creation of a contextual overview and a scope and content note of the collection materials in its entirety, thereby keeping the collection together rather than scattered throughout the catalog.

There was resistance to proceeding in this direction, as a significant weakness of traditional archival description is a lack of direction in the creation of access points for works.[13] Since the emphasis is on the creators or provenance of the materials, the focus on choice of access points is naturally on the persons or corporate entities responsible, even if the materials are primarily related to the creation of known works. A classic example is an author's collection of source material used during the course of writing a book. For example, at the UCLA Library Department of Special Collections, a manuscript collection containing drafts and other documents related to the writing of two of Ansel Adams's books, *Born Free and Equal* (1944) and *Sierra Nevada: The John Muir Trail* (1938), are simply described as "Papers" with Adams traced as the primary access point.

However, access points are lacking for the works that each of these sets of documents is related to, possibly under the assumption that a user would most likely come across these papers by way of the creator's name.

The problem with this methodology is that the creator alone does not identify the work.

Granted, archival description is not as tidy as bibliographic description, but when there exists a mechanism to gather works together, especially works of performance that are chiefly characterized by title, an alternative arrangement should be considered, even if it means physically breaking up the collection.

In the case of the Ansel Adams papers, one method of getting to the work entity would be to create subject added entries for the authorized form of the name-title references, since the papers are *about* two specific works. Name-title references have chiefly been utilized in traditional library catalogs as a mechanism to uniquely identify works.

Another example is the University of North Carolina at Chapel Hill's collection description for the records and production elements of Florentine Films. Florentine Films was founded in 1976 by documentary filmmaker Ken Burns and others. The archival collection came to the university in response to a request to acquire production materials related to Burns's seminal documentary *The Civil War* (1990) for the university's Southern Folklife Collection. The agreement reached was for Burns to deposit archival records and film footage not only for *The Civil War* but for all of the works produced by Florentine Films. This was a significant undertaking by a repository that did not have expertise in moving image preservation and access, so, predictably, all the collection materials were arranged and described as a single provenance based collection. From a moving image repository perspective, there are a number of issues with this approach that make this organizational model less than optimal. Not only does each production described contain its own documentation that is distinctly separate from materials created for another production, but the completed works contained within can stand on their own, as each is characterized by title, broadcast date, production credits, and so forth.

For preservation purposes, discrete items are more usefully described within the context of the *work* as a whole, as materials may be borrowed or donated to the archive for preservation or restoration by different and sometimes anonymous sources.

Within the structure of the finding aid where discrete items are often not described, these assembled materials would lose their context and provenance.

Archival institutions in general have in the past held on to the view that, since their institutions are small and collect unique material, standardized cataloging practices would be economically unfeasible. However, this viewpoint is being challenged as more archival institutions, particularly those that collect moving image materials, discover that their institutions do collect similar, if not duplicate, materials.

Lisa B. Weber notes that "the purpose of archival description and library cataloging is the same: to provide access to materials."[14] Even if library descriptive practices differ in form and content from those of archival practice, organizing principles could be adapted. In the case of moving image collections, Martha M. Yee argues that near-equivalents could be cataloged using one record if the only difference is in its physical format. Therefore, a video of *Gone with the Wind* containing the identical ideational content of the 35mm film could be attached to the same holding through the use of a hierarchically structured single record to show differences in physical format. And if, as Yee suggests, "all institutions were to decide to create new records only when [a] significant difference in either intellectual or artistic content or identification occurs, codification of this practice would help to standardize it."[15]

Another significant difference among archival institutions and libraries is that the former are oriented more toward the preservation of their collections than on how their collections are being used. Library catalogs use a system of a common language and authority control through a regulation of terminology used as access points in catalog records—by distinguishing terms, showing relationships, and documenting decisions. By using these data value standards, library catalogs prescribe to the concept of Cutter's famed objects: (1) enable users to locate a particular work by author or title, (2) locate all works of an author, (3) locate all the editions of a work, and (4) locate all works of a particular subject.

Although archival materials can be identified through the subject content and descriptive characteristics of the material, the question of authorship is not clearly defined.

Additional thought must be given to the concept of provenance — to improve access points to the corporate entity or entities that created the material.

By doing so, how users search a collection becomes a major consideration. Since the primary reason for collecting material is to provide description and access, understanding how an archival collection is used provides a basis for implementing standards so that it can be adequately accessed by those most likely to use it. A major criticism of Encoded Archival Description (EAD), which is a mark-up language used to deliver archival finding aids on the World Wide Web, is that user studies were not conducted before the standard was formalized.[16] As a result, researchers have difficulty navigating the hierarchical layers, since they do not necessarily understand the relationship between the creator and the materials.

REPRESENTING THE WORK

The importance of creators in traditional archival description must not be underestimated. As Daniel Pitti explains from a strictly archival perspective, the description of creators "is an essential component of the preservation of the documentary evidence of human activity. . . . Records, broadly speaking, encompass both the narrower archival definition, but also artifacts, whether created as by-products, or as intentional products. "'Anything made by human art and workmanship' is thus a record: books, articles, movies, sound recordings, paintings, sculptures, collections of natural objects, and so on."[17] This is an important concept to acknowledge when developing a structure for a collection of unidentified or ephemeral materials that are not known works.

Even though (generally speaking) works can be discovered through the use of creator access points, what is often overlooked in archival description is the predominance of a formal title in identifying works of performance. The archival community is currently developing a standard for creator description: Encoded Archival Context (EAC). EAC is intended to complement Encoded Archival Description (EAD) by allowing repositories to share costly creator descriptions, thereby minimizing duplication of effort. No provisions are being made for those institutions that place a strong reliance on title as the primary access point, which breaks from the one-to-one correspondence between the description and creator. It should be noted, however, that traditional library authority control, which is a methodology used to control headings, does not routinely identify works either. FRBRization of existing catalogs may remedy this situation, as it will be essential to create work identifiers to differentiate among expressions. Even with this recognition, as Martha Yee summarizes, "most of the FRBRizing projects so far have seemed determined to work with nothing but bibliographic records, with little recognition that it is the authority record that represents the work."[18]

Primarily due to this lack of collocation on the work entity, the UCLA Film & Television Archive subscribes to an analytic collection level approach inspired by the

FRBR conceptual model. FRBR is expected to be at the heart of an update of the *Anglo-American Cataloguing Rules* titled *Resource Description and Access*. Jennifer Bowen explains that the proposed new rules for constructing headings will be not only at the work level but at the expression level: "A cataloger would create an expression level heading by adding expression level attributes or other identifiers for the expression to a uniform title for a work."[19] Like multilevel description in more traditional document archives, this model is not *always* ideal for a moving image archive, where not all physical holdings may contain a title, as numerous holdings may be unedited materials or outtakes that were never distributed commercially. However, for completed moving image works containing title and credit screens, FRBR has much potential as an organizational principle. As Bowen explains, "Headings for expressions may be particularly useful when a library owns extensive materials in a specific area, especially when the collection contains many expressions of the same work or many manifestations of the same expression."[20] This same principle can be extended to moving image works where it is not uncommon that a single exemplar of a work be released in numerous versions (or expressions)—e.g., the original release version, the director's cut, the airline version, and so on—and exist as multiple manifestations—e.g., 35mm film, VHS, DVD, and so on. Logically the FRBR model fits snugly with the way that an archivist works with related resources within a collection. An example based on the FRBR conceptual model is the UCLA Film & Television Archive's record for the restored version of the first Technicolor two-color silent feature, *The Toll of the Sea* (1922).

AN ANALYTIC CASE STUDY: *THE TOLL OF THE SEA*

The Toll of the Sea was for many years considered lost, as no prints of the film survived. However, Technicolor Corporation, which produced the film to highlight the company's new two-color subtractive process, came across the rare original camera negative and placed it on deposit with the UCLA Film & Television Archive in 1985.

The two-color Technicolor subtractive process utilized a beam splitter prism that exposed two standard size frames simultaneously, one through a red filter and the other through a green filter. The film was advanced two frames at a time so that, at normal camera speed, twice as much film was used as was for black-and-white photography, resulting in the creation of a one-strip film.[21] The two corresponding frames were positioned toe to toe. Registration of the red and green elements was produced optically and controlled by an accurate positioning of the sprocket holes. Using a special printer, separate prints were made from the red and green filter negatives on relief print film half the thickness of ordinary motion picture positive film, then cemented together (emulsion side out) so that the prints could be projected conventionally. The side printed from the red filter negative was then dyed blue-green and the side printed from the green filter dyed red-orange. This system differed from the later Technicolor imbibition process in that matrices were used for direct screening rather than as a method for transferring the dyes onto a release print.

The principle employed in the subtractive color process was simple. If each negative recorded one part of the color spectrum and then was superimposed on the screen through its own corresponding filter, the original scene would be reproduced.[22] Subtraction from white light will yield primary colors—cyan, which is minus the red filter, combined with yellow (or minus blue) will produce green; and yellow, which is minus the blue filter combined with magenta (or minus green), will produce red. Although the two-color subtractive process had yet to incorporate the blue part of the spectrum, the two-color system was enough to re-create decent flesh tones and natural foliage.

According to Robert Gitt, who oversaw the restoration of *The Toll of the Sea* for the UCLA Film & Television Archive, the camera negative arrived shrunken, brittle, torn apart, and with many fragments placed inside a paper sack.[23] Considering the film's importance in the history of color motion picture processes, preservation of the extant elements began almost immediately. The negative was cleaned, repaired, and spliced together in its original order using Frances Marion's original scenario as a guide. The final sequence did not survive, but Gitt and partner Richard Dayton of YCM laboratories were able to restore the final titles from the continuity script on file at the Library of Congress.

In what is considered artistic ingenuity by some and a question of ethics by others, Gitt and Dayton took an authentic two-color Technicolor camera to a beach near Santa Barbara and re-shot the missing ending of waves crashing onto the shore as the sun went down. All that was omitted was the film's star, Anna Mae Wong, who was seen walking into the breaking waves to her demise in the lost original.

After the reconstruction was complete, the UCLA preservation staff made master positive separations of the red and green elements. A printing negative was then produced from the separation elements to preserve the integrity of the restored original camera negative of the first two-color Technicolor subtractive process feature and what is considered the last—the camera negative of the new ending.

Although a complex restoration, *The Toll of the Sea* was more straightforward than many, as it is more common for a restored film to be pieced together from an array of the best surviving print material from different generations.

Anna Mae Wong in *Toll of the Sea* (1923). Courtesy of UCLA Film & Television Archive.

It is rare that the original camera negative survives, as it is usually either destroyed beyond repair or missing entirely. Therefore print elements are begged, borrowed, or rescued from trash bins of collections all over the world.

If a film preservationist is fortunate, these print elements will have been struck directly from the original camera negative.

Up until the early 1970s, it was a general practice among studios to make prints from the original camera negative, "subjecting the best element to the harshest treatment in handling, exposure to contaminants and mechanical stress."[24] Today, the traditional practice is to reserve the original negative for the production of secondary printing elements. If prints become worn out, damaged, or destroyed, the original camera negative remains intact and can be referred to later to re-create the original achievement.

Despite the good fortune of possessing a nearly intact original camera negative, the reconstruction of *The Toll of the Sea* posed serious questions about how the restoration was accomplished. The re-shot ending notwithstanding, Gitt himself admits that if the archive were to do the restoration over again, it would be done more along the lines of the archive's later restoration of *Follow Thru* (1930). "With *The Toll of the Sea*, we didn't even do a wet gate to diminish the scratches," Gitt recalls.[25] For the Technicolor two-color reconstruction of *Follow Thru*, where an original camera negative also survived, the separation master positives achieved more accurate hues by printing the elements with color light optically before creating the Eastman color internegative. And to be fair, since no original Technicolor prints survive of *The Toll of the Sea*, and at least one does of *Follow Thru*, a more accurate depiction of color hues could be achieved for the latter using the original Technicolor print as a guide. With *The Toll of the Sea*, it was all guesswork.

Placing original print materials on Eastman color low-fade stock rather than on true Technicolor dye transfer prints can also be viewed as unfaithful to the original release version of the motion picture. However, the Technicolor dye transfer process was discontinued in the early 1970s. The Technicolor Corporation at that time switched to Eastman color to cut down on operating costs. In the case of restoring a dye transfer two-color Technicolor film, part of the complexity in re-creating the illusion of the original two-color process was coming up with a compromise, as the process that originally printed the materials no longer was available in the United States. Additionally, the original release prints of *The Toll of the Sea* were printed on a nitrate base, with the red and green strips cemented back to back. Although the cemented-together strips could be projected in a standard projector, the prints were thicker than a standard black-and-white print. As a consequence, the original two-color Technicolor prints tended to buckle, scratch, and require more frequent replacement. It should not be surprising, then, that no original prints of *The Toll of the Sea* survive; nor should it be a surprise, considering the inherent technical inadequacies of this early attempt at the dye transfer process, that Gitt and Dayton did not choose to re-create exactly the original Technicolor two-strip printing process.

In documenting the preservation elements for *The Toll of the Sea* in the catalog, one bibliographic record is created describing the work, including a local note outlining its preservation history, while each element used in the restoration process is attached in a separate holdings record. A hierarchically structured document is thus created that will allow users to know immediately what version of the film the archive contains, as well as determine what elements were used in the restoration. Each separate holdings record is then attached to the bibliographic record and includes:

- number of reels
- description of the element using standardized terminology
- footage count (real or estimated)

- notes on reproductions (i.e., element was "Reproduced from a 35 mm. safety dupe pic neg")

- the laboratory where the elements were reproduced

- donor or depositor information

- whether the element is silent, sound, in color, or black and white

- notes on any restrictions for accessing the material

What is missing in the record is evidential documentation used in the restoration process, such as Frances Marion's continuity script—material that is probably not held by the archive.

It is not the traditional approach in an item level catalog to guide users to another institution's resources, but that concept is being challenged as more and more electronic resources are added to library catalogs.

In addition, recent content standards, such as *Describing Archives: A Content Standard (DACS),* provide direction on including related materials in overall collection descriptions.[26] It is thereby advised that related materials used in the restoration be added as part of an overall preservation history note in the bibliographic record.

In most instances, what a moving image preservationist attempts to restore or reconstruct is the original achievement. It is important, therefore, to understand and document the history of the film at hand to know how many versions exist. There may be foreign release versions, director's cuts, airline versions, and television broadcast versions, in addition to the original studio release version. A film may have been deliberately cut for censorship purposes at some point in its history. Distributors or producers may have sought to second-guess the censor or to avoid a possible public outcry by making their own edits in a film before releasing it to a new audience. The film may be shortened or altered on release, or re-release, as a result of critics' reviews or the comments of preview audiences. The film may be incomplete through accidental loss or damage— or, in the case of early film, due to physical deterioration in the film stock. Material from a private collector may have suffered intentional damage, such as removing the main titles to conceal a film's identity, when its acquisition by that collector had not been legal. Films may have pieces cut from the original for resale or reuse in compilations. Film may be re-released in a different manifestation (such as a colorized version) to appeal to a new generation, and it may be edited, panned and scanned, or even lengthened or shortened to accommodate a television broadcast schedule.

To examine the multiple versions issue further, the reconstructed *The Toll of the Sea* produced a DVD version included as part of the National Film Preservation Foundation's *Treasures from American Film Archives* (2000). Although the visual content is identical to the reconstructed version, complete with the new ending, there is a vital difference. The DVD version contains a score orchestrated by composer Martin Marks, adapted from the extant published full score originally compiled by composer Ernst Luz for the film in 1922. This significant difference between the two versions should be noted. Marks's new score, although reminiscent of the original, is by his own admission "my improvisatory liberties."[27] Differences in sound are important and often overlooked, but they should be documented, since how an audience experiences the film with a particular soundtrack can influence an audience's reaction to the film. In the case of silent films, especially, it was common that music and sound effects were added to or altered in later releases, and various performances of the same original score by different composers were added to a new soundtrack, as was the case with the DVD release of *The Toll of the Sea*.

THE COLLABORATIVE PRINCIPLE

Although it became evident at the UCLA Film & Television Archive that the primary access point for a collection of home movies, commercials, promotional, industrial, or educational materials could usefully be described based on provenance, that was not necessarily apparent for a collection of unedited materials from a particular film or television program. As David Miller and Patrick Le Boeuf elegantly point out in their analysis of works of performance, "the collaborative principle is so strongly assumed . . . that main entry under title is mandated even where a film is arguably the work of a single person."[28] Therefore, it can be surmised that a provenance based main entry or primary access point for a collection of unedited materials related to a commercially distributed motion picture or television program would be a poor choice.

Since the collaborative nature of creating a motion picture is so ingrained, singling out one individual or corporate entity to gather all materials together does not serve the end user well.

It was therefore decided that, for optimal access, production elements related to a single motion picture or television program would be described with title as the primary access point, with creators described as added entries. This flies in the face of traditional multi-

It's All True (1941). "Herois do Mar," D. I. P. Newsreel. Courtesy Cinemateca Brasileira, São Paulo, Brazil.

level archival description but suits the archive's needs better as a repository for preserving moving images, where titles often are more prevalent than creators of works.[29] To further illustrate this concept, Orson Welles's unfinished film, *It's All True* (1942) will be examined.

HIERARCHIC COLLECTION LEVEL CASE STUDY: *IT'S ALL TRUE*

In 1942, Orson Welles traveled to Rio de Janeiro to make what was initially envisioned as a four-part anthology, *It's All True,* for RKO Radio Pictures. The film was never completed or released and its aftermath is often cited as destroying Welles's credibility as a commercial filmmaker.

As part of this complex story goes, soon after Pearl Harbor, Nelson Rockefeller, working for the State Department and a major shareholder in RKO, recruited Welles as a special ambassador to South America with the purpose of making a film designed to improve pan-American cultural relations. Since Welles wished to take on a more active role in the war effort, he was willing to take on the challenge by reenvisioning a film he had already started titled *It's All True.* To do so, he would bring in a South American flair by eliminating an episode of the film centered around the origins of jazz. Instead, he would focus one of the stories on Carnaval and the origins of samba. Besides incorporating the episode already in production, "My Friend Bonito" (based on a story by Robert Flaherty), the final component would revolve around the true story of the *jangadeiros,* fishermen who sailed over a thousand miles on makeshift rafts to petition the president of Brazil for improvements in their working conditions. Welles came upon the true story while reading a magazine on his flight down to Rio.

Welles arrived in Rio in time to film Carnaval, but when word got back to RKO that the director was shooting footage in the shantytowns that cling to the hills around the city, executives at RKO became nervous.

Rumors of Welles's artistic license grew to mythic proportions, minimizing Welles's intent to link the music emanating from the surrounding hillsides as the preprint for the colorful and lively music of Carnaval. RKO executives, not particularly tolerant of the subtleties of other cultures, were unable to grasp the significance, especially since they had expected a sort of lighthearted Dolores Del Rio musical extravaganza.

Worse still, other complications mounted, particularly as Welles was filming the story of the *jangadeiros.* Tragically, one of the fishermen accidentally drowned during production. RKO's response was to pull the plug. Welles stayed behind with a skeleton crew in spite of the setback and finished shooting the story in honor of the local fisherman who had given his life to document the *jangadeiros'* remarkable achievement.

Welles commented on the debacle of *It's All True* to a *New York Times* reporter in 1963:

> I was to shoot, among other things, a giant Technicolor documentary on the carnival in Rio. No script, no story line, and a budget of a million dollars. A mammoth Hollywood crew and tons of equipment were shipped to Brazil and we started in recording the carnival, and documenting the samba. The material was interesting. But back in Hollywood . . . the film we were sending them looked fairly mysterious. No stars. No actors even. "Just a lot of colored people," to quote one studio executive, "playing their drums and jumping up and down in the streets." Meanwhile there'd been a great shake-up at RKO: Rockefeller's men were out. The idea was to make a case against the old administration, and my million-dollar caper in Rio, without a shooting script, made a perfect target. I never really lived that down.[30]

Welles never intended to abandon *It's All True.* He was forced to return the footage to RKO in 1945–46 when he was unable to complete payment for the rights. After this juncture, he lost contact with the project. RKO then classified the production elements as stock footage and repurposed some of the color footage from "Carnaval" in feature productions.

Fast forward to 1985, when a Paramount executive discovered an amazing cache of negative rolls from *It's All True* in a vault at the studio. Richard Wilson, who was Welles's associate in Rio, took this opportunity to finish the episode re-creating the heroic journey of the *jangadeiros* titled "Four Men on a Raft," which had been completely shot.

Before the find in Paramount's vaults, an RKO inventory from November 1952 (considered to be the last inventory taken of the footage before the Paramount discovery) indicated that the studio retained twenty-one reels (16,793 feet) of nitrate positive and corresponding negative from "My Friend Bonito," fifteen reels (13,978 feet) of positive nitrate and corresponding black-and-white negative from "Four Men on a Raft," plus the existence of seven reels of black-and-white positive footage (approximately 6,500 feet) printed from Technicolor negative, one reel (5,481 feet) of Technicolor positive, and some 200,000 feet of unprinted Technicolor negative, along with 50,000 feet of music sound negative from "Carnaval."

In 1958, Desilu acquired RKO, and a few years later, Paramount took over all of Desilu's stored footage. During Paramount's custody, thousands of feet of the Technicolor footage were dumped into the Pacific Ocean, while the remainder was placed in vaults at Paramount. The whereabouts of the sound negative, apparently containing original recordings of Rio's top musical talent, remains a mystery.

When the extant footage was discovered, arrangements were made to donate it to the American Film Institute, which then arranged to store the footage at the UCLA Film & Television Archive. Money was raised to prepare the "Four Men and a Raft" episode for the festival circuit, as a method to raise money for preserving the remaining footage. In the early 1990s, the surviving rushes of *It's All True* were gathered by Wilson and film critics Myron Meisel and Bill Krohn, who edited the material and created a documentary, which was released in 1993.

Although Welles did not live to see his unfinished film, he did know that the extant footage had been recovered. His reaction, according to the Paramount executive who discovered the footage, was that the production had been cursed, so he had no interest in seeing it resurrected.[31]

The curse seems to still be in place, as organization of the material presents a significant archival challenge. Since the film was never completed, and a script never written, it is impossible to re-create Welles's intentions. Initially the rushes that were edited into the documentary were described by the UCLA Film & Television Archive at the item level, causing a search on *It's All True* to bring up hundreds of records that are virtually indistinguishable from one another. To complicate matters, after the records had been entered, further preservation work on the rushes was done, which so re-arranged the described elements that the inventory records that had been entered into the catalog immediately became obsolete. This is a perfect example of why bibliographic description, which relies on transcription from a chief source, is not always the best methodology to describe certain categories of moving image materials.

Catherine Benamou, a professor at the University of Michigan and a film scholar committed to seeing that all the production elements for *It's All True* are preserved, estimates that the UCLA Film & Television Archive contains fifty-two cans (approximately 75,145 feet) containing production elements for "My Friend Bonito," of which 7,000 feet have been preserved on safety positive. The extant footage of "Carnaval" consists of twenty-six cans (approximately 35,530 feet), of which 3,330 feet have been preserved. Of the Technicolor footage, only about 5,481 feet remain; of this color footage, approximately 2,750 feet of safety color interpositives were processed for use in the 1993 documentary. All of the Technicolor footage remains in vaults at Paramount. The remaining footage from "Four Men on a Raft" consists of fifty-two cans (63,950 feet), of which approximately 15,450 feet has been preserved. Color footage shot for this episode is likely included among the "Carnaval" footage located at Paramount.

Clearly the project's incompleteness and transfers of ownership, along with the fact that the few who physically handled the production materials over the years did not have enough familiarity with the scope of the project to accurately identify and arrange the footage, all add to the present challenge of adequately organizing the material. Following on the initiative of Richard Wilson, who carefully identified most of the footage that has been preserved to date, Benamou is committed to identifying and grouping the remaining footage by scene, episode, and shooting location, based on a close viewing of the nitrate, checked against her knowledge of shooting locations, surviving script materials, correspondence, and testimony of the film's surviving participants.

As the process of sorting out the materials continues, it is important to understand the underlying collaboration that organizing the extant footage requires. Collection level arrangement and description cannot be adequately accomplished in isolation.

Organization at the collection level often makes it necessary that scholars work alongside preservationists, archivists, and catalogers, with the realization that the record may change over time due to ongoing preservation activities, additional analysis, and other circumstances.

By the time Benamou sat down with a cataloger, the decision to abandon further item level control had already been made, through consultation with those who work closely with the materials and knew its context. The idea behind this decision was as much a practical one (so that if the rushes were again re-arranged, the preservationist could note what had been done on the inventory without disrupting the integrity of the catalog) as it was one to preserve the historical context and evidential value of the footage that remained.

In essence, a collection level description was created for each episode of *It's All True,* chiefly because each of the three parts had different casts and crews. The archive based these descriptions chiefly following the guidelines in *DACS* and supplemented by appendix C of *Archival Moving Image Materials,* second edition *(AMIM2),* so in the future, a direct search in the archive's catalog on the title *It's All True* will bring up fewer records.

The collection description is composed of these primary components:

- title of the work in its established, authoritative form followed by a form identifier

- part designation for each episode[32]

- date of production or release

- historical overview of the production

- scope and content of the collection

- topic/genre headings

- access points for the primary creators

Besides the prevalence on title, this form of access is preferred since (generally speaking) the source of the materials may be questionable (some elements could have been retrieved from a dumpster by a collector) or they may have come from multiple sources. Due to the collaborative nature of works of performance, it would also be confusing to organize a collection of unedited materials related to a single motion picture or television program that wasn't based on title,[33] since no matter which creator is chosen, according to traditional archival arrangement and description, that creator would then be the subject of the biographical/historical overview.[34] Since these production elements are the extant records of a motion picture *work,* it would be more appropriate to provide a contextual analysis emphasizing the history of the unfinished production.

As Catherine Benamou suggests, *It's All True* is beneficial for a variety of research purposes.[35] The project greatly contributes to film history since the extant footage portrays inter-American relations and social realities distinct from those in the work of Walt Disney and other "Good Neighbor" directors and producers. Portions of the project anticipate Italian neorealism and Brazilian *cinema nôve* in style and strategy. Individual shots and scenes record Welles's approach to shot composition, choreography, and visual narration. Beyond the importance of *It's All True* in the Welles's oeuvre, the fact that most scenes were shot on location means that they are a record of places, people, and popular cultural practices linked to specific locations in Mexico and Brazil. Therefore, providing a contextual analysis becomes vital if the footage is to serve as a historical record.

CONCLUSION

Although *The Toll of the Sea* is cataloged based on the traditional item level approach pioneered in libraries, the decision to link each manifestation to a corresponding expression level record can be referred to as an analytic grouping of materials. In this analytic approach, the bibliographic record becomes part of an overall structure that conveys meaning as to the relationship between the whole and its corresponding items.

Other forms of collection level description can be incorporated to convey different relationships, but, like the analytic approach that has become the focus of descriptive practice at the UCLA Film & Television Archive, traditional groupings more common in the descriptive practices of document archives are underused.[36] As Howard Besser suggests,

"Archivists need to shift from a paradigm centered around saving a completed work to a new paradigm of saving a wide body of material that contextualizes a work."[37]

Besser further emphasizes that "the [World Wide] Web and enhanced DVDs have created a world where all kinds of ancillary materials have become important parts of an enhanced production, and where viewers want to see small fragments of a work almost as much as they want to see a work in its entirety."[38] And as burgeoning materials form collections that merge text, audio, and image, the digital aggregate encapsulating the items increasingly becomes the authentic record.

Since the advent of digital libraries has focused on aggregates of material, moving image archives can use collection level description for a variety of purposes:

- to provide an overview of groupings of otherwise uncataloged items

- to allow researchers to discover the existence of a collection first and then to target their queries to selected items

- to support controlled searching across multiple collections and to assist users by reducing the number of individual hits returned to an initial query

- to support cross-domain resource discovery, since researchers want to discover and access resources drawn from across the collections of diverse institutions

Description at the aggregate level is a fundamental part of traditional archival descriptive practice. The traditional archival community has well-established national and international standards for collection level description, where hierarchical description often stops at the level of individual items, particularly where there are multiple instances of the same type of item. This could be a problem for moving image archives with a preservation mission, since they depend on discovering the best available source material of specific film elements for a restoration project. If that source material is not adequately identified, it may be overlooked.

Collection level description offers significant advantages over item level description in certain circumstances. Cataloging backlogs can build up, because there are not the resources for describing everything at the item level. Even if holdings are fully cataloged at the item level, there may be dissatisfaction with the results, as researchers may be interested in locating unknown or untitled moving image material contextually. This is particularly true with aggregates of home movies from a particular family or individual, outtakes from a particular film, or even unidentified or poorly described episodes from a specific television program.

Archivists describing collections of manuscripts or other unique materials have used collection level description for decades. Catalogers in moving image repositories such as the Library of Congress use collection level description to link to aggregates of online moving image surrogates or for groupings of commercials or home movies. Collection level description under these circumstances is a promising means of providing access to large collections of materials, especially those that are anonymous or ephemeral in nature.

Cataloging materials at the collection level does not mean settling for low standards of description. Rather, it is a way to provide access to a range of materials in cases where the title of a work is less important than both the content and context of its creation, which conveys to users its impartiality and authenticity as evidence. Moreover, it addresses the fundamental shift in the perspective and methods researchers bring to their studies as popular culture receives more attention as a means to gaining insight into the social and political context of historical events.

APPENDIX

Key to Primary Standards Used

Data Content Standards: *Anglo-American Cataloguing Rules,* 2d ed., rev. *(AACR2R); Archival Moving Image Materials,* 2d ed. *(AMIM2); Describing Archives: A Content Standard (DACS)*

Data Value Standards: Library of Congress Subject Headings (LCSH); Library of Congress Authorities (http://authorities.loc.gov)

Data Structure Standards: UCLA Film and Television Archive uses the MARC21 bibliographic and holdings formats (http://www.loc.gov/marc/), but, for the purposes of illustrating ideational content, the MARC21 tagging is omitted in each example, as it is recognized that other repositories may have adopted their own local standard or another structural standard such as Encoded Archival Description.

Figure 1. Analytic collection level record for *The Toll of the Sea* (1922)

Standards used: *AACR2R, AMIM2, LCSH,* Library of Congress Authorities

Title/description: Toll of the sea / Technicolor Motion Picture Co. ; director, Chester Franklin ; story, Frances Marion.

Release date: 1922.

Version: UCLA reconstruction, including one scene reshot by UCLA Film and Television Archive staff at end of film based on Frances Marion's original scenario.

Cast: Anna May Wong (Lotus Flower); Kenneth Harlan (Allen Carver); Beatrice Bentley (Barbara Carver); Baby Marion (Little Allen); Etta Lee, Ming Young (gossips).

Credits: Director of photographer, J.A. Ball.

Summary: Lotus Flower rescues an American man washed up on the seashore. They fall in love and marry, but he returns to the United States without her, while she bears his son. When he returns, he is accompanied by his American wife.

Local Note: PRESERVATION HISTORY: Preserved at the UCLA Film & Television Archive. Preserved from the original 35 mm. nitrate two-color Technicolor camera negative. Final sequence missing from the original camera negative re-shot by UCLA staff using a 2-color Technicolor camera. Master positive separations were created from the camera negative. Then red and green printing negatives on Eastman color low-fade stock were created from the master positive separations.

Topic/genre heading: Runaway husbands—China—Drama.

Topic/genre heading: Single mothers—China—Drama.

Topic/genre heading: Miscegenation—Drama.

Topic/genre heading: Features.

Topic/genre heading: Silent films.

Topic/genre heading: UCLA preservation.

Credits heading: Franklin, Chester M., 1890–1954. direction

Credits heading: Marion, Frances, 1888–1973. writing

Credits heading: Wong, Anna May, 1905–1961. cast

Identifiers: Physical elements:*

1. M31841 10 reels of 11 (ca. 10,000 ft.) : si., 2-col. Technicolor ; 35 mm. nitrate SEN orig pic neg.

2. M32337 2 reels of 3 (r1-2) (ca. 4000 ft.) : EC (col.), low-fade ; 35 mm. safety prsv dupe pic neg.

3. XFE4738 1 reel of 1 (ca. 150 ft.) : EC (col.), low-fade ; 35 mm. prsv pic neg. PART/ELEMENT: Credit logo and introduction titles created at Title House.

4. XFE547 1 reel of 1 (ca. 400 ft.) ; 35 mm. safety prsv pic neg. PART/ELEMENT: Red and green printing neg for new ending, 1985. NOTES: 2 rolls in 1 can.

5. XFE77 -80 4 reels of 4 (ca. 4000 ft.) : green ; 35 mm. safety prsv pic masterpos.

6. XFE81 -84 4 reels of 4 (ca. 2000 ft.) : red ; 35 mm. safety prsv pic masterpos.

*Partial list of physical elements used in the restoration.

Figure 2. Top-level description for each episode of *It's All True* (1942)*

Standards used: *DACS, AMIM2* Appendix C, *LCSH,* Library of Congress Authorities.

NOTE: Brackets [ ] indicate that the formal title and credits are supplied, rather than transcribed directly from the chief source.

Title/description:	[It's all true (Motion picture) — rushes. Episode 1, My friend Bonito] / [Mercury Productions for RKO Radio Pictures, Inc. ; director and producer, Orson Welles ; codirector (location), Norman Foster ; screenplay, John Fante and Norman Foster ; associate producer, Jesús "Chucho" Solorzano].
Production date(s):	1941–1942.
Extent:	approximately 75,145 feet of film.
Source:	Episode based on a short story by Robert Flaherty.
History:	My friend Bonito was originally part of a four-part film based on real-life stories set in North America. After Orson Welles's appointment as goodwill ambassador to Latin America in early 1942, the episode became part of a four-part semidocumentary dedicated to the improvement of inter-American relations. Jesús "Chucho" Solorzano was chosen as lead bullfighter for the episode in the summer of 1941, John Fante and Norman Foster wrote the screenplay, and roughly two-thirds of the episode was shot on location in Mexico under the codirection of Norman Foster and Orson Welles between late September and mid-December of 1941. Production headquarters and lodging for the cast and crew were at the Hotel Francis in Aguascalientes and at the Hotel Ritz in Mexico City. Filmed in various locations in Mexico between September 25, 1941, and December 18, 1941. Scenes of the bull and boy at play and tientas (or bull tests) shot in Jalisco near Aguascalientes. Scenes of the blessing of the animals and cow tientas shot in Tlaxcala. Scenes shot at Atenco Ranch in Mexico State during November 1941. Attempts to shoot birth of a bull scenes shot at Maximino Avila Camacho's ranch. Bull-fighting scenes shot at Guadalajara and at Plaza el Toreo in Mexico City. Cast includes Jesús "Hamlet" Vasquez Plato (Chico); Domingo Soler (Miguel, the caporal); Carols

Villarias (Don Luis, the hacienda owner); Jesús "Chucho" Solorzano (first matador); Silverio Perez (second matador); Fermin "Amillita" Espinosa (third matador); Conchita Cintron (matador, rejoneaddora); Ramon Macias (bullhand); Pedro Chavez (bullhand). Welles planned to finish shooting for the episode after his return from South America in August 1942 and continued to make plans to complete it until 1946, but abandoned the project when he was unable to secure the backing of a major studio.

Scope and content: Scenes of bull raising, branding and bullfighting as well as a religious ritual. Consists of approximately 75,145 feet of black-and-white nitrate film rolls in 52 cans, of which 7,000 feet has been preserved on safety positive film.

Topic/genre heading: Hacienda de Atenco (Mexico).

Topic/genre heading: It's all true (Motion picture).

Topic/genre heading: Bullfighters—Mexico.

Topic/genre heading: Bull rings—Mexico.

Topic/genre heading: Jalisco (Mexico).

Topic/genre heading: Tlaxcala de Xicohténcatl (Mexico).

Topic/genre heading: Mexico City (Mexico).

Topic/genre heading: Guadalajara (Mexico).

Topic/genre heading: Unedited footage.

Credits heading: Welles, Orson, 1915–. direction, production

Credits heading: Foster, Norman, 1900–1976. direction, writing

Credits heading: Fante, John, 1909–. writing

Alternative title/description: My friend Bonito.

Title/description: [It's all true (Motion picture)—rushes. Episode 2, Carnaval, or, The story of samba] / [Mercury Productions for RKO Radio Pictures, Inc., with the collaboration of Cinédia Studios, Inc., Rio de Janeiro ; director, producer, screenwriter, Orson Welles ; executive assistant and associate producer, Richard Wilson ; screenwriter, Robert Meltzer].

Production date(s): 1942.

Extent: approximately 41,011 feet of film.

History: In December 1941, Orson Welles was asked by John Hay Whitney of the Office of the Coordinator of Inter-American

Affairs to serve as goodwill ambassador to Latin America. Part of Welles's duties were to include the filming of Rio Carnaval at the request of the Brazilian Department of Press and Propaganda. As a result, "My friend Bonito" was suspended, director Norman Foster recalled to Hollywood to direct Journey into fear and the finishing touches were put on shooting for The magnificent Ambersons, all in time for Welles and a twenty-seven-member RKO/Mercury crew to begin shooting Carnaval in early February 1942. After documenting the festivities in both Technicolor and black and white, laboratory tests were done of the Technicolor footage in Argentina. Given the positive results, the black-and-white crew was assigned to shooting locations around Rio and the Easter festivities in Ouro Preto, in the nearby state of Minas Gerais. The Technicolor crew was assigned to shooting fictional re-enactments of musical actitivies associated with Carnaval preparations and celebrations at the local Cinédia Studios, starring Sebastião Bernardes de Souza Prata ("Grande Othelo") and Pery Ribeiro, son of samba star, Dalva de Olveira and composer Herivelto Martins, who assisted Welles with choreography and set design. In the meantime, preparations were made to begin shooting the arrival of the jangadeiros in Rio de Janeiro in both Technicolor and black and white. Following the "accidental" death of jangadeiro leader, Jacaré, in mid-May 1942, Welles's production budget was severely cut, and after the shooting of the Orca Cassino scenes the first week of June, most of the RKO/Mercury crew was sent back to Hollywood. Very little of the Technicolor footage was printed, and most of both the Technicolor and the black-and-white footage remains in nitrate form. Some shots of the fictional material were used by RKO in films in the mid- to late 1940s. Although nearly all of the black-and-white footage has survived, vast amounts of Technicolor footage were disposed of by Paramount / Gulf + Western after its acquisition from Desilu

Studios of It's all true as part of the RKO library in 1967. According to the November 1952 inventory at RKO, 7 reels or 6,500 feet of black and white positive footage exists printed from Technicolor negatives, 1 reel or 5,481 feet of Technicolor positive and 200,000 feet of Technicolor negative, along with 50,000 feet of music sound negative, which possibly contains the Rio Technicolor scenes from Jangadeiros.

Scope and content: Documentary footage of people celebrating Carnaval in the streets and nightclubs of Rio de Janeiro, along with re-enacted scenes of samba practice and performance filmed at Cinédia Studios. Featured songs include Ave Maria no morro, Batuque no morro, Carinhoso, Escravos de jó, Lamento negro, Lero-lero, Nega do cabelo duro, Nós os carecas, Nós os cabeleiros, Panamérica e folgo nego, Praça onze, Saudades da Amélia, Se alguém disse, Um a zero. Consists of approximately 35,530 feet of black-and-white nitrate negative film rolls in 26 cans, of which 3,330 feet have been preserved. Of the Technicolor footage, approximately 5,481 feet remain, which is most likely the nitrate positive film referred in the 1952 RKO inventory.

Topic/genre heading: It's all true (Motion picture).

Topic/genre heading: Sambas.

Topic/genre heading: Carnival—Brazil—Rio de Janeiro.

Topic/genre heading: Unedited footage.

Credits heading: Welles, Orson, 1915– direction, production

Alternative title/description: Carnaval.

Alternative title/description: Carnival.

Alternative title/description: Story of samba.

Title/description: [It's all true (Motion picture)—rushes. Episode 3, Jangadeiros, or, Four men on a raft] / [Mercury Productions for RKO Radio Pictures, Inc., with the collaboration of Cinédia Studios, Inc., Rio de Janeiro ; director and chief writer, Orson Welles ; associate producer, Richard Wilson].

Production date(s): 1942.

Extent: approximately 63,950 feet of film.

History: While flying to Rio in February 1942, Orson Welles read about the heroic voyage of four jangadeiros on a raft to Rio de Janeiro in the fall of 1941. He was intrigued both by the jangadeiros' courage and initiative and by the implications of this voyage for the future of Brazilian democracy. An admirer of Robert Flaherty, Welles also saw the opportunity to experiment with ethnographic documentary. After documenting Carnaval in February 1942, and meeting the jangadeiro leader Manoel "Jacaré" Olimpio in Rio, Welles traveled to Jacaré's native city of Fortaleza in the state of Ceará, Brazil, to scout locations with screenwriter Robert Meltzer and cameraman Eddie Pyle. Originally intending to shoot the entire episode in Technicolor, Welles was limited by RKO to shooting only the jangadeiros' arrival in Rio de Janeiro in Technicolor, while all of the re-enacted and documentary scenes shot in the northeast (Fortaleza, Recife, Itapóa, and Salvador) between mid-June and late July 1942 had to be shot in black and white using a skeleton crew. The three surviving jangadeiros starred in the episode, along with the deceased Jacaré's brother, João "Jacaré" Olimpio Meira, Jeronimo's nephew, José Sobrinho, and a young fisherman's daughter, Francisca Moreira da Silva. A love story between Sobrinho and Francisca was created to replace the planned dialogue with Jacaré and to provide the pretext for documenting scenes of daily life in the jangadeiro community. All of the essential scenes were shot and the footage sent back to Hollywood in late July, where some of it was processed and printed. A rough assemblage of a small portion of the footage survives and Welles reported to the primary cinematographer, George Fanto, that he was pleased with the footage. However, its whereabouts remained unknown until a Paramount executive, Fred Chandler, located the black-and-white elements in a Paramount vault in 1980. The footage to this episode forms the focus of the short preliminary documentary directed by Richard Wilson titled "Four men on a raft," as well as the film, It's all true: based on a unfinished film by Orson Welles, directed by Richard Wilson, Myron Meisel, and Bill Krohn, produced by Les films Balenciaga, and distributed by Paramount Pictures in 1993. Shot on location in Rio de Janeiro, Brazil mid-March to late May 1942 and in the Northeastern region of Brazil mid-June to July 24, 1942. According to the November 1952 RKO inventory, 15 reels or 13,978 feet of positive nitrate and corresponding black-and-white negative exists.

Scope and content: Black-and-white and Technicolor footage featuring the reenactment of the heroic voyage of four raftsmen (or jangadeiros) to Rio de Janeiro to petition the Brazilian president, Getulio Vargas, for inclusion in his new social security legislation, along with documentary scenes of everyday life in the Mucuripe fishing community on the northeast coast of Brazil. Consists of approximately 52 cans or 63,950 feet of black-and-white nitrate negative film rolls, of which approximately 15,450 feet have been preserved. Color footage shot for this episode is probably included in the Carnaval section.

Topic/genre heading: It's all true (Motion picture).

Topic/genre heading: Fishers—Brazil—Social life and customs.

Topic/genre heading: Unedited footage.

Credits heading: Welles, Orson, 1915–. direction, production

Alternative title/description: Jangadeiros.

Alternative title/description: Four men on a raft.

*Each record would link to an inventory list of individual items.

NOTES

My sincere gratitude to Robert Gitt, Ross Lipman, and Catherine Benamou for sharing their insights and expertise.

1. Randall C. Jimerson, "Archival Description and Finding Aids," *OCLC Systems & Services* 18, no. 3 (2002): 125–29.

2. The final report of IFLA's *Functional Requirements for Bibliographic Records* (K. G. München: Saur, 1998) is available at http://www.ifla.org/VII/s13/frbr/frbr.htm.

3. To learn more about MPEG-7, refer to the overview available at http://www.chiariglione.org/mpeg/standards/mpe-7/mpeg-7.htm. For an overview of the ISAN, visit the ISO ISAN Web site at http://www.isan.org.

4. Leonardo Chiariglione, "Introduction" in *Introduction to MPEG-7: Multimedia Content Description Interface,* ed. B. S. Manjunath, Philippe Salembier, Thomas Sikora (New York: Wiley, 2002), 4.

5. *Cataloguing Cultural Objects: A Guide to Describing Cultural Works and Their Images* (February 28, 2005, draft), 14. http://www.vraweb.org/CCOweb/.

6. Michael Heaney, *An Analytical Model of Collections and Their Catalogues,* 3d ed., rev. (January 2000). UKOLN/OCLC. http://www.ukoln.ac.uk/metadata/rslp/model.

7. See definition for archival description in Richard Pearce-Moses, *A Glossary of Archival and Records Terminology* (Chicago: Society of American Archivists, 2005), 25.

8. Refer to the appendix on collection level cataloging in the Library of Congress, Motion Picture, Broadcasting, and Recorded Sound Division. AMIM Revision Committee, *Archival Moving Image Materials: A Cataloging Manual,* 2d ed. *(AMIM2)* (Washington, DC: Library of Congress, Cataloging Distribution Service, 2000).

9. Margaret F. Nichols, "Finding the Forest among the Trees: The Potential of Collection Level Cataloging," *Cataloging and Classification Quarterly* 23, no. 1 (1996): 65.

10. For a discussion of archival values, refer to L. J. Smart, "OAIS, METS, MPEG-21, and Archival Values," *The Moving Image* 2, no. 1 (Spring 2002): 107–29.

11. Marketing material for a single motion picture could contain more than one version of a theatrical trailer, a TV spot, and a teaser, in addition to an electronic press kit.

12. Although it should be noted that works associated with a titled work are always supplied by attaching a form identifier to the title proper. See *AMIM2,* 1F1.1.

13. *Describing Archives: A Content Standard (DACS)* (Chicago: Society of American Archivists, 2004) makes the distinction between supplied and formal titles and refers to the rules for transcribing formal titles to the appropriate chapters in *AACR2R* (see *DACS* 2.3) but lacks direction in the creation of uniform titles or work identifiers.

14. Lisa B. Weber, "Archival Descriptive Standards: Concepts, Principles, and Methodologies." *American Archivist* 52 (Fall 1989): 44.

15. Martha M. Yee, "Manifestations and Near-Equivalents of Moving Image Works: Theory, with Special Attention to Moving-Image Materials," *Library Resources and Technical Services* 38, no. 3 (1994): 252.

16. Articles that examine the difficulty of EAD as a standard for resource discovery and interoperability include Elizabeth J. Shaw, "Rethinking EAD: Balancing Flexibility and Interoperability," *The New Review of Information Networking* (2001): 117–31; Kristi Keisling, "Metadata, Metadata, Everywhere—But Where Is the Hook?" *OCLC Systems & Services* 17, no. 2 (2001): 84–88; Christopher J. Prom, "Does EAD Play Well with Other Metadata

Standards? Searching and Retrieving EAD Using OAI Protocols," *Journal of Archival Organization* 1, no. 3 (2002): 51–72; Matthew Young Eidson, "Describing Anything That Walks: The Problem behind the Problem of EAD," *Journal of Archival Organization* 1, no. 4 (2002): 5–28; Jihyun Kim, "EAD Encoding and Display: A Content Analysis," *Journal of Archival Organization* 2, no. 3 (2004): 41–55; and Christina J. Hostetter, "Online Finding Aids: Are They Practical?" *Journal of Archival Organization* 2, no. 1/2 (2004): 117–43.

17. Daniel Pitti, "Creator Description: Encoded Archival Context," *ICBC* 33, no. 2 (April/June 2004): 32.

18. Martha Yee, "FRBRization: A Method for Turning Online Public Finding Lists into Online Public Catalogs," *Information Technology and Libraries* 24, no. 3 (June 2005): 81.

19. Jennifer Bowen, "FRBR: Coming Soon to Your Library?" *Library Resources and Technical Services* 49, no. 3 (July 2005): 177.

20. Ibid., 178.

21. Roderick Ryan, *A History of Motion Picture Color Technology* (London: Focal Press, 1977), 79.

22. Ibid., 14.

23. Robert Gitt, presentation on motion picture color processes, James Bridges Theater, UCLA, May 16, 2001.

24. Michael Friend, "Film, Digital, Film," *Journal of Film Preservation* 24, no. 50 (March 1995). http://www.cinema.ucla.edu/fiaf/journal/html50/film.html.

25. Gitt presentation.

26. See *DACS* 6.1–4.

27. See notes for *The Toll of the Sea* contained as part of the DVD collection, *Treasures from the American Film Archives* (National Film Preservation Board, 2000).

28. David Miller and Patrick Le Boeuf, "'Such Stuff as Dreams Are Made On': How Does FRBR Fit Performing Arts?" *Cataloging & Classification Quarterly* 39, no. 3–4 (2005): 157.

29. The importance of title as the primary access point is so ingrained in the moving image archival community that it is the suggested main entry for collection level cataloging in AMIM2.

30. Clinton Heylin, *Despite the System: Orson Welles versus the Hollywood Studios* (Chicago: Chicago Review Press, 2005), 144.

31. Stephen Farber, "1942 Welles Film Footage Recovered," *New York Times*, August 28, 1986, C19.

32. *AMIM2*, appendix C, provides guidance in the creation of whole/part designations.

33. In the *DACS*, chapter 9 commentary, it is stated that the primary relationship that exists between records and the organizations or individuals associated with them is "for the creation, assembly, accumulation, and/or maintenance and use of the materials being described."

34. In the *DACS*, chapter 10 commentary, it states that "information about the corporate body, person, or family that created, assembled, or accumulated, and/or maintained and used the materials being described may be incorporated into the description."

35. Catherine Benamou in a memo to Ross Lipman, film preservationist at the UCLA Film & Television Archive, 2000.

36. According to a survey of twenty archival repositories that collect moving images, the creation of hierarchical finding aids is not a standard practice. Refer to Abigail Leab Martin, *AMIA Compendium of Moving Image Cataloging* (Chicago: Society of American Archivists, 2001), 34–36.

37. Howard Besser, "Digital Preservation of Moving Image Material?" *The Moving Image* 1, no. 2 (Fall 2001): 44.

38. Ibid., 52.

AMATEUR VIDEO MUST NOT BE OVERLOOKED

JUDI HETRICK

In early September 2003, the *New York Times* revealed that an amateur video from September 11, 2001, that showed both planes hitting the World Trade Center had surfaced. It is the only footage that does so. In the two years after it was shot, however, the tape had "bounced around" the apartment of its maker, Pavel Hlava, an immigrant from the Czech Republic. Once, he found his young son with the camera, erasing the tape. He got the camera away before any harm was done, the *Times* reported. *Times* editors headlined the story, by James Glanz, "A Rare View of Sept. 11, Overlooked."

"Looking at the overlooked" is how Warren Roberts frequently described the academic field of folklore. For Roberts, who in 1953 became the first person to earn a folklore PhD in the United States, "the overlooked" referred to modest houses, tools, and other everyday artifacts that can reveal how the majority of pioneer Americans—people he called "the 95 percent"—had really lived. He believed that historians and others had more than sufficiently documented the wealthy and influential 5 percent. Folklorists, on the other hand, were called to seek out and deeply understand artifacts of the 95 percent that were not often prized or widely seen as valuable.

Artifacts made today by the 95 percent include technologically advanced texts such as digital video. The events of September 11, 2001, are among the most infamous newsworthy images ever captured by an amateur videographer, but they were not the first and will certainly not be the last. Amateur moving images have literally changed the way we see the events of our time. As Jan-Christopher Horak, the editor of *The Moving Image,* wrote not long after the attack:

> One heard it over and over again: it was like a movie. Indeed, humanity all over the globe experienced this catastrophe in real time like no event before, thanks to the advent of the digital video camera. That invention has allowed every amateur moving image maker to deliver broadcast-quality tapes of events that previously we could have only heard about or at best seen in a still image. (vi)

But camcorders are not reserved for times of national crisis. Members of the 95 percent all across America record community events ranging from more small-scale disasters, such as tornadoes and snowstorms, to the traditions of parades and festivals that mark the cycle of the civic year. In the small groups that view these tapes, they are one way people come to know their neighbors. Yet it is a rare tape that is made public to a larger audience, as was Hlava's remarkable recording. Journalists value amateur tapes only when they major record events missed by professionals. And amateur video is only slowly entering the awareness of many of those whose mission is to record and preserve the artifacts of our time. Still, the existence and use of amateur videotape outside profes-sional circles sparks questions about community epistemology:

Who is empowered to tell the stories of our communities, both to insiders and to those outside the group? Who should be empowered with that storytelling mission?

The 95 percent should share that storytelling mission, and their videos can be a major contribution in every community. This is in line with the Library of Congress's Television/Video Preservation Study, which has called on archivists to "identify home video as a potentially valuable source of social documentation" (Murphy 1997). Archivists

Amateur videographers recording parade. Photo courtesy of Judi Hetrick.

should pursue partnerships and community outreach to identify and select amateur community video for archiving. This article suggests some preliminary criteria for identification and selection of such video, and also recommends expanding and adding detail to the ways home movies and video are categorized by creating a new genre called "community vernacular video." Finally, a movement to save these videos is urgently needed, as the change from tape to digital formats endangers many original video documents.

BROAD-BASED COLLECTION TEAMS

Because community video is a democratic and locally specific resource, its selection is best determined through democratic and locally specific partnerships and processes. These include:

- partnerships with local clubs, librarians, folklorists, and so on

- involvement with the community through programs such as home movie days and hometown motion picture awards

- cooperation with the reformatting industry and others advising people on format transfers.

If they have not already done so, archives and other institutions that hold television and video should act now on the 1997 Library of Congress Television/Video Preservation Study recommendation to form advisory groups. Those groups can be customized for each institution and each community, and should include academics and professional archivists, amateur archivists and historians, and also makers and viewers of the amateur video itself. A broad-based group will help professionals find and identify video that may be suitable for preservation. People distribute community video outside the family to interested small groups or communities that can range in size from a handful of neighbors to a religious congregation to an entire county or even to uncounted, self-selected Web surfers. These videos will rarely be put up for sale. In his book *There's No Place Like Home Video,* James M. Moran points out, "home mode artifacts circulate as symbolic statements about membership, identity, and lifestyle within a private sphere of gift, rather than exchange, relations" (58). Even though community video is a part of the public sphere, its exchange often follows the gift ethic as rooted in the private sphere. This means that the tapes must be actively sought through contacts with the small groups they portray. Such contacts also can help identify those members of the community who, while still amateurs, have built reputations as good and dependable videographers. Such people are usually avid video hobbyists or active club or community members who donate their time on evenings and weekends to making the video record. Some started in still photography or home movies and have added new recording technology as it was introduced. Others came to the task of community documentation only when family events—often the birth of a child or grandchild—sparked the purchase of a camcorder, and the photographer's interests eventually moved from family to the larger community.

Clubs, including but not restricted to local historical societies, are one set of institutions that can help identify these folks. So are religious communities, where video documentation can range from professional quality at large, technologically savvy congregations to occasional amateur shoots in smaller groups.

If professional folklorists work within the community, they could become important members of the selection team. Their work, as Tom van Buren wrote for the Westchester County Business Journal, is to "research and highlight the [area's] many diverse cultural traditions," so their contacts are likely to be broad, and their eye focused on bringing to public attention cultures that might otherwise remain hidden. Likewise, if there are folklore archives within a community or state, their archivists are natural allies in the push for identification of suitable video.

Amateur videographers recording parade. Photo courtesy of Judi Hetrick.

Although folklorists do not work in every community, almost every town has a public library, and almost every library has a media section. Some public libraries already have community video in their collections. Sometimes the librarians themselves have produced community video, which often depict programs hosted at the library.

Moreover, representatives from all these groups should both advise archivists on the selection of video and be advised by archivists on the preservation of video already in community collections. Making and keeping multiple copies is part of the nature of video, and few active organizations are likely to donate master copies of their materials. Still, in exchange for professional advice on duplication and preservation, many groups and videographers will not only share copies of their work, they may well eventually donate originals for safekeeping.

In addition to networking within small groups in the community, public calls for contributions can place more community video squarely in the public realm. One such call, "The Hometown Motion Picture Awards," was made by the public library in the small southern Indiana town of Mitchell in 1998. It yielded video that ranged from a junior high school local history project to decades-old movie footage of local hero and original Mercury astronaut Gus Grissom visiting his hometown in the 1960s. Moreover, a public program in which excerpts from all the entries were screened and the public was asked to vote for the winner helped increase awareness of the importance of both home movies and amateur video. Both the small local newspapers and a larger regional television station ran stories on the competition.

The AMIA-sponsored Home Movie Days could themselves serve as collection points for video or serve as models of successful grassroots collection campaigns.

Open workshops in which professionals teach amateur videographers how to preserve images in their private archives are another means to the larger goal of saving amateur video, and at the same time fosters communication between amateur videographers and professionals.

The history of the home-movie preservation movement holds a lesson for video archives. In the early 1990s, many families had their films transferred to video and discarded the originals. A similar technological shift is happening today as video is transferred to digital formats. Numerous thriving small businesses throughout the United States offer videotape to digital transfer services. Other businesses offer instruction or equipment that allow people to complete the transfers themselves at home. These entrepreneurs are potentially vital allies in the movement to preserve amateur video, as they are in a position to educate people about the value of video archiving and could serve as liaisons between the video-making public and archivists and other preservation professionals.

CRITERIA FOR VIDEO SELECTION

Advisory groups can simplify the task of identifying which videos to archive by noting one simple fact of content: some recordings are restricted to the private, family realm, while others record activities of groups larger than a family and that take place in public or civic arenas. These latter videos may have been made by private citizens, but they record activity in the public sphere.

Unlike family-based home movies where people have some expectation of privacy, motion pictures made outside the home are often of people participating in civic events or engaged in public performance.

And the events recorded need not have the drama that Hlava captured to be of historic importance. In discussing the move to preserve regional moving images in the United Kingdom, Heather Norris Nicholson noted,

Regionally derived moving imagery provides an important source of historical and geographical narratives about locality, community, and nationality. The routine visit by an eminent individual—government minister, member of royalty, or in more recent time, sports or media celebrity—to somewhere in the provinces becomes something special at the local level and an excuse for bringing out the camera. Recorded moments of shared celebration or commemoration that usually warrant little if any national comment provide valuable counternarratives to the more broadly based official versions of historical experience. Such imagery is saturated with socially and culturally constructed ideological meanings. (153)

In the United States, much vernacular film and some video has been collected and archived as a way to expand the regional historic record. Northeast Historic Film in Maine was a pioneer in this area. "From the start (1986), Northeast Historic Film has taken on the task of preserving amateur films and videotapes that record the life of the Northeast in detail and from perspectives nowhere else available" ("Archiving Home Movies," 1). Home movies are similarly valued in collections documenting areas and peoples as varied as those in the American South,[1] Hawaii, and Nebraska.

Although moving images from the domestic sphere—the majority of home movie subjects—are important elements of the social record and worth preserving, amateur video allows a new a focus on collective or civic content of the type Nicholson describes and more. The portability and ease of operation of video cameras has meant a burgeoning number of recordings made in this larger public sphere. While home movies of public-sphere images are occasionally found in film format, they are far more frequent in video. Moreover, makers of public or community amateur video often intended it for viewing outside the home. These public videos include recordings made at civic events such as county fairs and town festivals, documentation of community problems such as hurricanes and tornadoes, and activities of the small groups, clubs, and religious congregations. Again, the content of such tapes will vary from community to community. Diné College in Tsaile, Arizona, holds tapes of powwows and native culture instruction in its archive. The public library in Cleveland, Ohio, has videos of its Christmas concert and of lectures about American European immigrant literature.

Common to all these public-sphere videos is that they show community activities literally through the eyes of community members. If the only difference between amateur and professional video were that point of view, it would be reason enough to preserve them and add the amateur vantage point to the record. But amateur tapes also frequently vary from professional products in how they are shot and put together. People

Parade participant video-recording spectators. Photo courtesy of Judi Hetrick.

outside the socialization of professional television or documentary filmmaking will not often emulate professional forms, even though they are familiar with them. Rather, as studies in visual anthropology have shown, different groups use different aesthetic systems for different types of creative expressions, including film.[2]

Just because amateur video doesn't look and sound the same as a professional recording does not automatically mean it's bad, but it does mean that it is different.

A study of more than one hundred of these amateur community videos made across the United States shows that they very often have key characteristics in common.

- They are usually made by one person and with community-based motivation and purpose.

- They usually show events in chronological order, in real time, and are only edited in camera.

- They show spatial context for the activities being documented.

- They base camera choices on respect and compassion toward individuals depicted or affected by the events shown.

- They are not narrated or are minimally narrated on the video audio track, leaving aural "space" for narration and comment when the video is exhibited.

Instead of emulating television news or movies, with emphasis on sound bites and quick cuts, amateur community videographers strive for complete and holistic depictions. These characteristics are not accidental, but they are not emulations of professional aesthetics. What Susan Sontag wrote of still photography applies as well to video:

> In deciding how a picture should look, in preferring one exposure to another, photographers are always imposing standards on their subjects. Although there is a sense in which the camera does indeed capture reality, not just interpret it, photographs are as much an interpretation of the world as paintings and drawings are. Those occasions when the taking of photographs is relatively undiscriminating, promiscuous, or self-effacing do not lessen the didacticism of the whole enterprise. (6–7)

Additionally, like professionals, many amateurs care deeply about production values, even if their equipment is not professional grade. They eschew the shaky camera work and constant prattling commentary that are stereotypes of amateur work. Indeed, in many small communities, amateur videographers develop reputations for the good quality of their videos and are frequently asked by other community members to record events. Archivists should seek amateur video that has high production values, as judged against other amateur video.

Once tapes are acquired, adequate documentation of amateur video shares the problem that Rosemary Bergeron has pointed out for certain small-gauge films:

> The identification of the George W. Fisher footage is problematic because there is no information from the creator about the contents of the footage other than very cryptic titles scribbled on the small 9.5mm reels. In this respect it is typical of much amateur footage and family snapshots. . . . Without the value added by this work of identification and documentation, small-gauge footage risks remaining marginalized, unused, and unpreserved. (27–28, 39)

How fully a recording can be documented is one selection criterion that can help determine which videos to save. Many documentation problems can be avoided by identifying and collecting video while its creators can still be involved in the process.

Additionally, supplemental and supporting information can be gathered to accompany videos: ephemera such as event programs and newspaper clippings could become part of a video donation. If the video recording is one that contains "aural space," a recording could be made of the maker narrating the tape, or the person could be asked to write supplemental explanatory text.

Dividing amateur video by its public or private content is, of course, a task of broad categorization that will need to be refined and polished. The two realms interpenetrate in many activities and topics. In testimony as part of the Library of Congress Television/Video study, scholar Deirdre Boyle said,

> Imagine if you will now a documentary producer 100 years from now who is interested in making a documentary about the recent Gulf War. She would need to have access to videotapes; not just those broadcast as news by CNN or NBC, but those exchanged by military personnel and their families during the war.

Selecting video that illuminates public issues such as war but which was shot for use within the family means that issues of privacy come into play. Permission will be needed from both videomakers and their subjects for private tapes to enter the public realm of the archive. As with audiotaped oral histories, options for release include having

Two amateur videographers (one partially hidden) recording a patriotic ceremony. Photo courtesy of Judi Hetrick.

the recording sealed for a certain number of years to avoid infringing on the privacy of those depicted while still preserving valuable documentation about larger public issues from a personal point of view.

EXPANDED CATEGORIZATION

In these early years of the twenty-first century, video is woven into our collective social history, and as we step up efforts to preserve it, we will also need to develop terminology for discussing it. The term "community vernacular video" describes the recordings this article has discussed with more precision than the language that is currently in use.

Amateur video is often called "home video," and that term's parallel to "home movies" makes it very attractive. But "home video" has come to mean everything from footage of family gatherings to rental DVDs of Hollywood B-movies. And as Snowden Becker has pointed out,

> "Home videos"—home movie documents originally created on videotape ... belong to an entirely different class of technical concerns, use a substantially different visual language, and largely come from a different period in the history of amateur films, among other distinctions. (89)

The vast majority of camcorder use is domestic—as were most "home movie" productions—but the word "home" is limiting and can lead to lack of distinction among very different types of tapes. Images of a child's birthday party and of destruction following a hurricane can both be termed "home video." Replacing the term "home" with "amateur" does little to clarify the categorizations. Nonfiction family home movies and video are amateur, but so are amateur fictional moving pictures that emulate Hollywood standards and techniques or that take an artistic stand with the avant-garde.

The more precise descriptive term "home mode" has been used to describe both still and moving amateur photography since visual anthropologist Richard Chalfen published *Snapshot Versions of Life* in 1987. "Mode" is also the terminology preferred by Moran, who, in *There's No Place Like Home Video,* says that "mode" looks at external cultural functions such as persuasion and serves as a more useful form of classification— and one that more easily accommodates amateur film and video alongside professional documentaries (68–69). Moran distinguishes between "mode" and "genre," restricting genre characteristics to patterns inside a text—such as thematic conflicts.

To folklorists, who frequently classify all types of creative expressions created by the 95 percent, the concept of genre is a complex one that can relate to subject, form, function, and performance, among other variables, some of which include elements of what Moran calls "mode." Folklore genres can reflect literary or ethnographic orientations, and they can be identified from the outside, by scholars, or from the inside, by the people who create the expressive forms being classified and categorized (Ben-Amos 1976). The amateur video discussed here is set apart from other forms by who makes it, by the equipment they use, by the ways they construct the recordings, and by the videos' subject matter. Adopting terminology that is in the spirit of folklore genre classification seems appropriate to the form and all its many manifestations. Hence,

the term "vernacular video" can be used as a new and more precise category to describe nonfiction videos made by untrained camera operators who attempt to realistically reflect life around them.[3]

"Vernacular" is from the phrase "the electronic vernacular," which folklorist Barbara Kirschenblatt-Gimblett introduced in 1995 to describe informal Internet culture. As Kirschenblatt-Gimblett has noted, "The operative term is *vernacular*. It will focus on what ordinary people are doing with the medium" (emphasis added). Vernacular's meaning as "a language or dialect native to a region or country rather than a literary, cultured, or foreign language" helps clarify the term when it is used in relation to video. These recordings are similar to a dialect of the larger language of moving pictures, but it is a dialect at the opposite end of the spectrum from the "literary" or "cultured" expression of a Hollywood epic. The videos relate to a specific place, region, or country. In a similar way, vernacular language has long been among the "overlooked" subjects adopted by folklorists for serious study.

And while "video" may seem to require no explanation as an appropriate term, technology is changing so fast that "video" already has numerous meanings and connotations, less than fifty years after its invention. Video—moving pictures captured electronically on tape or in digital form instead of chemically on film—has in its short history evolved from three-quarter-inch analog tape reels to half-inch consumer cassettes to minicassettes, then to digital tape and digital discs to digital data stored on hard drives of computers or transmitted only in electronic form. Video telephones—a staple of science fiction for decades—are now a reality and are still using the term "video" for the pictures they transmit. "Video" has remained the constant appellation for all these technologies and has even been applied retroactively. After people had old home movies transferred to tapes in the 1980s and '90s, many began calling them "videos"—although they usually qualified it with terms such as "old" or "my dad's." So a phrase like "I think

I have that in an old video" can mean "I think I have that on one of my home movies transferred to videotape."

All of today's video formats may quite soon be made technologically obsolete by digital developments, just as the video revolution quickly shelved home movie technology. The video documents discussed here may be near the end of their historic period of creation, making a conversation about their selection and preservation all the more urgent.

"Vernacular video," then, can more clearly identify a broad genre of moving pictures identified primarily by the status of the creator, by the equipment used, and the recording's content. Adding the modifier "community" to "vernacular video," clearly signals the movement of the "home movie" phenomenon into the public, social, and civic realms, depicting life away from home, outside the family and outside the private realm.

Taken all together, "community vernacular video" describes electronic moving pictures, made by people not trained professionally and not using professional equipment, that document the activities of various communities outside the family. The community members who make them rarely employ professional moving picture conventions, and the category can include video by people from outside a community who are invited in to create community video and who follow the community's aesthetic standards. The tapes are about activities important to that community. Depending on whether they are shown soon after the event or at a later time, the tapes serve as documents of grassroots news or history—stories that are told through the eyes of community members.[4]

If we agree with the UK Film Council that "film and moving image are the single most important source of education, information, and culture in the world today" (Nicholson 2001, 153), then we should insist that moving images created and used by the 95 percent be no longer overlooked but instead take their place in our institutions of safekeeping.

NOTES

1. "Picturing Home: Family Movies as Local History," a community education project of the Center for the Study of Southern Culture at the University of Mississippi, has sixty collections that include not only family events but also "depictions of everyday life singular to the South." The collections come from white families who employed black workers and servants, so that "woven throughout white, Southern home movie footage is a visual record of African American life in the South."
2. See Sol Worth and John Adair's landmark study, *Through Navajo Eyes,* for more on visual anthropology.

3. Although I did not see it until several years later, in the January/February 1995 edition of *Columbia Journalism Review* (33, no. 5), Patricia Aufderheide used the term "vernacular video" (46) very broadly in an article about all types of small-format video. Editors also used the term in the headline: "Vernacular Video: For the Growing Genre of Camcorder Journalism, Nothing Is Too Personal."

4. Community video can be professional and not vernacular. This is the case when a chamber of commerce hires someone to make a promotional video for industrial recruitment, or even when a cable-access station uses staff members to record activities at a fair or festival and then edit it into an hour-long program. These two tapes will look radically different, but both can be placed on the continuum from vernacular to professional closer to the standard, professional visual dialect of our day; they are shot and edited by people who are paid because of their knowledge of professional standards and composition.

WORKS CITED

"Archiving Home Movies." 1990. *Northeast Historic Film Moving Image Review* 3, no. 1 (Winter): 1.

Becker, Snowden. 2001. "Family in a Can: The Preservation of Home Movies in Museums." *The Moving Image* 1, no. 2 (Fall), 88–106.

Ben-Amos, Dan. 1976. *Folklore Genres.* Austin: University of Texas Press.

Bergeron, Rosemary. 2002. "Identifying and Documenting the Small Gauge Film: Researching Rare Footage of a First Nations School in the Canadian West." *The Moving Image* 2, no. 2 (Fall), 25–40.

Boyle, Deirdre. Testimony before the panel of the National Television/Video Preservation Board, March 1996 at the Sheraton Hilton New York Hotel. http://lcweb.loc.gov/film/hrng96ny.html.

Chalfen, Richard. 1987. *Snapshot Versions of Life.* Bowling Green, OH: Bowling Green State University Popular Press.

Glanz, James. 2003. "A Rare View of Sept. 11, Overlooked." *New York Times*, September 7. www.nytimes.com.

Horak, Jan-Christopher. 2002. "Editor's Foreword." *The Moving image* 2, no. 1 (Spring), vi–ix.

Kirschenblatt-Gimblett, Barbara. 1995. "The Electronic Vernacular," Phi Beta Kappa lecture delivered at Indiana University, November 19. Transcript from private recording, made with permission.

Moran, James M. 2002. *There's No Place Like Home Video.* Minneapolis: University of Minnesota Press.

Murphy, William T. 1997. *Television/Video Preservation Study, Volume 1: Report.* Washington, DC: The Library of Congress. http://lcweb.loc.gov/film/tvstudy.html.

Nicholson, Heather Norris. 2001. "Regionally Specific, Globally Significant: Who's Responsible for the Regional Record?" *The Moving Image* 1, no. 2 (Fall): 152–63.

"Picturing Home: Family Movies as Local History." 1996. The Center for the Study of Southern Culture, University of Mississippi. http://www.cssc.olemiss.edu/sma/picthome/picthome.html.

Roberts, Warren. 1988. *Viewpoints on Folklife: Looking at the Overlooked.* Ann Arbor, MI: University of Michigan Press.

Sontag, Susan. 1977. *On Photography.* New York: Delta Books.

Van Buren, Tom. 2003. "Folk Arts of Mexico Take Root in Westchester: A Profile." *Westchester County Busines Journal.* April. http://www.findarticles.com/p/articles/mi_go1587/is_200304/ai_n7521263.

Worth, Sol, and John Adair. 1972. *Through Navajo Eyes.* Repr. Albuquerque: University of New Mexico Press, 1997.

STORYTELLING AND ARCHIVAL MATERIAL IN *THE TROUBLE WITH MERLE*

MAREE DELOFSKI

Between 2000 and 2002, I researched, wrote, and directed a tele-

vision documentary about Merle Oberon, the Hollywood star of the

1930s and '40s. The film, *The Trouble with Merle,* explores various

competing stories and claims made by different groups for Oberon's ethnicity and na-

tionality: that she was either born in India of Anglo-Indian ancestry or that she was

Tasmanian-born of Chinese ancestry. In the process of uncovering these stories, the film

reflects on celebrity and memory, and the way racism can shape a life.

Merle Oberon's provenance and early life story have been a matter of some

contention among those interested enough to discuss such things—particularly in Aus-

tralia, where numerous individuals have claimed a family relationship to her. In the

course of researching *The Trouble with Merle,* I uncovered different accounts of Oberon's

Dark Angel (1935), directed by Sidney Franklin, with Merle Oberon and Fredric March. Courtesy Janet Schirn Collections.

early years and nationality, family histories that led me from Australia to the United States, India, and Canada. As a filmmaker interested in storytelling, picking through these narratives offered an opportunity to consider their cultural function and specifically, given that my film was about a historical figure, how both nonfiction and fiction archival film material might be used in the film along a spectrum from the evidential or empirical to the expressive. One challenge was to develop a structure for the film that might allow the telling of these different "Merle" stories while at the same time providing some insight into the pleasures of storytelling itself, and into the way a set of questions about race, class, and celebrity attached to the "idea" of Oberon. I envisaged a film that could contribute to a discussion that illuminated the tension that often exists between empirical notions of historical evidence and the significance of oral histories and myth in people's lives. And, of course, the film's title, *The Trouble with Merle,* is intended to suggest this very tension.

Desmond Bell, discussing documentary filmmakers' use of archival film footage in the representation of history and popular memory, has posed the following questions:

How should we as documentary filmmakers picture the past, how should we conduct the struggle for memory? Should archival images be dealt with as primary evidence and mute testimony to an unattainable past or as narrative resource capable of releasing the submerged voices of history and attending to their story? (5)

Similar questions informed the research for and production of *The Trouble with Merle*. The archival footage in the film includes Oberon performing as dramatic characters in her fiction films together with actuality footage of her as a celebrity film star. Early archival images of Tasmania, newspaper clippings, family photographs, and archival Australian television footage are also used. The potential of the archival material to function as both indexical evidence and story element is what interested me.

In television documentary film biographies, a life story is often constructed along a chronological grid using interviews with the subject and their peers, together with archival footage and illustrative material presented with a voice-over.

Recent examples of this style of biography might include *Stanley Kubrick: A Life in Pictures* (2001), a documentary about the late film director. The film is narrated[1] by another Hollywood star, Tom Cruise, who describes Kubrick's life from his birth onward. Interviews with Kubrick's wife Christiane and a range of those who knew and worked with him combine with archival material such as family photographs and extracts from the director's films to illustrate or substantiate the truth of the commentary. In a documentary biography of this kind, truth often becomes an unassailable monolith, represented by a seamless lack of conflict. Documentary theorist Bill Nichols has described a variety of categorical possibilities for the documentary form: the expository, interactive/participatory, observational, reflexive, and performative. Nichols's categories are conceptualized as a kind of historical narrative for documentary's formal development, where "new forms arise from the limitations and constraints of previous forms and in which the credibility of the impression of documentary reality changes historically" (32).

Nichols's discussion of the expository mode suggests that it is characterized by the use of voice-over — "speaking for, or on behalf of, someone or something" (34) — or, in its earliest form, intertitles. In contemporary documentary, Nichols's modes may often be discerned in different combinations in a single work and thus should not necessarily be considered as discrete categories of films; nevertheless one could describe a documentary like *Stanley Kubrick: A Life in Pictures* as "classically" expository in that its commentary addresses the viewer directly and is the shaping device for the film. Traditionally, the narrating voice in such films has been male, authoritative, and middle class, although there is a growing body of contemporary documentary narrated by the female voice. The voice may be anonymous or, as in the film on Kubrick, that of a celebrity who brings his authority as a Hollywood "A-lister" to the task of rendering the subject's life on screen. Yet, there are other examples of expository documentary films that are more textually open, despite their use of commentary, such as playfully reflexive works like Chris Marker's *Letter from Siberia* (1956) or, more recently, Tony Harrison's *Maybe Day in Kazakhstan* (1993).

In *Letter from Siberia* Marker replays a sequence of Siberian road workers mending a road three times consecutively, using different commentaries, performance styles, accompanying music, and sound effects each time. In so doing, he demonstrates the power of commentary to inflect the image and thus the arbitrariness of documentary truth.

Maybe Day in Kazakhstan, a film about the disintegration of the former Soviet Union, uses a rhyming narration that infers that the images we are seeing in the documentary are shot in a market place in Kazakhstan. By the film's conclusion, however, it becomes apparent that the market is in fact in Greece, that the traders who sell their goods there are in fact exiles, and that their "Kazakhstan" may be more of a memory than a physical place.

In conceiving *The Trouble with Merle,* the competing truth claims for Oberon's life story attracted me, as they made possible a documentary film that explored the desire underpinning those claims and, ultimately, the power of story itself. Many Tasmanians of a particular generation have an emotional and cultural investment in their stories of Oberon—and it was this I also wanted to represent. Thus, constructing a linear, causal chronology of a life based on archival material used only as illustrative or evidential footage with a seemingly transparent connection to a historical reality did not appeal. Instead, I cast myself as an "epistemically hesitant" detective/inquirer[2] attempting to explain an enigma, a narrating voice that, unlike Cruise's, is *not* always replete with knowledge. In this I was exploring the possibilities of constructing a meta-account of the Oberon life stories that might direct an audience away from an idea of documentary biography as a historically transparent given, toward the particular desires embodied in the range of claims on Oberon's provenance.

There are, of course, other precedents for this kind of strategy. For example, British filmmaker Isaac Julien's poetic account of writer Langston Hughes, *Looking for*

Langston (1988), mixes nonfiction archival footage with stylized black-and-white recon-structions. It is as if Julien's intention is to represent not so much an "actual" Harlem of the 1920s as to express something of the nature of male desire. In Australia, writer-director Kriv Stenders has explored the idea of memory and its relationship to autobiog-raphy in his documentary film *Motherland* (1993). In his autobiographical account of his childhood and his relationship to his beloved Latvian grandmothers, Stenders refuses the use of actual archival material. Instead, he elects to create a set of dramatized faux-archival memories that are so excessive in their representation of an idealized past, so "golden" and strangely florid, even as expressive black-and-white re-creations, that their status as unproblematic or transparent reconstructed memories becomes heightened and thus questionable. In another Australian documentary, Tony Ayres's *Sadness* (1998), the narrator, William Yang, explores a broader meaning of family, steering the audience be-tween archival photographs of his natural family and archival photos of his family of gay friends suffering and dying from AIDS. These images are intercut with a dramatized mem-ory of an unsolved family murder delivered *Rashomon*-like from various storytelling posi-tions. In Ayres's film, there is a tension between the actual or evidential status of the family stills and the fictionalized, reconstructed accounts of mystery, the indexical character of the still images with their historical claims to authenticity slugging it out with the (clearly) con-structed and thus potentially "unreliable," yet visually pleasurable, memory sequences.

Each of these documentary films approaches questions of history, biography, and their construction on film from a position that implicitly questions notions of a trans-parent documentary realism or the documentary tendency, as described by Michael Renov, "to preserve or record" (25).[3] Rather, in these explicitly authored works, an expressive representation of a past appears to interest the filmmakers.

One of the aspirations that *The Trouble with Merle* shares with the work of these filmmakers is the desire to explore the tension between the evidential and the expressive as an element of storytelling itself.

Like these films, *The Trouble with Merle* is a hybrid, combining a number of Nichols's modes, and is an authored work. By authored documentary, I am describing a subset of documentary that has been evolving since the mid-1980s. Works of this kind are not intent on maintaining the illusion of an apparently unmediated or direct relationship with "the real." Instead, they are often hybrid forms drawing on a range of techniques with which to represent or infer the filmmaker's or author's negotiation with the socio-historical world. These techniques may include the explicit presence of the author onscreen, as in the works of Nick Broomfield, Ross McElwee, or Michael Moore, or, as in the works of Julien and Stenders, the use of more experimental or fictional strategies that signify the intervention or controlling presence of the filmmaker, what John Grierson terms "creative treatment of actuality" (13).

BACKGROUND TO THE FILM

Like many Australians, I had grown up believing that Merle Oberon was an Australian film legend. The story was well known: Oberon was born in Tasmania, the tiny island state at the bottom of the map of Australia, like another Tasmanian film star, Errol Flynn. Each had somehow traveled to Hollywood and, in local parlance, made it big. Oberon had been nominated for an Academy Award and was written up in Australian newspapers and magazines as "the Tasmanian-born Hollywood movie star." Australian writer Hal Porter notes in his overview of Australian stars of the stage and screen,

> Merle Oberon (Estelle Merle O'Brien Thompson) was born on February 12, 1914, at St. Helens, a village overlooking the black mud flats of St. George Bay on the north east coast of Tasmania. She lived in Tasmania until she was seven. She was taken to live in Bombay, India, where her education was continued and completed in Calcutta. As an adolescent she displayed an enthusiasm for acting . . . (265)

Oberon was particularly famous during the 1930s and '40s in the United Kingdom and the United States. She starred in many films with such leading men as Gary Cooper, Lawrence Olivier, Robert Ryan, and Leslie Howard. Her best-known films include *The Private Life of Henry VIII* (1934) and *Wuthering Heights* (1939). Others, of course, may have their favorites.

For my mother's generation it was as if Tasmania, famous for its apples, was also a breeding ground for film stars.

Of course there were in fact actually only two stars, but for a country that had so few "international" celebrities at that time it must have seemed as if Tasmania had something rather special going for it. It is important to note here that Tasmania is separated from the mainland of Australia by a wide stretch of water, Bass Straits, and that south, beyond the island, is Antarctica. To a large degree, many older Tasmanians' views of themselves were shaped by their geographical relationship to an idea of the center — conceptualized in relation to Australia as either Sydney or Melbourne, and in the broader worldview, as Europe or America.

Sometime in the 1980s, I learned that Oberon may not have been Tasmanian after all, rather that she was Indian and that her Australian provenance may have been a masquerade. To be honest, I hadn't thought about her much until then, and beyond a kind of "so what" response to this news, I didn't think about her again for another twenty years or so, until, by chance, a curious piece of information came my way. It seems that the star, who died in Los Angeles in 1979, had come to Sydney in 1978 as a guest of the local film industry. She had been invited as special presenter for a film awards ceremony, the Sammys. The organizers had been looking for a presenter with special significance for Australia, and

Oberon was one of the few international stars alive at the time who had any Australian film industry connection. The fact that she could be billed as "an Australian star from the golden period" rendered her celebrity status even more alluring.

Glen Kinging, a former television executive, organized the invitation to Merle to attend the Sammy Awards:

> To make a point of difference, we wanted to have an Australian, international star, if possible, and obviously there weren't too many. Also, we didn't want it to be like a pop star. To be honest, we wanted someone who was a little more of a legend, for what it was worth, and Chips Rafferty wasn't around, so I thought "Merle Oberon." I was watching her in a movie, and I thought, "Oh yes, she's Australian . . ." As far as I was concerned, she was Australian and she was just delightful.[4]

Learning that she was on her way to Australia, the Lord Mayor of Hobart, the capital city of Tasmania, issued an invitation to the star to visit her birthplace and attend a special reception in her honor at the town hall. Discovering so many years later that Oberon had accepted this invitation and had actually gone to Tasmania for the reception, I was intrigued. If she were from India, why would she do such a thing? It seemed both odd and foolhardy to carry the identity masquerade into the heart of the lie. This tantalizing scrap of information catapulted me into the research for the film. What also attracted me in this initial stage of the research was the potential for a film that explored Tasmania's relationship with Oberon, that understanding this relationship might provide a way of discussing our fascination and desire for connection with celebrity in general and Tasmanians' view of themselves in the world in particular. Tasmanian-born writer and historian Cassandra Pybus has remarked on Tasmanians' sense of isolation and their corresponding fascination with Merle Oberon as a sign of a cosmopolitan world that seemed to exist just beyond their physical grasp: "We all tell stories to prove we exist. Tasmanians tell stories to prove that we have not slipped off the edge of the world."[5]

Charles Higham's 1983 biography *Princess Merle,* which he wrote with Roy Moseley, first asserted that Oberon was not Tasmanian but Anglo-Indian, that she was born Estelle Thompson in Bombay. According to Higham and Moseley, Oberon's Tasmanian provenance was concocted by British film producer Alexander Korda in London after she had arrived there from India with her mother. The racism of the period meant that Korda's studio regarded her mixed-race background as a major obstacle to her becoming a star. Tasmania in the 1930s must have seemed a perfect place to bury an inconvenient Anglo-Indian identity. It was conservative, resolutely British (read: white), and so remote that it was sometimes dropped off the map of Australia entirely. It was also a long way from the United States and Europe, so the likelihood of the deception being discovered was minimal; a letter might take more than six weeks to travel to Australia from the northern hemisphere in the 1930s. Certainly the fact that there was a community of Indigenous people on the island was irrelevant to the studio. Thus it seems Estelle Thompson, an Anglo-Indian from Bombay, transformed into Merle Oberon, a white upper-class Hobart girl who moved to India from Tasmania with her mother only after her distinguished father, an officer in the Colonial Service, died in a fox hunting accident. As Charles Higham has commented, the fact that there are no foxes in Tasmania did not appear to bother the studio.

While *The Trouble with Merle* focuses on the star's 1978 visit to Hobart as both an emblematic and enigmatic event, the significance of which the audience is invited to consider, Oberon's biographers refer to it only briefly in their account of her life. Higham and Moseley assert that Hobart Council, which had issued the invitation to Oberon as a famous Tasmanian "returning home," discovered prior to the reception that there was no record of her Tasmanian birth:

> What . . . Merle did not know was that the Registrar of Births, Deaths, and Marriages in Hobart had already established that Merle had not been born there and that her civic welcomers went through the ceremony as an artificial courtesy to her. (292)

However, traveling to Tasmania to research Oberon's visit nearly twenty years after the publication of this biography, I discovered that some Tasmanians who had attended the reception, including the lord mayor's secretary, believed Oberon was most definitely one of them (and indeed, continue to do so). There were also several completely different versions of her birth and early life in Tasmania—stories that were the antithesis of the studio story in terms of Oberon's class and race. Where the studio had promoted her as the progeny of an upper-class white colonial family, many Tasmanians believe she was the illegitimate daughter of a poor Australian-Chinese chambermaid from the remote northeast of the island, a woman from a family called Chintock. The woman, Lottie Chintock, had become pregnant by the wealthy, married Anglo hotelier for whom she worked.

According to this version of Oberon's life, Lottie Chintock had been forced to relinquish Merle and through various pathways in different versions of the story, the little girl had made her way to India and later to Europe where she became a star.

Between 2000 and 2002, when I was researching and filming this documentary, different versions of this story were still in circulation in Tasmania.

Yet, in a kind of parallel universe, research revealed that there were individuals in India and Canada who also claimed a relationship to the film star and who had different stories to tell—stories of poignant family relationships and family secrets where Tasmania didn't rate a mention. Captain Harry Selby, an Anglo-Indian originally from Bombay, had been Charles Higham's informant for Oberon's biography and had claimed at that time that he was her nephew. During filming for the documentary he came forward and revised his relationship to the star stating he was her half-brother. They shared the same mother, Constance Selby. Constance had relinquished her daughter to her mother who had raised the child. Due to family sensitivities Captain Selby had chosen not to reveal this to the biographers at the time of *Princess Merle*'s publication in the 1983. Now his family was grown up, he believed he could, backed by a birth certificate and correspondence.

A FICTIONAL ARCHIVE

As I have indicated, in Tasmania, some remain passionately committed to the idea of Oberon as Lottie Chintock's daughter. Consistent in each Tasmanian version of her life is her leaving the island at the age of seven to travel to live in India—sometimes with a British Indian Army officer, sometimes with an Indian silk merchant, and once with a troupe of traveling Irish actors called O'Brien. But there is no documentary evidence of her travel arrangements or of the existence of these people. For the Tasmanian story-tellers, there is no factual documentation of Merle's early life there—no birth certificate, no family photographs of Merle as a small girl. Unlike Oberon's Indian biography, which includes a birth certificate, baptism certificate, letters from the star to family members, and so on, all the Tasmanians had were family and community stories about Merle and her Tasmanian mother Lottie Chintock, and equally important, the body of fiction films she starred in. For those committed to the idea of Merle as a Tasmanian-born Australian-Chinese, her feature films may have become a kind of family archive of images—documentation that proved the validity of their claim on her.

Lottie Chintock was from a little village in northeast Tasmania and, although she'd been dead for fifty years, her memory was still very strong in the state. Family members had photos of Lottie and stories about her longing for her lost daughter, Merle Oberon. Yet in the state archives of Tasmania there was no official record for anyone who could remotely approximate to Oberon, or for a daughter for Lottie. Did Lottie have a little girl? Was she taken from her? What happened to her? Lottie is said to have made the long trip from the northeast to Hobart to see each of Oberon's films. Her nephew, Peter Lawrence, remembered her yearning after one such trip, "I saw my girl on the screen, I saw my girl on the screen."[6] Could each screening of an Oberon film in Tasmania have provided an opportunity to scan the star's face for evidence of her Tasmanian heritage? Can fictional film deliver a documentary moment? U.S. documentary filmmaker Ross McElwee has reflected on this in his recent film *Bright Leaves* (2003). McElwee's family myth maintains that the Hollywood feature film *Bright Leaf* (1950) is a fictionalized account of his great-grandfather's life as a tobacco plantation owner in the American South. In his documentary, McElwee refers to the fiction film functioning for him like "a surreal home movie enacted by Hollywood stars." How much more directly may Tasmanians have connected to their archive of fictional images of Oberon—perhaps as Cathy from *Wuthering Heights*? Were there resonances of her lost child for Lottie Chintock when Cathy tells Heathcliff, as they stand in the wild world of the Yorkshire moors, how she longs for "music, parties . . . the world"? Did this explain something of Oberon's glittering journey through life? Did William Wyler's pictorial representation of the Yorkshire moors speak to Tasmanians of the rugged northeast landscape where their Merle was born? Or perhaps there were clues in Oberon's scornful speech as Georges Sand in *A Song to Remember* (1945), where she tells of the struggle she has endured as a woman in a man's world? Did these images of the star chart the trajectory of her life for many Tasmanians until her death in Los Angeles in 1979, when newspaper banners proclaimed, "Tasmanian-born Movie Star Dies in the U.S."?

The Trouble with Merle is structured as prologue, exposition, journey, denouement, and epilogue. The opening of the film is perfectly conventional, as it illustrates the range of personae that Oberon embodied, the images on screen comprising a montage of studio publicity stills and moving images of the star as various characters in her fiction films together with actuality images of her as a celebrity. However, archival fiction footage is also used to indicate that the distinctions between categories in the film may not be so rigid. A kind of slippage is suggested when a fictional Merle, Jane Benson in *Over the Moon* (1939), reads from a book about the "oriental set" of someone's eyes: "his eyes smouldered with all the passion of the Orient, flickered with unsated desire." This moment is intended to prefigure the discussion of race running through Tasmania's claim on Oberon, and the film's strategy of appropriating fictional material in order to transform it into narrative and expressive elements in the film. The prologue is also intended to set up the double function of factual evidence and story element that archival images will perform throughout the film. The archival material used in the Tasmanian section of the film is constructed to move between the denotative and connotative function: while some archival material is used in an evidential or illustrative fashion, other material is used to signify or express "something more."

The Tasmanian stories are explored in the first half of the film. They are preceded by a short informational section that sets up the historical background to Oberon's stardom: her role as Anne Boleyn in *The Private Life of Henry VIII* (1934) and her marriage to British producer Alexander Korda. Archival fiction footage of the actress as Anne Boleyn together with nonfiction stills of Oberon and Korda combine with a commentary that essentially outlines "facts." We are told that the studio hid Merle's Anglo-Indian background and chose Tasmania as her new birthplace. Biographer Charles Higham confirms this story with further detail. The style in this section of the film is authoritative and expository, typical of a conventional biographical television documentary; images serve the commentary in an unambiguous and direct way, providing an apparently unproblematic access to history.

Yet, as I have already noted, one of my aims in making *The Trouble with Merle* was to suggest the seductiveness of story and myth. Myth, of course, cannot necessarily be "proven" by documentation; its validity lies in the way it satisfies a culture's needs.

By exploring myth we can begin to understand people's desires. As narrative theorist Peter Brooks has written,

The narrative impulse is as old as our oldest literature: myth and folktale appear to be stories we recount in order to explain and understand where no other form of explanation will work. (3)

The Tasmanians' stories of Oberon's upbringing had been, in the main, second- or third-hand accounts exchanged across generations and, generally, outside the lived experience of the storytellers. Ultimately, their significance lay more in what they revealed about the tellers' struggle for identity than as authenticated information about Oberon's provenance. Australian historians Paula Hamilton and Kate Darian-Smith have commented on the way individual memories, once articulated, can enter the realm of the collective and be transmitted across generations:

> As we share those memories that are perceived to be relevant to our own identity, we are also incorporating a memory of events which are outside our lived experiences but are deemed to be central to the identity of our society. In this way, for example, we can "remember" people we have never met, places we have never been to, and events we had no part in.... It is through these collective—and indeed imaginative—memories that we structure our world and understand our past. (1–2)

In the section of the film that describes my journey of inquiry in Tasmania, the time frame moves from past to present to past and, for the first time in the film, archival fiction footage is introduced not in order to illustrate a factual aspect of Oberon's career but rather to suggest something of the relationship between the star and her Tasmanian audience. Thus footage from *Lydia* (1941) performs a number of functions. Importantly, it allows us an opportunity to "look" at the star, perhaps in the same way that some Tasmanians may have "looked" at Oberon in the cinema in 1941 when this film was released, perhaps projecting their desires and hopes onto her screen image.

The sequence where material from *Lydia* first appears begins with an exterior wide-angle shot of Hobart Town Hall shot in 2001. The town hall is a typical nineteenth-century civic building. Inside the building an elegantly dressed Pamela Archer is sitting in the room where the reception was held. A guest at the 1978 reception, she relates how exciting it was to meet Merle Oberon: "Being in Tasmania, you don't see many famous people, and so consequently this invitation to meet Merle Oberon was wonderful, it was just so exciting."[7] In another corner of the reception room, sitting under an official portrait of Queen Elizabeth, Doone Kennedy, a former lord mayor of Hobart, confirms the sense of anticipation that prevailed in Hobart before the reception:

Lydia (1941), directed by
Julien Duvivier, with Merle
Oberon, Edna May Oliver, and
Joseph Cotton. Courtesy Janet
Schirn Collections.

We had this thing about Errol Flynn being a son
of Tasmania and Merle Oberon being a daughter of Tasmania, so we had a few famous names
and people felt that this was going to be something really good to actually have
her come here and meet us.[8]

The scene now shifts to the town hall's grand mahogany staircase. As the camera begins to float up the staircase, we hear Oberon's voice as Lydia: "I entered the room
as if in a dream, walking on air." Following this, the actual town hall staircase dissolves
into the fictional staircase of *Lydia* as a glorious young Merle/Lydia in a white ball gown
glides up the stairs toward a ballroom where dancers are swirling across the floor. Back
in the Hobart Town Hall, Pamela Archer recollects, "She looked very, very charming, she
was very quiet, I think she would have been a little afraid of us all."[9] The scene cuts
again from the present to the fictional world of Merle/Lydia, who appears to look appre-
hensive at Pamela's remarks. Re-inscribing these images from *Lydia* in a new narrative
context, that of Oberon's 1978 visit to Hobart, I hoped might contribute to a rereading of
them, inferring something of Oberon's vulnerability at the time.[10]

The relationship between Tasmanians and Oberon's screen image is also suggested when small moments from *I, Claudius* (1937) are appropriated in the documentary. This Alexander Korda–produced film, in which Oberon starred as Messalina, was never actually completed. However, for my purposes, there is something "knowing" in the exquisite images of the (then) very young star. Although, ironically, most Tasmanians would never have seen Oberon's performance in this role (unless they saw the documentary on its making, *The Epic That Never Was* [1965]), the images made possible a screen dialogue between the actress and her Tasmanian public. For example, when Claudius (Charles Laughton) agrees with Caligula (Emlyn Williams) that Messalina is "fantastically beautiful," it is as if he is a star-struck fan, perhaps like the Tasmanians were in this period. In response to Claudius's gushing praise, Merle/Messalina glances over her shoulder triumphantly and, as I argue, knowingly; she appears to have no doubts about her power over either Claudius or her audience.

Voice-over, as I have discussed earlier, has a powerful capacity to inflect the meaning of images that I hoped to use in *The Trouble with Merle* During the film, one particular image from *I, Claudius* is used twice. A close-up of Merle/Messalina is structured into the unfolding narrative as a response to statements made by different Tasmanian storytellers. In the first instance, Merle/Messalina appears to respond to a rather bald claim made by Barbara Knight, former Secretary to the Lord Mayor, that "the story was that Merle Oberon was born in Tasmania, that she was of mixed parentage, that she was illegitimate."[11] Merle/Messalina appears to look slightly hurt by this revelation. Later in the film, the same shot is edited into an exchange between myself and Maxine Green, a Tasmanian storyteller who claims to know where proof of Oberon's Tasmanian birth lies but refuses to divulge its whereabouts. As she tells me, "I have to keep that, that's mine,"[12] Merle/Messalina's expression is inflected differently. Instead of appearing hurt as she did in the earlier sequence, now it is as if she shares Maxine's secret and, perhaps, is bemused by her refusal to part with it. Music, in both instances, assists in suggesting these readings of the star's expression.

A NONFICTION LANDSCAPE

The conflicting stories of Oberon's past are represented through a re-creation of my research journey as both a literal and a figurative journey through the Tasmanian landscape, and there are varying treatments of nonfiction archival Tasmanian footage shot in the northeast at St. Helens where Tasmanian Merle is said to have lived as a child. Although footage appears to be used here in an apparently illustrative fashion in order to

Edyth Langham, interviewed in New Zealand about Merle Oberon. Courtesy Australian Film Commission.

describe St. Helens around the time of Oberon's alleged birth and early years there, there is an odd disparity between the emptiness of the images on screen and storyteller Edyth Langham's claims that "St. Helens was very much like the Gold Coast of today, it was where everyone went for holidays, it was quite social."[13] Despite Langham's claim, the archival images we see reveal a sparsely populated landscape with a few houses near a deserted beach. To further develop the idea that nonfiction archival material present in the film might not always function as a literal representation or confirmation of information given on the voice track, images of a "generic" ocean liner leaving the harbor at Hobart are used three times from three different angles in relation to the three different stories of Merle's departure. For example, Rosina Mayhead, who claims to be the daughter of the Tasmanian midwife who delivered Oberon to Lottie Chintock, tells how an Indian silk merchant adopted Oberon and took her to India:

> And then she went to the old model school until she was seven and that's when she went. He decided to take her back to India . . . but she was never what they said she was, she was not Indian, she was Chinese.[14]

Under Mayhead's voice, a ship's foghorn sounds as a grainy black-and-white archival image of an ocean liner leaves the dock and sails down the Derwent River from Hobart toward the sea. People are waving to the ship from the banks of the river as it sets off on its long voyage. Later in the film, Edyth Langham claims Oberon was taken to India by an Indian Army officer:

> They adopted her and took her to India because they were, I believe, in the Indian Army. And that was how she made that great trip to India and how the Indian story came about.[15]

A ship's foghorn also interrupts Edyth's story, and more archival footage of the same ocean liner sailing down the Derwent appears. This time, it's much smaller, viewed from a grassy hill overlooking the bay. The final image of the ship occurs during genealogist Evan Best's account of Oberon's journey to India as a child in a company of traveling players named O'Brien:

> These O'Briens asked her father, Gimlet Thompson, whether they could take her with them and eventually got his permission to take her overseas, and they took her to India.[16]

The ship is now a tiny speck on the horizon. It is the same ship we have seen each time—not the *actual* ship of course, because we do not know whether in fact Oberon traveled by ship from Tasmania to India. It is the image of *a* ship, intended to connote the "idea" of Oberon's ship from the Tasmanian storytellers' perspective, and that I hoped might indicate my own perspective on the conflicting elements in their stories.

Similarly, the status of archival photographic stills varies during the film. In an early section discussing the Tasmanian stories, an archival photograph of the midwife who is said to have delivered Oberon is presented as unproblematic factual evidence that the woman, Philadelphia Flynn, existed. However, later in the film, when publicity stills of Oberon and photographs of her Tasmanian mother, Lottie Chintock, are compared for evidence of their mother-daughter relationship and as a relative's proof of the family resemblance, the publicity stills' status as photographic evidence is weakened—for it becomes obvious that Oberon, like a chameleon, had many fictional appearances. Three different studio photographs of the film star in various roles, the kinds of photographs that fan magazines would have published and to which Tasmanians might have had access, are offered to support the claim by Oberon's Tasmanian nephew Peter Lawrence that there is an obvious family resemblance between Oberon and Lottie Chintock. But in each photograph, the star looks remarkably different, even unrecognizable. The photos of Lottie, family snapshots that are offered as a comparison, are themselves fuzzy and indistinct. It is almost impossible see Lottie clearly or to hazard a guess as to whether these two women could be related. But such is the power of his desire for connection that the nephew says, "I've got no doubts in my mind that Merle is Lottie's daughter because of the likenesses in the photographs, if you compare the photographs . . ."[17] I hoped the juxtaposition of photographs might encourage the audience to question both the status of the archival evidence and their own desire for proof.

JUST ANOTHER STORY

The Trouble with Merle is one more story to add to the set of tales that have attached to Merle Oberon over the past thirty years. One of the great ironies of the stories out of Tasmania is that, in creating them, Tasmanians returned Oberon to the circumstances the studio had presumably attempted to disguise — poverty, mixed race, and illegitimacy. Like the Tasmanians and the studio, I also attempted to create a Merle story, one that raised questions as it tried to answer them and tried to make sense of the sea of stories — not necessarily with a definitive answer but the possibility of answers. This approach does not satisfy every audience. A prominent Australian film critic writing of the documentary criticized its knowledge strategies precisely because the film, as he said, "raised more questions than it answered." I was rather pleased with his response.

NOTES

1. In this discussion "narrated" refers to voice-over.

2. British filmmaker Nick Broomfield has performed this kind of documentary persona in films such as *The Leader, His Driver, and the Driver's Wife* (1991). In the film, Broomfield appears to be trying unsuccessfully to gain access to the political leader Eugene Terre Blanche while at the same time offering insights into the nature of right-wing activities in contemporary South Africa.

3. Renov offers four documentary tendencies: "to record, reveal, or preserve; to persuade or promote; to analyse or interrogate; to express" (25).

4. Glen Kinging, interviewed by Maree Delofski, Sydney 2000.

5. Cassandra Pybus, interviewed by Maree Delofski, Lower Snug, Tasmania, 2001.

6. Peter Lawrence, Lottie Chintock's nephew, recounted this in an interview with Maree Delofski, Tasmania, 2001.

7. Pamela Archer, interviewed by Maree Delofski, Hobart, Tasmania, 2001.

8. Doone Kennedy, interviewed by Maree Delofski, Hobart, Tasmania, 2001.

9. Pamela Archer interview.

10. Various guests at the 1978 Hobart reception noted that Oberon appeared strangely nervous during the event and that she became faint at one point and had to leave the room.

11. Barbara Knight, interviewed by Maree Delofski, Tasmania, 2001.

12. Maxine Green, interviewed by Maree Delofski, Tasmania, 2001.

13. Edyth Langham, interviewed by Maree Delofski, Hobart, Tasmania, 2001. The Gold Coast that Langham refers to is a densely populated coastal area in Queensland, Australia, where international and local tourists stay in hotels and apartment blocks.

14. Rosina Mayhead, interviewed by Maree Delofski, Hobart, Tasmania, 2001.

15. Edyth Langham interview.

16. Evan Best, interviewed by Maree Delofski, Sydney, 2001.

17. Peter Lawrence interview.

BIBLIOGRAPHY

Bell, Desmond. 2004. "Shooting the Past? Found Footage, Filmmaking, and Popular Memory." *Kinema,* Spring. http://www.kinema.uwaterloo.ca/bell041.htm.

Brooks, Peter. 1992. *Reading for the Plot: Design and Intention in Narrative.* New York: Vintage Books.

Grierson, John. 1966. *Grierson on Documentary.* London: Faber.

Hamilton, Paula, and Kate Darian Smith, eds. 1994. *Memory and History in Twentieth-Century Australia.* Melbourne, Australia: Oxford University Press.

Higham, Charles, and Roy Moseley. 1983. *Princess Merle: The Romantic Life of Merle Oberon.* New York: Coward McCann.

Nichols, Bill. 2001. *Introduction to Documentary.* Bloomington: Indiana University Press.

Porter, Hal. 1965. *Stars of Australian Stage and Screen.* London: Angus and Robertson.

Renov, Michael, ed. 1993. *Theorizing Documentary.* New York: Routledge.

FILMOGRAPHY

Bright Leaf (Michael Curtiz, USA, 1950).

Bright Leaves (Ross McElwee, USA, 2003).

The Epic That Never Was (Bill Duncalf, UK, 1965).

I, Claudius (Joseph Von Sternberg, UK, 1937).

The Leader, His Driver, and the Driver's Wife (Nick Broomfield, UK, 1991).

Letter from Siberia (Chris Marker, France, 1956).

Looking for Langston (Isaac Julien, UK, 1988).

Lydia (Julien Duvivier, USA, 1941).

Maybe Day in Kazakhstan (Tony Harrison, UK, 1993).

Motherland (Kriv Stenders, Australia, 1993).

Over the Moon (Thornton Freeland, UK, 1939).

The Private Life of Henry VIII (Alexander Korda, UK, 1934).
Sadness (Tony Ayres, Australia, 1998).
A Song to Remember (Charles Vidor, USA, 1945).
Stanley Kubrick: A Life in Pictures (Jan Harlan, USA, 2001).
The Trouble with Merle (Maree Delofski, Australia, 2002).
Wuthering Heights (William Wyler, USA, 1939).

Audiovisual Archiving and the World of Tomorrow

Explorations into Accreditation and Certification

EMILY STARESINA

This article explores if and how accreditation and/or certification of audiovisual archival education may strengthen the identity of the field as a recognized profession in its own right. By analysing the results of the case study, it examines the function of accreditation and certification within the traditional[1] archiving profession and aims to uncover the feasibility of implementing accreditation and/or certification as a method of educational standardization within the audiovisual archiving profession.

CONTEXT

A profession is a body of people in a learned occupation who agree upon and maintain codified values, ethics, and practices within their field, which in turn safeguard the integrity of the profession. Professionals require a specialized education in which these values, ethics, and practices are taught. Professions require a forum in which these values, ethics, and practices are debated. Thus, professionals compose a professional community, but they also give back to the community. As such, professions are widely recognized by the general public, the government, and the private sector, who all hold the professions accountable for the actions of all their practitioners. The presence of accountability—both internally and externally—is integral to a profession, as it indicates that a profession has a function in and a responsibility to society. Among the common elements that inform a profession are work autonomy; a specialized core body of knowledge, ethics, principles, and values defined and upheld by committed individuals and organizations; a body of literature; and control of a job market. In order to synthesize all these elements, there must exist a standardized method of educating a profession's practitioners.

The type of education may vary from internships, workshops, individual courses, and long-distance training to college diplomas, advanced university degrees, examinations, and certifications. In most professions, such as law, medicine, and accounting, the successful completion of one or a combination of these options is required before a practitioner may legally commence working. Standardized education is used as a tool to ensure that would-be practitioners share the essential background knowledge and skill sets to perform their job according to a set of established standards. One method of standardizing education is through the process of accrediting professional or specialized graduate-level education. Accreditation refers to the recognition process whereby a governing body—usually part of an existing association—outlines standards in graduate education and has the power to accredit programs that meet established criteria. A second method of standardizing education is through certification, whereby an individual is recognized as possessing defined skills and knowledge to perform required tasks in accordance with minimum standards set by one or several governing bodies or institutions.

It has been more than one hundred years since Boleslaw Matuszewski wrote his futuristic text "A New Source of History" and the first paper prints of films were deposited in the Library of Congress. In terms of being a professional field, however, audiovisual archiving has yet to mature. One factor contributing to this state of affairs is that audiovisual archiving has lacked a formalized method of educating its practitioners. Throughout the 1970s and 1980s, such education was largely a matter of on-the-job training supplemented by occasional workshops and seminars.[2] During this period, there were limited forums for discussion outside of a handful of institutions, such as the International Federation of Film Archives (FIAF), and professional literature was scant. There existed neither codified values nor standards by which the community of audiovisual archivists could work or be identified. The 1998 UNESCO publication *Philosophy of Audiovisual Archiving: Principles and Practices* was one of the first attempts to codify values and standards within the audiovisual field. Its author, Ray Edmondson, observed that the field and its practitioners lacked a clear identity and recognition within the collecting professions, the government, the audiovisual industries, and the public as a whole. He noted that a lack of synthesized values, ethics, principles, and perceptions created a vacuum at the profession's core.[3]

Today, however, the outlook is less bleak. Best practices and standards in every aspect of the field—from preservation to cataloging to access—are beginning to emerge. The Moving Image Collections (MIC) initiative is an example of organizations and individuals both within the audiovisual archiving field and in related fields creating and sharing cataloging and access standards. Opportunities for community discussions and lobbying have increased with the proliferation of professional associations such as the Association of Moving Image Archivists (AMIA), the International Federation of Television Archives (FIAT), the International Association of Sound Archives (IASA), and the Audiovisual Archiving Philosophy Interest Network (AVAPIN). There exists a rapidly growing body of literature in journals, books, and on the Internet in which both audiovisual theory and practice are addressed. Perhaps most notably, however, is the growth of educational opportunities in the form of graduate degree programs.[4] In the second edition of the UNESCO document, however, Edmondson acknowledges that there is little evidence that such growth has translated into formal recognition of the profession by governments and employing authorities.[5] Thus, despite these recent advances, including the cocktail of educational choices,

the field lacks a defined set of educational standards or curricula that are an integral aspect to many professional vocations. What, then, will it take to turn the audiovisual archiving field into a viable and recognized profession?

One can make a case for focusing on the education of its practitioners. With the paradigm shift from preservation alone to preservation and access, as well as the introduction of digital technology into the mainstream, audiovisual archivists increasingly must make complicated and crucial legal and ethical decisions in areas where precedents are few. Moreover, when one looks at comparable professions, such as librarianship, one sees that education plays a vital role in the development, growth, and accountability of those professions and their practitioners. The presence of a profession among other professions and the notion of accountability are key factors underlying the strength of any profession—and standardized education is one building tool.

There is a tendency to think of audiovisual archiving as a field separate from what Edmondson calls other "collecting professions," such as traditional archiving and librarianship. Even within the field is a divisive tendency to break off into media-specific compartments, such as sound archives or film archives. On the one hand, this division seems redundant. A pediatrician is just as much of a doctor as a geriatrician, despite the fact that their specialities require specialized training. It is obvious that we are not librarians, but by how far do our goals, practices, or ethics differ from those held by traditional archivists, who deal with both static and electronic media? At the foundational level, the two groups share similar goals, mainly to preserve and provide access to archival materials. On the other hand, the ways these duties are performed is where the similarities begin to breakdown. The three pillars of archival science—provenance, respect des fonds, and original order—cannot, to a large extent, be applied to audiovisual archives, as they do not always fit the challenges of preserving audiovisual media. For one, the tumultuous relationship between studios, archives, and private collectors often led archivists to accept films of uncertain provenance, an issue still dealt with today. Despite the differences dictated by physical media, both groups approach their respective media with an interdisciplinary nature, seeking information from other fields such as history, ethnography, and art to complete their tasks.

The similarities between archiving and audiovisual archiving extend beyond shared core goals. The field of traditional archiving struggled to create its own professional identity outside of the work of academics and historians. Many archivists and historians have written about the difficulty of establishing a definition of their profession and of developing standards, let alone pursuing research and theory.[6] Integral to the search for identity within the archival field was the role of education. In the same vein, audiovisual archiving is struggling to define its professional parameters and public identity. It is constructive, then, for audiovisual archives to look to the traditional archiving field to note how the standardized educational framework developed.

ACCREDITATION

Professional associations play a key role in the education of practitioners. Although there may be various associations or organizations within any one profession, only a select few will mature into the profession's flagship institutions. One such association is the American Library Association (ALA). Since its inception in 1876, the ALA has taken a leadership role in the librarian profession by creating and enforcing standards from best practices and values to education. Similarly, the archival field in the United States has its own flagship institution, the Society of American Archivists (SAA). Two significant factors led to the birth of the SAA in 1936. Within the American Historical Association developed subgroups that were primarily archival in focus. As a result of the visible activities of these subgroups, the U.S. Congress established the National Archives as an independent federal agency in 1934. Congress's recognition lead archivists to feel the need to articulate a professional distinction between themselves and historians and scholars and that an association was necessary to aid in the growth and advancement of the archiving profession.[7] Both the ALA and the SAA, as flagship institutions of their respective professions within the United States, have been heavily

involved in the education of their professionals—albeit with different approaches.

The field of audiovisual archiving has its own share of associations and organizations that have played and continue to play a role in the education of its practitioners. Since the 1970s, FIAF has offered summer-school training workshops. AMIA hosts workshops at its annual conference. Various other workshops and seminars are hosted worldwide. Gregory Lukow, chief of the Motion Picture, Broadcasting, and Recorded Sound Division of the Library of Congress, in an overview of the education options for audiovisual archivists, notes that "such narrowly defined modes of archival training have generally excluded the complex social, philosophical, and cultural contexts in which modern, professional archival practice is grounded."[8] Since the 1990 UNESCO publication of *Curriculum Development for the Training of Personnel in Audiovisual and Recorded Sound Archives,* the first publication of its kind on the subject, there has been a shift, as Lukow points out, from training to educating practitioners in the field.[9] The creation of educational standards is a critical step in the growth of any profession, so why do none exist in the audiovisual field? The difference between the library or traditional archival professions and the audiovisual field, however, is that the latter's abundance of professional associations yields less a united front that a fragmented statement.[10] There exists no association, such as the ALA or SAA, to represent the field as a whole, or at least no existing organization has yet taken a leadership role in investigating educational standards.[11] Is standardizing education a task that comes up only after a profession or a professional association has reached a particular age or plateau? Educational standards imply that there are codified practices, values, and so on that should act as the foundation of the education of its practitioners, yet the audiovisual archiving field has yet to develop such fundamentals. What signals that a field is ready to begin standardizing the education of its practitioners? To get a better understanding of the climate in which this may occur, let us take a look at the experiences of the SAA.

The SAA has been instrumental in the creation of formalized educational standards for archivists. "Guidelines for a Graduate Program in Archival Studies" is its official document in which the elements of standardized education are laid out. Qualifying graduate archival studies programs (which are differentiated from a more general information science program or a specialized historical manuscripts program) must follow core curricula and must supply the appropriate administration, faculty, and infrastructure as outlined in the SAA guidelines. The goal of these guidelines is to improve the quality of archival studies graduate programs by establishing minimum expectations for students and universities, thereby encouraging the development of more comprehensive programs to improve the profession by better educating archivists.[12] Today's SAA guidelines are a product of multiple revisions since the 1970s, and at one point they were under consideration for accreditation purposes. One should note, however, that the SAA's guidelines are just that — guidelines for graduate archival programs, as opposed to a formal accreditation of programs. Is this merely a question of semantics or are there tangible differences between the two methods of standardizing education? Does one method translate into more benefits over the other, and if so, in what capacity? Does it stand to reason that guidelines are a stepping-stone to accreditation? To answer these questions, let us look at the how accreditation operates within the comparable profession: librarianship.

If the goal of the SAA's graduate archival guidelines is to create minimum educational standards with the purpose of strengthening the field by better educating its archivists, what is the goal of accreditation?[13] Accreditation is a tool used to uphold minimum standards outlined by a governing body that institutions or programs must meet to be accredited. Accreditation is a voluntary system in which a higher education program or school is self-evaluated and peer assessed to determine whether it meets appropriate standards of quality and integrity on a continual basis. In the library profession, self- and peer evaluation occurs via the ALA's Committee on Accreditation (COA). Through accreditation the ALA-COA hopes to

assure the educational community, the general public, and other agencies or organizations that an institution or program (a) has clearly defined and educationally

appropriate objectives, (b) maintains conditions under which their achievement can reasonably be expected, (c) is in fact accomplishing them substantially, and (d) can be expected to continue to do so.[14]

Like the SAA's guidelines for graduate archival education, a library program seeking accreditation must meet the ALA's outlined mission, goals, and objectives, which are applied to curriculum, faculty, students, administration and financial support, and physical resources and facilities. Although the goal behind the criteria used by an accrediting agency such as the ALA and goal behind the guidelines for graduate archival education are similar, the former is legitimized not only internally but also externally. ALA's accreditation policies and procedures are recognized by the Council for Higher Education Accreditation (CHEA), the largest U.S. institution to approve the quality of regional, national, and specialized accrediting organizations.[15] In addition to being recognized by CHEA, the ALA also belongs to the Association of Specialized and Professional Accreditors (ASPA).[16] To be a recognized professional or specialized program, a governing body (such as the ALA-COA) must belong to either CHEA or ASPA.

Among the benefits accrediting agencies that belong to CHEA or ASPA share are professional development and networking opportunities. One could argue, however, that similar benefits can be provided by nonaccrediting agencies such as the SAA by way of conferences and workshops. The main difference, then, between offering guidelines and offering formal accreditation services is that the latter's actions are scrutinized by an external agency. The benefits implicit in this difference are obvious: for one, external scrutiny ensures that the accrediting agency is responsible for keeping up with broader accreditation trends and practices; for another, the onus of constant review of the quality of the program is placed on the program itself, which in turn increases the accountability of the program and thus ensures that its graduates have a defined level of knowledge as they enter the workforce, which may affect an employer's hiring decision. Still, one must wonder what tangible benefits manifest from accreditation?

In 1983, archivist Fredric M. Miller wrote an article assessing the current state of SAA's efforts to standardize graduate archival education. To explain why accreditation never came to fruition, despite various attempts since the 1970s, he offered the phrase, "if it ain't broke, don't fix it." By that he meant that (a) students shopping around for a strong, worthwhile education could compare educational offerings in SAA's published directory of programs without accreditation, and that (b) there did not seem to be a monetary argument for accreditation. He offered as example the salary of medical librarians—a specialized group requiring a master's degree, an examination, two years of experience, and certification—noting that it was similar to that of an archivist in 1982. He also noted that accreditation in a field that was predominantly female would do little to drive up salaries.[17] Today, however, this outlook is considerably different. According to the U.S. Department of Labor, the median annual salary for an archivist in 2002 was $35,270.[18] In contrast, the median annual salary of a librarian in the same year was $43,090. Results from a recent Canadian study on government salary comparisons for the same year yielded similar results. An archivist working for the federal government was paid $52,846 Canadian (US$33,307) while the entry-level librarian was paid $66,312 Canadian (US$41,795).[19] Are salaries an important indicator of the maturity of a profession? Although more research is needed to prove a direct correlation between accreditation and salaries, consider this: the Canadian study found that archivists, whose skills are highly transferable, are leaving their positions for more lucrative positions both within the government and outside it. The same study voiced concern that the profession—where highly educated people are needed to perform the challenging tasks of archiving in today's world—may be in jeopardy of losing its integrity if it cannot retain the level of highly educated archivists it needs. As a result of their findings, it found that a raise in salaries was justified. Similarly, a recent survey of graduates of archival education programs in the United States found that the most frequently cited reason for leaving the archival profession was a poor salary but that building a stronger and better-educated profession depended on the retention of graduates from graduate archival programs.[20]

There are other reasons the SAA's 1980s efforts to implement accreditation failed. Miller came to the general conclusion that the guidelines could not justify the effort needed to overcome the inherent difficulties in accreditation. He illustrated several specific issues. First, he noted that there was a lack of commitment from the community to pursue accreditation. Some perceived accreditation as an elitist act and the SAA as an elitist organization for pursuing it. Others attributed it to a lack of money, that the SAA was seen as too poor to take on accreditation and that the idea of raising membership dues to pay for accreditation was not popular.[21] The job market was another influence; the indifference toward archival education shown by major employers such as the Library of Congress and major historical societies made it difficult to for the SAA to know what employers needed in terms of an archival curriculum from future employees.[22] To some academics, the current guidelines, which were revised in 1994, were inefficient—too rigid and practical in their application, which did not (and does not) reflect the realities of promoting an archival program on a shoestring budget.[23] Thus, the SAA's attempt at accreditation failed because of a culmination of political, social, and economical problems.

Today, however, the profession has made substantial gains in practice and theory, which can be seen in the growth of graduate archival programs. These positive developments lead one to wonder if the SAA will once more attempt accreditation. According to Solveig DeSutter, the SAA's director of education, the Society is not working toward accreditation but instead continues its efforts to encourage development of archival education programs that comply with the guidelines. When asked what benefits exist for students to attend graduate archival programs that follow the SAA's guidelines, DeSutter pointed out that some professional organizations include as part of their criteria for awards attending a school that conforms to the guidelines. When asked what employers think of the guidelines, DeSutter offered that, while there were no hard rules, as the oldest association for archivists with a roster of respected archivists, it cannot hurt a prospective employee to make a potential employer aware that he or she has graduated from a program that follows the guidelines.[24] Certainly, the recognition of the guidelines by other associations in the field proves that the SAA is the flagship institution in the field, but as salaries for librarians demonstrate, accreditation is a method by which outside recognition takes concrete form.

CERTIFICATION

Professional certification[25] is another method of implementing a standardized education for practitioners of a profession. Certification is either mandatory, as is the case with medical librarians, or voluntary, as is the case with accountants. Like accreditation, certification may be administered by a professional organization. It may also be administered by a governmental body. Certification communicates that the holder has obtained a widely recognized and accepted level of professional competence as outlined by the administering certifying agency. Like accreditation, certification also undergoes a reflection process whereby holders often have to recertify. Unlike accreditation, which is institutionally based, certification is granted to individuals who have successfully met the criteria laid out by a credentialing agency. Example criteria include passing one or a series of exams, having several years of practical experience, or having a certain level of education such as a master's degree. In that sense, graduating from an accredited institution or program may be one of several requirements for certification, or it may not matter at all. In professions such as accounting or records management, certification guarantees that the holder is eligible for promotions or positions with greater responsibility. The extent to which certification benefits the holder depends on the legitimacy of the certifying organization within and outside the field. It also appears that the more difficult obtaining a certification is, the more favorably it reflects upon the profession. For example, if a candidate in the accounting profession in Canada fails to successfully complete the credential process within four attempts, he or she cannot ever reapply. This method ensures that only those candidates who meet the profession's rigorous standards

are credentialed. In effect, this process promotes a level of accountability and prestige that is associated both within the profession and to the general public.

Along with experimenting with accreditation during the 1970s, the SAA launched a campaign to establish credentials for archivists. In 1987, the Society formed an Interim Board for Certification (IBC) to determine qualifications and standards by which practitioners could be tested for certification. As a result, the Academy of Certified Archivists (ACA) was born and has for more than fifteen years been issuing the designation of CA (Certified Archivist). Although the SAA and ACA today remain independent of each other, the latter grew out of the SAA's observation that certification would strengthen the field. The SAA supports the actions of the ACA by holding exams in conjunction with SAA's annual conference, in order to reduce travel costs for members. The support of the flagship institution in the field provides a certain amount of validity to the ACA's operations. To be eligible to write the examination, potential members must meet defined criteria, which are broken down into several options. Option 1 demands that potential members have a master's degree with a concentration in archival administration plus one year of qualifying professional archival experience. Option 2 requires a master's degree plus two years of qualifying professional archival experience. Option 3 concerns previously qualified archivists whose certification has lapsed, and option 4 is for recertification of previously certified archivists. An outside option for students and recent graduates is to take the exam, which ensures that they are provisionally certified, and allows a three-year window in which to obtain the qualified archival work experience. Recertification after five years is mandatory by taking the exam or by petitioning. Petitioning involves a points system where the candidate must outline, on paper, how they have professionally developed. Person who take certain courses offered by the SAA earn certification points. There is no fee for recertification, although there are annual dues and exam and certification costs.[26]

How does certification benefit its holders in the real world? The core mission behind the ACA's actions is to take a leadership role in supporting and promoting the highest level of professional archival practice, and they achieve this mission through certification and through promoting the employment of certified archivists. In 2002, the U.S. Department of Labor reported that there were approximately 22,000 persons in archival, curator, and museum technician jobs. Of these 22,000 individuals, how many were certified archivists? According to the ACA's 2004 membership roster, approximately six hundred practicing archivists are certified within the United States, with an additional eighteen international members.[27] By the numbers, it appears that the CA is a designation only a minority of archivists possess, which suggests that the CA is not a major factor affecting employment in the archiving world or outside it. In addition, the certification is not mandatory, so what, then, are the tangible benefits from the ACA's certification process?

There is evidence to suggest that the ACA credential is valuable to employers. For example, the University of Missouri, in its 2004 Governance System for Librarians and Archivists, requires that to obtain a level-four archivist position, a candidate must have either a CA or a CRM (certified records manager). The Denver Public Library boasts that, out of a team of nine, four are certified archivists. Organizations such as the SAA and the Society of Southwest Archivists offer courses that reward participants recertification points. A further way to judge the certification designation is to consider academics' opinions on the subject. Some programs or institutions, such as Temple University, provide information for students wishing to obtain a CA. Like accreditation, however, certification requires an agreed-upon skills set and body of knowledge to be successfully implemented. Some academics have boycotted certification as a "dumbing down" of educational requirements for being a professional archivist. Others found it problematic that the grandfather clause—which allowed those with certain title, years of education, or professional experience to be credentialed—permitted individuals with little or no archival experience or education to slip in.[28]

What function would either accreditation or certification have in the audiovisual field? How would it be implemented, and by whom? How could it be enforced? Could the field avoid some of the pitfalls that the SAA faced and continues to face today?

ACCREDITATION AND/OR CERTIFICATION FOR AUDIOVISUAL ARCHIVISTS?

Audiovisual archiving as a profession lacks the public recognition that other, more established professions share. Despite recent attempts by Edmondson and others to codify archival principles, practices, and values, the overall acceptance and recognition of such fundamentals remains in a premature state. At this point, it would appear that jumping into either accreditation or certification of educational standards may be premature as well. At the same time, however, is it difficult to assess whether educational standards are born of codified practices or the other way around. In this vein, the audiovisual archiving field can glean much from the experiences the traditional archiving profession has had with accreditation and certification, especially when one considers the difficulties the traditional archival field had—much like audiovisual archiving has today—in establishing itself as a profession. Standardized education plays a key role in the strengthening any field, and the audiovisual archiving field is no different.

Most individuals attracted to careers in audiovisual archiving do not pursue it for the promise of lucrative salaries. Yet, there is a market for graduate audiovisual archival programs—and soon these graduates will be searching for employment. If they cannot secure employment that recognizes their level of education—as compared to other collecting professions such as librarianship and to a lesser extent traditional archiving—they may opt for more lucrative employment elsewhere, as the results of the Canadian and U.S. studies cited earlier indicate. The potential drain of specially educated people in the audiovisual archiving field is alarming, considering it has only just begun to form in an organized fashion. It is too early, though, to discern if the profession will suffer "brain drain." The fact remains that there is a strong argument for standardized education. But is graduate-level education necessary or even desired by the field as a whole?

Key questions and concerns must be addressed before considering either accreditation or certification as viable options for the audio-visual archiving field. The traditional archival field currently has guidelines for graduate archival programs, which are recognized by various educational institutions and organizations within the profession. Yet, archivists still earn substantially less then librarians, and many are leaving their positions to pursue better paying careers. Although more research needs to be conducted to prove or disprove the link between salaries and accreditation, the external recognition of accredited programs by agencies such as CHEA or ASPA may give the accreditation option an edge over guidelines. If the audiovisual archiving field decides to move toward accreditation, would creating guidelines, such as the SAA's, be the first prudent step in accomplishing this goal?[29] Will an existing organization such as AMIA offer to incur the financial burden and political pitfalls of accreditation? How would audiovisual technicians who have backgrounds in chemistry instead of specialized graduate degrees fare if accreditation were imposed? Similar concerns surround the certification option. If, on the one hand, one interprets the traditional archival field's forays into certification as the failed result of accreditation, is there a reason for the audiovisual archiving field to pursue this educational option? If, on the other hand, one sees certification as a valid and enforceable method of educating practitioners, promoting an understanding of employers' needs, and strengthening the entire field, how would it be implemented in the audiovisual archiving profession? Would certification apply to audiovisual technicians and other similarly educated and non-formally educated individuals? Would there be a grandfather clause? What would be the ramifications, if any, for misconduct? Would—could—both academics and practitioners work toward creating mutually agreeable certification standards? Would the implementation of either or both accreditation and certification meet the needs of the audiovisual archival community? Would one be more feasible over the other? Could it and would it be enforced? How can we pursue either endeavour while at the same time addressing the complexities embracing the audiovisual archiving profession?

This article is intended to uncover the function and feasibility of accreditation and certification standards within the audiovisual archiving profession. While there are no firm answers, the benefits and complexities of both options have been outlined. By analyzing the SAA's experiences with accreditation and certification, the audiovisual archiving field has a reference point from which to glean valuable insight.

The underlying moral of the SAA's experience is that there must exist a need and a desire that fuels a long-term commitment by the professional community to both implement and enforce standardized education. To judge if such a need or desire exists, there must be an investigation into the social, economic, and political spheres in which the audiovisual archiving field revolves. Thus, as archivists in a burgeoning field, we must ask ourselves some serious questions about the role of education in the field. Currently, some efforts are being made to assess the function and quality of education within the field of audiovisual archiving. An example is the "Comparing Curricula: Programs in Moving Image Archiving and Preservation" panel session held at the 2003 AMIA conference.

It is evident that standardized education within a professional field lends a level of accountability and integrity to a field, and it also generates a professional presence. From this point of view, then, standardized education is a topic that our evolving field cannot afford to pass up. Whether or not one embraces some form of standardized education in the audiovisual archiving field, it is evident that, with formal educational options for audiovisual archivists on the rise, a comprehensive and critical inquiry into the feasibility of standardized education is in order.

NOTES

1. Within this text, the phrases "traditional archiving," "traditional archival profession," and "archiving" are employed to differentiate between the audiovisual archiving field (and audiovisual archivists) and the traditional archiving field (or archivists). For purposes of simplicity, the "traditional" profession is that which grew from the preservation of static documents, such as manuscripts, papers, and so on, but also includes electronic documents.

2. This is noted by Gregory Lukow in his overview of audiovisual education in "Beyond 'On-the-Job': The Education of Moving Image Archivists—A History in Progress" (*Film History* 12, no. 2 [2000]: 134–47).

3. Ray Edmondson, *Philosophy of Audiovisual Archiving: Principles and Practices* (Paris: UNESCO, 1998; 2d ed., 2004).

4. In addition to the existing workshops and seminars, there are several specialized master's degree programs, including one at the University of California, Los Angeles and one at New York University.

5. Edmondson 2004, 3.

6. This observation was made by archivist Fredric M. Miller in his article "The SAA as Sisyphus: Education since the 1960s" (*American Archivist* 63, no. 2: 224–36).

7. For an overview of the development of the SAA, please refer to their Web site, http://www.archivists.org.

8. Lukow, 137.

9. Ibid.

10. See Edmondson.

11. This is only partially accurate. AMIA is taking some form of credentialing under consideration (see the education committee's meeting minutes), but thus far no deliverable guidelines have been realized. At the last couple of conferences, there have been panels comparing curricula of existing educational programs within the field. For a look at the minutes, visit http://www.amianet.org/committees/CoB/Education/minutes.html.

12. The SAA's official Web site, http://www.archivists.org, provides a detailed explanation of the impetus behind the guidelines, as well as the guidelines themselves.

13. There are three types of accreditation: regional, institutional, and specialized or professional. Regional or institutional accreditation agencies accredit an institution that meets educational quality standards. Within the United States, there are six regional bodies that govern accreditation within their geographic boundaries. Specialized or professional accrediting agencies recognize specific programs within institutions that meet educational standards outlined by accrediting agencies (such as the ALA), which in turn meet the standards set by organizations such as CHEA and ASPA (see notes 15 and 16). This article explores only specialized or professional accreditation.

14. See ALA's Web site (http://www.ala.org/ala/accreditation/accredstandards/index.htm) for more detailed information.

15. CHEA is an American organization that coordinates accreditation activities. Its membership boasts more than sixty national, regional, and specialized accrediting organizations, including the ALA. For more information on CHEA, visit http://www.chea.org.

16. Like CHEA, ASPA also recognizes specialized or professional programs.

17. See Miller.

18. It is important to note that, along with archivists, this statistic includes the earnings of curators and museum technicians, and varies depending on the type and size of an institution.

19. For comparison, archivists working in the United States for the Federal government, in nonsupervisory, supervisory, and managerial positions, claimed an average annual salary of $69,706; librarians at the same level claimed $70,238. Canadian statistics were taken from the Professional Institute of the Public Service of Canada's report, *Why Pay Archivists and Historians More? Compensation, Recruitment, and Retention of Historical Researchers in the Research Group* (Ottawa: The Professional Institute of the Public Service of Canada, 2004). The Canadian salary figures were converted into U.S. dollars at the rate of exchange for October 1, 2002.

20. Elizabeth Yakel, "The Future of the Past: A Survey of Graduates of Master's-Level Graduate Archival Education Programs in the United States," *American Archivist* 63, no. 2 (2000): 301–21 at 310.

21. For example, the current fee structure for ASPA membership is broken down into two sections: there is an annual flat fee of $3,180 and an additional $5.45 for each institution that sponsors member-agency accredited programs with a cap at $500.

22. See Miller.

23. In e-mail correspondence (January 17, 2005) between the author and Anne J. Gilliland, associate professor at UCLA's Department of Information Studies, Gilliland expressed that this was her own view on the guidelines, yet it is not difficult to locate additional supporting literature to support this viewpoint. For example, Richard Cox, in his article "The Society of American Archivists and Graduate Education: Meeting at the Crossroads" (*American Archivist* 63, no. 2 [2000]: 368–79), states that the responsibility for the development of graduate archival education is and should be shifting from the SAA to the educators.

24. As told to the author in personal e-mail correspondence with Solveig DeSutter, January 17, 2005.

25. Not to be confused with certificate courses or programs in which once completed the student receives a certificate.

26. For a more detailed account of the ACA's methodology, visit their Web site at http://www.certifiedarchivists.org.

27. The ACA's membership roster can be found at http://www.certifiedarchivists.org/html/pdf/2004%20directory.pdf.

28. Gilliland, personal e-mail correspondence. Gilliland states that these are her own personal views as someone who has written the exam and felt that it was written by practitioners and not academics and that the "correct" answers to the questions were not the ones the authors of the test were looking for.

29. It might. Greg Lukow, in a phone interview (January 31, 2005) with the author, adds that the simpler first phase would be a sharing of information of the current educational offerings' basic core competencies for audiovisual archivists.

The Use of Digital Restoration within European Film Archives:

A Case Study

ARIANNA TURCI

INTRODUCTION

This article is based on my thesis, *Digital Restoration within European Film Archives,* which was written for the Professional Master of Arts Program "Preservation and Presentation of the Moving Image" at the University of Amsterdam during the 2003–2004 academic year. My research examines the role of digital restoration in European film archives, specifically to identify the use of digital technology in European film archives and to offer some observations about the prevalence of digital restoration in Europe.

Before I describe my research methodology, I want to emphasize that this case study is a snapshot of a particular moment in time and should be regarded only as a description of contemporary digital practices. Digital applications are constantly changing because the technology is evolving incredibly quickly. At the same time, digital technology is still a fairly recent innovation with lots of attending problems. In particular, the language describing the technology and its applications is not yet well defined and the ethical issues posed by digital restoration have not yet been adequately addressed.

I began interviewing European film archivists about digital restoration because I felt that there was a lack of information about contemporary practices in different archives. Although there are various journals, articles, and Web sites dedicated to the topic, there is very little comparative information about the practical experiments and ethical standards at work in different archives. Nor is there a detailed reference framework about the state of digital restoration in the archives.

I conducted a series of interviews with different European film archivists and used the data from these interviews to compare how the archivists are not only implementing their digital capabilities but also reflecting on their use. I examined how these archives are currently coping with the practical and ethical problems posed by digital restoration. My research also studied the similarities and the differences in approach at different European moving image archives. The following steps outline my research trajectory:

- developing the questionnaire
- researching appropriate responders at different archives
- sending the questionnaire via e-mail or meeting responders for live interviews
- analyzing the responses
- comparing different answers and forming conclusions

This research is not exhaustive because it presents the practices at only eight European archives. Yet, for purposes of general comparison, these archives provide a good overview of the European situation.

While I was studying in Amsterdam, I had the opportunity to participate in an internship at the Nederlands Filmmuseum. My affiliation with the Filmmuseum greatly facilitated my access to and knowledge of the different European archives represented here.[1] Of the nine archives I contacted, eight agreed to participate in my study. I had not expected such a positive response, and I was encouraged by it. In determining the archives to contact, I was guided by two criteria: their degree of involvement with digital restoration and the possibility of contacting them through the Nederlands Filmmuseum.

The interviews, conducted orally with Giovanna Fossati and Davide Pozzi and in writing with the other interviewees, were based on the following questions:

1. What is the approach of your archive toward digital restoration? Do you use digital restoration merely as an advanced tool to help the traditional restoration process or do you already restore (some or all) films entirely digitally?
2. What kind of scanner, software, and re-recorder do you use?
3. What do you find are the advantages and disadvantages of using these instruments?

4. Do you send films out to laboratories for any part(s) of the restoration process? If so, in what way do you monitor the job they do?
5. Do you think that digital restoration could one day replace traditional restoration completely?
6. What do you think about storing films on a digital format for preservation purposes?

The following case study describes my findings at individual European moving image archives.

ARCHIVES FRANÇAISES DU FILM DU CENTRE NATIONAL DE LA CINÉMATOGRAPHIE (CNC), BOIS D'ARCY, PARIS

The Centre National de la Cinématographie holds more than 300,000 reels of film. Restorers are slowly working their way through the collection. The collection includes films from 1892 to 1952, and most of these have not yet been cataloged. The CNC in France uses digital tools to restore parts of films, as in the case of their restoration of *The Crime of Monsieur Lange* (*Le crime de Monsieur Lange* [Jean Renoir, 1936]). This film archive is also one of the few archives that has already restored entire films using digital means exclusively. For example, *Bucking Broadway* (John Ford, 1917), which was restored in 2003, was just another anonymous silent film (the title on the print was *Drame du Far West*) until the actor Harry Carey was recognized in the print and archivists set out to identify the original title. The discovery of *Bucking Broadway* at the Archives Françaises du Film was a double victory: it is one of the rare surviving silent films made by John Ford, and it was the first feature film restored by the Archives du Film exclusively using digital technologies.

The archive's nitrate print was a tinted French version distributed in four color reels in 1918. This copy was very damaged: the frames were unstable, the image had deteriorated, and there were grading problems. The image appeared grainy and scratched, frames were missing, lots of splices had been made, and there were traces of mold. The intertitles showed early stages of decomposition, so they

were removed to avoid contaminating the image. Initially, a color duplicate was made from the nitrate materials using traditional means, but none of the print damage was corrected. However, John Ford's name was enough to justify a more in-depth restoration, and thus digital restoration seemed an appropriate course of action. At the time (2003), the cost of digital restoration was decreasing, thus opening up the opportunity for the CNC to use the new technology.

From the beginning, people involved in the restoration work realized the necessity of reference documents that would help to manage the creation of digital artifacts. The term "digital artifacts" refers to everything that is erroneously created by digital means. Digital artifacts are the changes made by computer programs when they erroneously interpret different parts of the image as imperfections and seek to "correct" them. As protection against digital artifacts, a black-and-white work print containing all the original flaws was struck, and a complete storyboard was created from the film's digitized images. Comparison of these reference documents to the digital output helped to identify and rectify the mistakes that occurred during digital duplication (such as inverted images and missing or incomplete scenes). During the scanning phase digital artifacts can also be created if the film fails to run perfectly through the mechanism or if there is faulty adhesion in the gate.[2]

The most serious flaws (torn perforations, visible splices, unstable images, deep scratches, spots, and so on) were first identified in the work print and then noted on the storyboard. Starting from these notes, the technicians (at a workstation set up inside the archive) responsible for the image manipulation made all the necessary corrections, which were then submitted to the restoration team for approval.[3] Digital artifacts were also created during the image manipulation phase: examples included the accidental deletion of outlines of doors and furniture, the elimination of a hat thrown into the sky by a cowboy and the disappearance of a horse in a distant landscape.[4] The restoration work was accomplished with the technical support of Centrimages-Paris.[5] Christian Comte, restorer at the film archive, highlights the many possibilities of digital restoration, including the opportunity to solve problems like grain-density modification, cracks, and loss of image information due to degradation of the emulsion, problems that can't be solved with traditional photochemical tools.[6]

For the film scanning process, this film archive works together with other laboratories. The archive chooses laboratories that have scanners equipped with wet gate elements because, in their opinion, it is the best method to delete scratches. They transfer the digital data files produced during scanning onto film stock in order to check the quality of the scanner's output. The film rerecording phase is carried out by external laboratories that use Celco and Solitaire film recorders. In general, they are satisfied with the quality of the duplicates that are produced by these rerecorders.

The other phases of digital restoration take place inside the archive, because they have different tools that allow them to work directly on their materials:

- Adobe Photoshop software is used to work manually on the images.
- Discreet Combustion software is used for image stabilization and to recreate intertitles.
- High-definition Replay is used for monitoring on visual screen the digital process at 2K resolution and in real time.
- Retouche (developed at the University of La Rochelle) and Diamant software are both used in order to automatically delete dust and scratches and to treat flickering and loss of image information.

Christian Comte suggests that these software applications have the advantage of being specifically conceived and produced for digital restoration of films. However, he also says that they are still too slow. He is also perfectly aware that these software packages allow every small part of the film to be repaired. Because of time constraints, he believes it necessary to limit the correction to the damages.[7] He is also convinced that digital restoration will take the place of photochemical restoration, once the production of film stock is discontinued.[8]

CINEMATECA PORTUGUESA/MUSEU DO CINEMA, LISBON

The Cinemateca Portuguesa has never restored, either in its entirety or in part, a film using digital restoration. This film archive uses digital technologies only for sound restoration. The reasons for their resistance against digital tools for moving image restoration are principally financial: at present they are investing funds in their own photochemical restoration laboratory. They intend to test digital restoration eventually and confirm that such a project will be undertaken in the near future.

With regard to the shift from film stock to digital formats, Luigi Pintarelli, laboratory technician at the Cinemateca Portuguesa, believes that this transition will surely happen in the next few years, because of the huge improvements in technology. He shares the concern about the lack of knowledge presently available regarding digital preservation strategies. He also suggests, ironically, that maybe this last barrier will be overcome by commercial manufacturers when they stop the production of film stock.[9]

CINETECA DEL COMUNE DI BOLOGNA (ITALY)

The Cineteca del Comune di Bologna has been involved in digital audio restoration for several years, using their own laboratory, the Immagine Ritrovata 2. In contrast, almost all films are restored in Bologna using photochemical restoration technologies rather than digital moving image restoration technology. At present, Davide Pozzi, restorer at the Cineteca di Bologna, and his staff of technicians have had three experiences with digital film restoration. However, these digital restoration efforts only involved a few selected film shots, rather than an entire film.

The first two films that they restored using digital technology were *The Kid* (Charles Chaplin, 1921), and *The Circus* (Charles Chaplin, 1928). In the case of *The Kid,* restored in 1998, they worked with the laboratory Dyt of Naples in order to repair some damaged shots. During the restoration of *The Circus,* in 1997, they used digital tools to reconstruct the film credits.

The third experience concerned the restoration of the film *Before the Revolution* (*Prima della rivoluzione* [Bernardo Bertolucci, 1964)].[10] The restoration work on *Before the Revolution* was accomplished in 2004 by Ripley's Film of Rome and Cineteca del Comune di Bologna. The restorers began with an original picture and separate track negative, both now stored in the archives of Ripley's Film. The alternation of sequences in black and white with shots in color in this film required two separate image restoration procedures, instead of traditional restoration methods. These processes were carried out in different laboratories. The restoration of the black-and-white picture negative on cellulose triacetate, which accounts for the greater part of the film, consisted mainly of repairing the physical damage and curing the emulsion. The particles of dirt and dust that had been completely absorbed by the emulsion over the years were removed manually because, during projection, they created annoying little white dots, mainly at the beginning and end of each reel. Furthermore, the film had surface cracks on both sides (emulsion and base), which were removed by wet gate printing the preservation fine grain.

The four-color shots that come at the end of the first half of the film, notwithstanding their short duration (59 seconds) required tricky digital restoration. The digital process allowed elimination of a series of flaws that could not be removed using traditional restoration techniques. The restoration and renewal of the color shots in *Before the Revolution* were an essential measure because, over the years, only copies in black and white had been circulated. This practice was contrary to the intentions of the director. Of the four-color shots, three had a mask, intended to create the effect of a viewfinder on an "optical camera." This effect was created in postproduction by placing backings during an additional pass through a Truka printer, a well-established and very common procedure. Consequently, the shots had been handled many times, thus increasing the number of scratches (some photographed) and traces of dirt "absorbed" by the emulsion.

In addition to these difficulties, there were other problems related to preserving the color negatives. The color negatives were chemically unstable with a subsequent loss of image steadiness and color fidelity. Digital Film Lab in Copenhagen digitally corrected all the aforementioned flaws that interfered with the original look of the film. This laboratory works with a Spirit telecine unit at 2K resolution and with an Arrilaser rerecorder. The flaws in the four-color shots were eliminated by scanning the color camera negative at a definition of 2K and by working both automatically and manually with the restoration program Inferno.

The work done on the mono sound of *Before the Revolution* was just as important. A wet gate print of a positive soundtrack was made from the original negative soundtrack. This was done with the dual purpose of creating a sound preservation element and as a starting point for digital transfer and related audio restoration. Noise reduction was applied digitally to the original soundtrack to eliminate the background noise and other aural interferences that had resulted from wear. The sound restoration work, carried out at Lobster Films in Paris and Studio Sound in Rome, ended with the transfer of the new restored soundtrack to Dolby SR, "Spectral Recording."[11]

Since this film archive works with different laboratories in different countries, Davide Pozzi tries to be present during all digital restoration processes in order to supervise the technicians' work. In his opinion, digital restoration has in the past often been looked at with suspicion, because there are few rules in this domain. Today that situation is changing and an ethics of digital restoration is being developed. For this reason, he suggests that film archives think about using digital tools in a more sustained manner.

Concerning the possibility of storing films in digital formats, Pozzi affirms that it is surely a "good thing" when film materials stored digitally are already preserved in traditional photochemical supports. In any case, he underlines that digital storage practices are still eschewed by film archives, because of technical issues and because archival staffs are untrained in the work. In conclusion, he argues that one of the biggest problems mitigating digital restoration in Bologna is limitations on preservation budgets.[12]

FILMOTECA ESPAÑOLA, MADRID

The Filmoteca Española has not yet restored an entire film by digital means but only film fragments, despite the fact that they have many damaged films that require digital restoration. If in the near future more financial resources become available, they will commence with digital projects.

Today, they are slowly moving toward digital restoration along three paths. First, they are restoring film fragments that can't be repaired by photochemical means. For example, Madrid technicians are restoring a portion (27 meters) of *Don Quijote de la Manche* (Rafael Gil, 1948) that had suffered deep cracks in the safety emulsion, scanning the image at 4K resolution. After they kinescoped (to record in Ampex/television process) a duplicate, combining sound and image, they edited together images from the existent duplicate negative to a new duplicate, substituting the damaged shots. They also scanned a fragment of the film *Un chien andalou* (Luis Buñuel, 1929) at 2K resolution. This dupe positive fragment had been duplicated from the original nitrate negative, which contained numerous emulsion side scratches that could not be alleviated with traditional photochemical wet gate reproduction, forcing them to apply digital software that eliminated all scratches.

Second, they employ noise reduction and image manipulation software in order to obtain masters of films that are not slated for photochemical restoration.[13] For instance, they plan to scan two different prints of *Polizon a bordo* (Florian Rey, 1941) that both contained long severe scratches, using automatic software before editing them together, in order to obtain the best quality.

Third, they use digital techniques to generate video copies for access. Candidates for such a procedure are film fragments, technical/industrial documentaries, and home movies. The copies are used solely for access, since they are not going to be projected. In these cases, the original has been duplicated using the wet gate in order to obtain a good-quality duplicate for preservation purposes. Digital tools are used to correct scratches and dust still present after the photochemical process and to edit and to reintroduce color.

Alfonso Del Amo, restorer at the Filmoteca Española, believes that the main advantage of digital restoration is the possibility of improving image quality beyond photochemical methods. This technology also allows for low-cost improvements of video access copies. In his opinion, the main disadvantage of digital is the cost of the entire process. Presently, digital restoration is still much more expensive than photochemical processes, even at 2K resolution. He also underlines that 2K resolution is too low for obtaining a good-quality restoration image.

Furthermore, it is much more difficult to prepare a film for the scanning process than to make it readable for an optical printer. The scanners available today are not designed for restoration but for production, special effects, and postproduction manipulation. Accordingly, scanners are not always able to scan old damaged films, films in nonstandard formats such as 8mm, 9.5mm, and 28mm, films without perforations or with nonstandard perforations, as well as shrunken and fragile nitrate prints. When a film can't be scanned, it must first be duplicated by traditional means onto 35mm before it can be digitally scanned. In such situations, many of the advantages of digital restoration are lost before starting. Finally Del Amo points out that it is quite difficult to check the quality of the final duplicate negative. Most of the Spanish companies possessing good rerecorders only want to use Kodak color stock to transfer the digital data files back to film. This is acceptable only for films in color but a severe limitation for an archive that often preserves silent black-and-white films.

People involved in restoration at the Filmoteca Española work with commercial laboratories, because they don't have digital tools on site. Theirs is only a small laboratory for photochemical duplication. In their opinion, the only way to supervise the work executed by the outside laboratory is by projecting the final result. When possible, they project both the original film and the duplicate. When it is not possible, they check the duplicate's quality during projection, making notes of problems, then with a magnifying glass compare it with the original to detect density and contrast issues.

Alfonso Del Amo thinks that digital restoration processes and technologies will supplant traditional restoration technologies at some point. He also suggests that, as more films are made and projected exclusively using digital means, film archives will be responsible for discovering the consequences of such a change. He believes that the job of research represents the main theoretical work of people involved in this process.

Regarding the possibility of storing films in digital formats, he affirms that at present there is no digital archival support with the same characteristics of photochemical formats. He suggests that the manufacturers of digital carriers are not interested in developing a stable and durable support comparable to film bases, since there is no economic benefit to them in long-term preservation. Preservation is a cultural value that is not an objective for the commercial industry. Besides, he points out, the development of the digital technologies has not yet stabilized. Manufacturers have still not defined the standards of resolution necessary for distribution to movie theaters and for domestic use. Furthermore, standards for broadcasting and for editing and reproduction change continuously.

Consequently, film archives may preserve films in digital form, but they will not know how to preserve these supports. He is aware that, of course, this is a suicidal situation but "that's what we have now." To keep preserving films on photochemical support is the only thing that film archives can presently do.[14]

FONDAZIONE CENTRO SPERIMENTALE DI CINEMATOGRAFIA/CINETECA NAZIONALE/ SNC, ROME

The Cineteca di Roma started to use digital tools in 1992 for sound restoration and in 1998 for image restoration. For sound restoration, they try not to correct too much in order to respect the original soundtrack. They use digital restoration for images when they can't find a suitable solution using traditional methods. They usually use digital technologies only to restore film fragments.

The first film restored by digital means was *Nights of Cabiria* (Federico Fellini, 1957) in 1998. The film was scanned using a Cineon scanner. The most difficult part of this restoration was the reintegration of one part of the original film (which had been censored out in 1957) into the digital data files. The positive acetate fragment suffered from vinegar syndrome. In this case, only digital technologies could be employed. The project was handled by Laboratoire Eclair in Paris using an Inferno workstation.

In 2002, the Rome archive restored *L'avventura* (Michelangelo Antonioni, 1959) using digital restoration to repair several deep scratches, cracks, and loss of information in the emulsion. The original negative was scanned on a Genesis telecine at 2K resolution. Image manipulation involved varying software programs as needed. The digital data files were then transferred onto 35mm using an Arrilaser film recorder. All restoration was done at Cinecittà Digital Laboratory of Rome. In the same year they also restored *The Gospel According to St. Matthew* (Pier Paolo Pasolini, 1964), following the same path. The Pasolini film was less damaged. Furthermore Tonino Delli Colli, the film's cinematographer, supervised the restoration work, giving precious advice.[15]

In summer 2004, they finished their first fully digital restoration, *Io sono un autarchico* (Nanni Moretti, 1976). They scanned the original color acetate reversal (half Ektachrome, half Kodachrome) with a Data Spirit telecine at 2K resolution, then repaired the image using software before transferring the digital data files back to 35mm color film. All processes were carried out by Augustus Color Labs in Rome. Cineteca di Roma was quite satisfied with this first experiment, because the 2K resolution was sufficient for reproducing the characteristics of the original film stock. Furthermore, the film was in an advanced state of deterioration, which would have made restoration by traditional photochemical means prohibitively expensive and difficult given the fragile original.

The Cineteca di Roma doesn't have any digital tools, so restorer Mario Musumeci and his staff work with different laboratories, such as Cinecittà Digital. In order guarantee quality, Musumeci explains very precisely to the vendors what he wants before the process begins, then verifies the results of the rerecorded duplicate by projecting it. He'd like to do more research in this area but presently lacks funds. Regarding digital restoration replacing traditional methods, he thinks that it will happen when film stock production ceases and all film distribution goes digital. Finally, Musumeci argues that the option of long-term digital storage can't at present be taken seriously because there are no strong and durable digital formats.[16]

NEDERLANDS FILMMUSEUM (AMSTERDAM)

Since 1998, the Nederlands Filmmuseum has been actively experimenting with digital technology for film restoration. Thanks to the archive's involvement in a European Union–funded project (2000–2002), which resulted in the creation of the new Diamant image manipulation software, their knowledge and experience in this field has grown significantly.

The Filmmuseum's task in the project was to draw up user requirements for the software and to test the results. During the process they became more and more aware of the ethical issues involved in working with new digital tools. From the start, their main concern was not the technology itself, which keeps evolving, but rather the way film restorers use it; in other words, they had ethical questions about to how far restorers should go with a restoration.[17]

In October 2001, the Nederlands Filmmuseum set up a workstation for digital film restoration. The workstation consisted of a powerful PC equipped with the Diamant software, for semiautomatic image manipulation, and Photoshop, for manual image manipulation. According to Giovanna Fossati, curator at the Nederlands Filmmusem, the Diamant software has advantages, such as the fact that it can be installed on a preexisting workstation or network using Windows. Thus, it is cheap software, since it doesn't require dedicated hardware, as do other software programs such as Restore and DA VINCI. The software is easy to install and its interface easy to use. Furthermore, Diamant allows the restorer to apply the correction filter to discrete areas of the frame, the "regions of interest." This solution leaves the rest of the frame untouched. However, according to Fossati the disadvantage of this software is that it can't be used for color correction or for cutting in imported shots. As a result, Diamant must be used with other software programs.[18]

In 2002, the Nederlands Filmmuseum acquired a license for the Diamant software and has since been experimenting with it on a small number of projects, in close collaboration with external laboratories. The workflow is as follows: Scanning and rerecording are carried out at an external laboratory. Digital image

Les Lis du Japon (France, 1917; restored 2003). Courtesy of Haghefilm.

manipulation occurs mainly in house with the Diamant program. Some additional manipulation takes place at an external laboratory under the museum's supervision.

As in the case of traditional photochemical restoration, archivists selected laboratories based on their specialty within the domain of digital restoration, including Haghefilm in Amsterdam, a partner for many restoration projects, Digital Film Lab in Copenhagen, and others.

Fossati feels that this kind of workflow is the most suitable for a film archive. Leaving the scanning and rerecording processes to external laboratories seems to be logical, since the necessary equipment is so expensive. On the other hand, the restoration of the image can be done (at least partially) in house under the supervision of a film restorer. She emphasizes that one of the most delicate issues within such a workflow is the exchange of digital data files with a laboratory. Today laboratories use removable hard disks but they are aware that, while this might be a cheap solution on the short term, it is not a reliable and reasonable option in the long term.[19]

The Nederlands Filmmuseum started testing digital restoration capabilities in 1998 when they restored the faded colors of *Violette Impériales* (France, 1952). The restoration was redone in 2001, in order to test updated digital tools and compare the results. For both projects, the Filmmuseum worked with Digital Film Lab in Copenhagen. The second experiment netted better results than the first. In 1999, they restored the faded colors of the film *Jenny* (Netherlands, 1958), working with the Digital Film Lab in London. In 2002, they restored fragments of *Musica Eterna* (Netherlands, 1951), using their own Diamant software and again working with Digital Film Lab for the scanning and rerecording phases.

For the Diamant project, *Een Autotocht in de Pyreneeën* (France, 1910) was chosen as a test film. This title was a particularly interesting object for restoration, because it previously had been restored photochemically and therefore allowed for a comparison between the different methods applied. For this test Filmmuseum restorers worked with Alpha-Omega in Germany and with Laboratoires Neyrac in Paris for film scanning and rerecording. The digital restora-

tion gave better results, because the film suffered from numerous scratches that remained visible after photochemical restoration. In 2002, the Nederlands Filmmuseum restored the film *Zeemansvrouwen* (Netherlands, 1930), following the same path as with *Een Autotocht in de Pyreneeën*. External treatments were handled by Digital Film Lab in London and Haghefilm.[20]

Also in 2002, Dutch archivists worked on restoring *Visages d'enfants* (Jacques Feyder, 1925) on color 35mm film. The restoration of *Visages d'enfants* is a work in progress. Work had began in 1993 as part of the Lumière Project, an effort subsidized by the European Community that brought together many European film archives to secure silent films. The original restoration had been done by the Cinémathèque Francaise, Cinémathèque Royale du Belgique, and Gosfilmofond, Moscow.

The restoration was based on prints from two different negatives, resulting in a nearly complete version, although some minutes are still missing. Film historian Lenny Borger reconstructed the intertitles in Dutch and French with the help of previous prints and censorship records. But one huge disappointment in 1993 had been that three beautiful and atmospheric scenes in the film were so damaged that the images were almost completely lost. In 2002, it was decided to digitally process these damaged scenes.

The scenes were scanned from the duplicate negative at Haghefilm using an Oxberry scan at 2K resolution. Repairing these scenes—about five hundred frames in total—was done mainly by hand using Digital Fusion software at Haghefilm. The repair consisted of creating new shots from two previous undamaged shots, copying only the mountain in the original frame and then pasting them into the later shot. The digital data files were then transferred, using an Arrilaser at 2K resolution, onto duplicate color negative. However, it is still uncertain whether the outcome will be good enough to actually integrate into the restoration. Experiments are continuing with the Haghefilm laboratory.[21]

In 2003, the Filmmuseum restored *Drie dagen met Monica* (Wil van Es, 1956) with Haghefilm. This Dutch documentary was originally projected in wide-screen using a special lens, the "delrama," a kind of CinemaScope

Drie dagen met Monica
(Holland, 1956; restored 2003),
directed by Wil van Es.
Courtesy of Haghefilm.

lens made in The Netherlands. The documentary, an advertisement for the port of Rotterdam, was unprojectable, because it suffered from color deterioration: the blues had disappeared and only magenta was visible. Scanning the film on an Oxberry at 2K with a wet gate, archivists tested both photochemical and digital grading, but digital tools gave better results. In general, the problem with color restoration is that it is difficult to know how the original looked. Although the archive owned a color separation negative of one reel, the quality of the master was poor because it had been generated from a copy rather than the original. In any case, the Nederlands Filmmuseum printed this negative as a color reference. The grading was done with Digital Fusion software at Haghefilm, without using masks, so that some marks on the edges are still visible. A certain degree of flickering in the second reel was corrected with Diamant software, while simultaneously correcting the color stabilization.

In summer 2004, Nederlands Filmmuseum restored *Les Lis du Japon* (France, 1917), a 9.5mm Baby Pathé, using digital technology for all restoration steps in connection with the project Research and Development (2003). Originally shot on 35mm film stock, it was reduced to 9.5mm after the introduction of the Pathé-Kok format in 1922 and hand-colored. Scanned at 2K with an Oxberry wet gate, image manipulation was done with Digital Fusion software at Haghefilm. The problem here was that 9.5mm has a perforation in the middle, which was visible at the top and bottom of each frame, forcing restorers to crop the frame by eliminating

pixels. They decided on this method, rather than zooming, in order avoid further resolution problems. They also deleted scratches, dusts and spots; however, some marks are still visible because some surface scratches were not processed out by the software. The digital output was transferred to 35mm color negative from which a color print was generated. Demonstrating the "before" and "after" of this restoration is still causing headaches; unless the Filmmuseum thinks of something better, they will use stills from the 9.5mm to demonstrate the "before" and the new 35mm print to show the "after."[22]

Fossati points out that 95 percent of Nederlands Filmmuseum's preservation efforts are photochemical, because digital film restoration is still an experimental practice. She considers it extremely important, however, to keep up with this evolving technology and to be directly involved in its development. As film restorer, she must be responsible for the choices made during a restoration.[23]

Concerning the possibility of digital storage, she believes that at present digital technology does not offer stable support for passive preservation. Digital formats have a high risk of obsolescence and have an uncertain life expectancy. Furthermore, Nederlands Filmmuseum considers any film preserved in a format different from film just a copy for access. At the same time, Fossati points out, the Filmmuseum

Drie dagen met Monica, with
Ann Hasekamp and Flipvan
Santpoort. Courtesy of
Haghefilm.

produces digital data files, which should be
preserved somewhere and somehow. People
involved in this process are wandering in the
dark on this particular issue. They currently
keep DTF tapes of their projects but see this as
only a temporary solution. Fossati suggests
that digital restoration and storage will change
completely when film production and distribution is accomplished only in digital formats.[24]

SUOMEN ELOKUVA-ARKISTO, HELSINKI

The Finnish Film Archive does not use digital
techniques on a regular basis. They are exploring the possibilities offered by going digital,
but they mainly do tests to solve specific problems. In 2001, they used digital restoration to
preserve one of the earliest Finnish sound
films, from 1929 and featuring the popular
singer Rafael Ramstedt, in a restored version
in high definition with a soundtrack from the
original sound disk. In order to restore the
sound they used a ProTools workstation with
Waves plug-ins. Digital Film Finland was chosen as the partner in this pilot. The archive also
tested different approaches to color correct two
faded originals. In this case, the films were
scanned at 2K resolution and then transferred
onto film using high-definition film recorders.[25]
Recently they made a DVD production in low
definition from a 1938 feature film. They also
have plans to test digital restoration with a
full-length feature when they find one suitable.
    The archive buys all its services from com-
mercial postproduction companies, so they in
effect use the same equipment used for mod-

ern feature films. Neither the equipment nor
the work flows in these companies are especially designed for archival work, thus Mikko
Kuutti, deputy director at the film archive,
argues that they "kind of have to make do."
The equipment is geared more toward producing a new artistic experience than reproducing
an old original. The archive works with two companies in Finland, which each have a Spirit
telecine unit and a Celco film recorder. For
image manipulation processing, they use both
the Diamant and the Inferno workstations that
are supplied by their lab partners.
    About the future, Kuutti thinks there will
be a time when the best way to produce a new
duplicate will be by digital means. But that
time will not come for many years. Whether to
store films digitally, he thinks, is a tough call,
and no solution seems to be available yet. He
points out that, because preserving digital data
files interests many parties other than film
archives, that there will be a workable solution,
and archives alone don't have to invent it.[26]

THE DANISH FILM INSTITUTE ARCHIVE
AND CINÉMATHÈQUE, COPENHAGEN

The Danish Film Insitute Archive does not use
digital technology on a regular basis, but they
have undertaken some digital projects. They
digitally edit and insert new intertitles. Thomas
Christensen, curator at the Danish Film Archive,

suggests that this use is not fundamentally different than conventional analogue negative cutting, the main difference being the ease of use and possibility to edit and grade to the frame. Digital image repairs, if needed, are also possible.

In any case, restorers at the archive try to keep image manipulation to a minimum for several reasons. They emphasize the importance of retaining the original appearance of the materials. Furthermore, the filter for automatic image repair does not work perfectly, while manual image repair is both subjective and costly, especially in personnel hours.

Restorers use a Spirit telecine unit, an Inferno workstation, and an Arrilaser film recorder. Sometimes they work with a photochemical laboratory, Soho Images in London. All digital procedures, except the creation of titles, are outsourced to Digital Film Lab in Copenhagen. They observe the movement of the digital data files through A-D transfer and Inferno editing. The monitoring of all digital processes is performed by visual control on screen.

In 1998, the first test was carried out, the restoration of a small part of the black-and-white film, *Circus Sarrasani*. In 2001, the first full-length restoration, of *Nedbrudte Nerver* (A. W. Sandberg, 1923), used a combination of digital and photochemical techniques at Digital Film Lab in Copenhagen and Soho Images in London—a "hybrid restoration." In 2002, again working with Digital Film Lab in Copenhagen, they restored *Copenhagen by Night* (1910). Also in 2002, they produced *The First Film Archive,* a DVD production, which included scanning original nitrate film on a Philips Shadow telecine unit, handling material with up to 2 percent shrinkage. In 2002, the Danish Film Institute also restored *Once Upon a Time* (*Der var engang* [Carl Theodor Dreyer, 1922]).[27]

To the archive, the advantages of using digital tools are ease of use, such as editing and preview facilities, and the possibility of combining elements without generational loss. At the same time, Thomas Christensen notes that, with current resolutions, digital technology is not a preservation medium but rather a restoration medium, in which the new negative is the presentation and production element but not a preservation element. He suggests that it

is also difficult to control all processes in the digital domain, because it is a kind magic "black box." In his opinion, digital is no different from analogue; in fact, both photochemical and digital restoration tests are done on film, in order to choose the best way to make corrections. With these tests, the restorer can figure out what different changes to the image might look like. It is impossible, however, to predict the final result without completing a restoration process.

Concerning the possibility that digital restoration might replace traditional restoration techniques, Christensen is afraid that very soon digital will be the only option available. He thinks that people who fight digitality are doing so for the wrong reasons. Although he would also like see conventional film duplication remain, he thinks it will only survive another ten years. Digital projection will change everything, if it catches on.

Regarding the possibility of digitally storing films, Christensen considers the option problematic because current technology is driven by speed and high storage capacity, not by preservation issues. He suggests that there may be a digital archive format someday and that then film archives will use it, just as they use digital betacam for low-definition video today. In any case, his heart lies with film stock correctly stored and handled. He confirms that the Danish Film Archive will retain original film elements for many centuries to come.[28]

CONCLUSION

Summarizing current applications of digital technology in European film archives, I will offer some general observations about the present state of digital restoration in Europe. Digital restoration seems generally more advanced in northern Europe (where digital experiments started roughly six years ago) than in southern Europe (with the exception of the Cineteca di Roma). The high cost of digital restoration is clearly a significant barrier to its more widespread use. In contrast to image restoration, however, digital sound restoration has occurred in almost all European archives for a number of years. Lastly, digital restoration is generally employed to address problems that cannot be fixed with traditional photochemical restoration.

None of the archives surveyed use digital technology on a regular basis, and only three (CNC–Paris, Cineteca di Roma, Nederlands Filmmuseum) have restored an entire film using solely digital means.

At present, archives are still experimenting with digital technologies and testing the possibilities and limitations of this new kind of film restoration. The tests have not always yielded perfect results, but they have helped restorers to determine appropriate applications of the technology. The software used for image manipulation varies considerably among different archives (with the notable exception of the Diamant software, which was specifically designed for film restoration and which was developed by several European institutions). This same variation has been true of scanners, telecine units, and rerecorders, but the technology has become more consistent as archives realized the necessity of meeting certain standards. Most of the film archives interviewed now use the Spirit telecine unit and the Arri-laser rerecorder, because of their data processing speed. The Spirit telecine unit is preferred by most film archives because it can handle films with up to 2.5 percent linear shrinkage.

It is important to note that the choice of software, as well as the scanner and the film recorder, is determined by what the laboratories own. Restorers at the Filmoteca Española and the Finnish Film Archive pointed out problems using equipment that was not produced for restoration needs, but for postproduction and special-effects needs. The restorers at the Nederlands Filmmuseum, the Danish Film Archive, and the Filmoteca Española underline how the low resolution and overall low quality of the final duplicate is a pressing problem for digital restoration. Final duplicates produced through digital restoration are not of preservation quality.

Most restorers prefer to be present during the digital restoration process so that they can supervise the laboratory work. They are responsible for describing, in detail, the intended corrections to the technician who will work on the film. Many restorers also believe that the final duplication projection is one of the best ways to check the quality of the restoration work.

In the past, film archives created their own photochemical laboratories in order to handle shrunken materials or adjust nonstandard chemical processes, since commercial laboratories could not meet their needs. Many archives are working to set up their own digital workstations, so that they can better follow the digital process and make decisions about what has to be corrected and what has to be left untouched. Currently, only the CNC–Paris and the Nederlands Filmmusem have accomplished this goal. Since the majority of film archives do not have their own digital laboratories, the digital restoration process remains difficult for many restorers to supervise and control.

Many ethical questions are raised by digital restoration, because the technology offers so many possibilities. With digital restoration, a film can be repaired down to its smallest elements (of sound and image), so the restorer must specify what should and should not be done, according to basic professional ethics. Overall, restorers interviewed were most concerned about respecting the original film versions. Restorers felt that films should not be corrected to improve on original versions. The restorers at the CNC–Paris, Nederlands Filmmusem, and the Danish Film Archive noticed that digital tools can restore a film to the most modern and up-to-date standards. In their opinion, it is therefore necessary to set strict limits regarding the manipulation of the film. On the other hand, there are other film restorers who see digital restoration, more enthusiastically, as a new way of dealing with problems that are not resolved by photochemical methods.

Although restorers at the different archives approach their work in different ways, they all share the priority of saving as many films as possible. They are prepared to experiment with digital technology as long as the original version is respected. Restorers are more and more aware that digital restoration allows them to solve problems that cannot be solved using traditional restoration methods. Restorers are reluctant to predict that digital restoration will replace traditional restoration, but they know that the restoration landscape will completely change when raw film stock production ceases. It is possible that films will no longer survive on celluloid but exist solely in digital formats.

Archives are wary of storing films in digital formats, because they do not think that current digital technology offers a stable base of support for preservation needs. It is possible that current digital media carriers will become obsolete and most have an unknown life expectancy. Technical obsolescence is a central issue for preservation and an important concern for its economic impact on large digital collections. Migration of data to newer formats to circumvent obsolescence must be correctly evaluated in terms of cost and time management issues. European film archives are, however, using digital formats for access and distribution.

While digital technology is becoming a useful tool for the restoration and reconstruction of films, it has not yet provided any long-term solutions for the preservation of moving images in digital formats. This is due, in part, to the fact that there is no universally agreed-upon standard or method for preserving images in a digital format, at least none that matches the universality, functionality, and life expectancy of photochemical support systems. At this time, no digital format is as secure as film stock. Digital technology holds great potential for film restoration, but there is still a lot a work to be done in addressing the above-mentioned ethical and practical matters. In any case, digital restoration methods and technology are constantly evolving. Tracking the continual changes in digital technology and their practical applications in moving image archives, therefore, becomes a useful activity, because the field is moving with such amazing speed.

NOTES

1. I would like to thank Giovanna Fossati and Simona Monizza, curator and restorer respectively at the Nederlands Filmmusem, for their helpful suggestions about whom to interview at the different film archives.
2. Giovanna Fossati, "From Grains to Pixels: Digital Technology and the Film Archive" in *Restauro, conservazione e distruzione dei film/Restoration, Preservation, and Destruction of Films,* ed. Luisa Comencini and Matteo Pavesi (Milan, Italy: Il Castoro, 2001), 134.
3. Jean-Louis Cot, "*Bucking Broadway:* Historique d'une restauration," *Positif* 504 (2003): 90.
4. The operation of the elimination of scratches and dust is achieved by specific software for manipulation of moving images. This software sometimes presents application problems. The main problem is that analysis of movement, in which all the elements extraneous to the image should be recognized, sometimes does not work perfectly, as when elements that have the same appearance as a scratch are recognized as extraneous even though they make up part

of the image. Software to eliminate spots causes the same kind of problems because there are no simple rules for distinguishing spots from original image features. This software uses as reference the image in the previous or successive frame or the total of the digital data files scanned. If the images are really dynamic, the reference image can be too different from the image to be treated, which can create mistakes. For instance, a spot will not be detected if the previous image and the successive image contain in the same part of the frame an object similar in form and detail. Also, when an object moves really fast from one image to another, it could be mistaken for a dust particle and be removed. See *First Film Restoration and Conservation Strategies: State of the Art Report,* ed. Gabrielle Claes, (CD-ROM; Royal Film Archive, Brussels/Prod. Information Society — European Community, 2002), 161.
5. For more on these restoration works, see http://www.centrimage.com/page/bucking.htm.
6. *First Film Restoration and Conservation Strategies: European Film Heritage on the Threshold of the Digital Era. The First Project's Final Report, Conclusion — Guidelines — Recommendations,* ed. Gabrielle Claes (CD-ROM; Royal Film Archive, Brussels/Prod. Information Society — European Community, 2004), 158.
7. Ibid.
8. Information provided via e-mail by Christian Comte, restorer at the Archives Françaises du Film du Centre National de la Cinématographie, on August 12, 2004.
9. Information provided via e-mail by Luigi Pintarelli, laboratory technician at the Cinemateca Portuguesa/Museu do Cinema, Lisbon, on August 9, 2004.
10. From an interview with Davide Pozzi, restorer at the Cineteca del Commune di Bologna, Italy, on July 22, 2004.
11. This summary of the restoration of *Before the Revolution* was provided by Davide Pozzi.
12. From interview with Davide Pozzi.
13. *Master:* a term used for a duplicate positive used for printing and never itself projected.
14. Information provided via e-mail by Alfonso Del Amo, restorer at the Filmoteca Española, Madrid, on August 1, 2004.
15. Unpublished interview put at disposal by interviewees Mario Musumeci, restorer, and Aldo Strappini, expert witness for preservation and restoration, both at the Fondazione centro sperimentale di cinematografia/Cineteca Nazionale SNC, Rome, 2002.
16. Information provided via e-mail by Mario Musumeci, restorer at the Fondazione centro sperimentale di cinematografia/Cineteca Nazionale SNC, Rome, on June 17, 2004.
17. Giovanna Fossati, "Proposal for a Presentation at The Reel Thing (Vancouver 2003)," October 2003, unpublished.
18. *First Film Restoration and Conservation* (2004), 153.
19. Fossati, "Proposal."
20. For more on these restoration works, see *First Film Restoration and Conservation* (2004), 153–56.
21. See Nederlands Filmmuseum biennale Web site: http://www.filmmuseum.nl/biennale/html/index-101.html.

22. Fossati, "Proposal."

23. *First Film Restoration and Conservation* (2004), 153.

24. From an interview with Giovanna Fossati, curator at the Nederlands Filmmusem, Amsterdam, on July 5, 2004.

25. For more on these restoration works, see *First Film Restoration and Conservation* (2004), 164–66.

26. Information provided via e-mail by Mikko Kuutti, deputy director at the Suomen Elokuva-Arkisto, Helsinki, on August 10, 2004.

27. For more on these restoration works, see *First Film Restoration and Conservation* (2004), 155–57.

28. Information provided via e-mail by Thomas Christensen, curator at the Danish Film Institute Archive and Cinémathèque, on August 11, 2004.

REVIEWS

Books

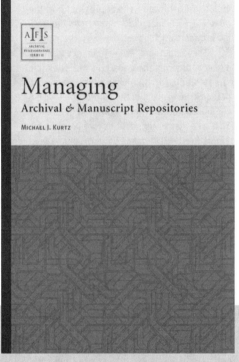

A|F|S
ARCHIVAL
FUNDAMENTALS
SERIES II

Managing
Archival & Manuscript Repositories
MICHAEL J. KURTZ

***Managing Archival and Manuscript Repositories*
by Michael J. Kurtz**
SOCIETY OF AMERICAN ARCHIVISTS, 2004

Janice Simpson

In the early 1990s, the Society of American Archivists (SAA) introduced their Archival Fundamental Series; a set of seven titles conceived and written to provide a foundation for modern archival theory and practice in North America. Like the Basic Manual Series that preceded it, this series was intended to have widespread application for a general audience within the archival profession. As the series editor, Mary Jo Pugh, explained, "the purpose was to strengthen and augment the knowledge and skills of archivists, general practitioners and specialists alike, who perform a wide range of archival duties in all types of archival and manuscript repositories." The past decade has witnessed significant changes in information technology and organizational complexity, and these developments have had an effect on the archival profession. Archival projects are getting more complicated and sophisticated, and archivists are fulfilling their traditional functions of appraisal, arrangement, description, preservation, and access in new ways. In response to these changes, the SAA has taken the initiative and updated the series.[1]

The purpose of the new series remains the same, but the individual texts are being rewritten in light of evolving standards and practices. *Managing Archival and Manuscript Repositories* by Michael J. Kurtz is one of the titles in the series; it updates the original publication by Thomas Wilsted and William Nolte published almost twelve years previously. The first chapter of Kurtz's text, "Management Theory and Practice," provides an introduction and context for the chapters that follow. This chapter defines management, emphasizes the importance of effective management, and provides a brief history of management theory. The chapter discusses how successful management techniques have evolved and describes management challenges peculiar to the current archival environment.

Chapter 2, "Leadership in Management," replaces what was only a paragraph in the Wilsted and Nolte text. Kurtz states that "the fundamental skill a good manager must possess is leadership" and that leadership and management are not distinct; there must be "leadership in management." Subsections of the chapter include vision, the value of self-knowledge, and mentoring. According to Kurtz, good leaders need to develop a vision of what they hope to achieve as individuals as well as a clear understanding of their institution's history and what their archives hope to achieve. They need a clear vision of the profession's goals and how their individual goals fit into these, and an ability to select a course of action that leads to achieving their goals. This chapter includes easy-to-read charts listing archival leadership skills, vision, and styles. What I found particularly interesting was the discussion on the roles and responsibilities of archival managers and how they have changed as part of the "information revolution." This is discussed in more detail in chapter 7, "Managing Information Technology."

A comparison of Wilsted and Nolte's chapter entitled, "Organizational Structure" with Kurtz's chapter entitled, "Organizational Complexity: A New Management Paradigm and Foundations of Organizational Success," demonstrates how drastically the working environment has changed in the past ten years. If what Kurtz says is true, the new paradigm is one of complex organizational relationships. Exploiting new technologies to build new relationships/partners, improving support structures, maximizing teamwork, and using new management techniques such as coaching and mentoring to achieve the desired results differs radically from traditional methods. Kurtz explores organizational theories, organizational culture, organizational relationships, and how the knowledge of these assists with better management. It is notable that a clearly written mission statement that outlines organizational placement, legal authority, defines collecting and access policy, and overviews staff accountability and responsibility is considered by Kurtz still to be the most critical component of a well-managed archive.

The following chapters address each of the areas a good manager should be concerned with: "Planning and Reporting," "Project Management," "Managing Information Technology," "Human Resources," "Communication," "Managing Archival Facilities," "Financial Man-

agement," "Fundraising and Development," and "Public Relations." All but the chapter on facilities is useful for a manager in any organization, however each chapter also uses examples that are pertinent to archives.

In the chapter "Planning and Reporting," Kurtz emphasizes the importance of an effective planning process designed to "drive" the budget, policies, and strategies of the organization. Once the necessary plans are in place, he states, implementation and regular reviews should follow. This chapter focuses on strategic planning for an archival program and the related operational plans required to integrate all program activities.

The chapter on "Project Management" is a new addition in the updated text but a topic all too familiar to archivists. Kurtz begins by defining the concept of the "project life-cycle," continues with a sample outline for a project plan, and makes suggestions for plan reviews, evaluation, and risk management. I particularly liked his "five factors for a successful project" that includes "mandate," "support/resources," "team leadership/facilitation," "communication," and "clear goals." Project management skills in archival work are essential, and most managers could use some improvement.

Information technology is constantly changing and significantly affects every archive, big and small. The chapter entitled "Managing Information Technology" addresses these issues and offers suggestions for planning, strategy, and tactics. Kurtz recommends partnering with in-house technical staff or contractors to ensure available resources are being used optimally to obtain and maintain the most efficient communication and asset management systems. Kurtz touches on the importance of staff training, integrating multiple systems, open versus proprietary systems, and developing an information technology product plan model. Kurtz recognizes this as one of the contemporary manager's biggest challenges.

While each topic is described as important, the section on human resources receives special recognition and is put on par with leadership. Kurtz states that "these two are inextricably linked and at the heart of organizational success or failure." The chapter provides basic recommendations on managing a staff large and small. It also covers recruitment, performance evaluation, training and development, and volunteer management. The information about communications is new. In addition to the basics, it includes a section on electronic communication tools and communication strategies. Kurtz states that the manager needs to "identify the basic communication needs of the archival unit and the parent institution, understand staff and public needs and create a process that enables effective decision making and policy dissemination; and, it must function accurately and consistently." A tall order, but one of the keys to guaranteeing productivity and performance.

The chapter entitled "Managing Archival Facilities" is the one most specific to archives. It discusses optimum environmental conditions for storing multiformat collections, space planning and design, space allocation, basic equipment, and supplies. There is also an interesting section on reviewing space needs, expanding a facility, working with architects and building contractors, and construction. The chapters on "Financial Management" and "Fundraising and Development" are basic but useful. They include tips for archivists such as a list of potential funding agencies and a sample grant application. The main body of the text concludes with a section on public relations which provides advice on establishing an image, developing constituencies, planning a PR program, and marketing archival services (and includes a sample press release), all of which are key factors in gaining support for programs.

As in the Wilsted and Nolte text, each of the chapters is followed by a list of suggested readings. At the end of the text, following a list of general management literature, Web sites, and professional associations (unfortunately there is no mention of AMIA!), Kurtz offers concluding thoughts. He describes archival management as a rewarding but admittedly challenging profession. He also recommends that managers pursue continuing education opportunities (to stay current with new management practices), network, share knowledge with other professionals, and keep up with the professional literature.

Relevant for archivists working in both large and small repositories, *Managing Archival and Manuscript Repositories* is of value to both the beginning archivist and the seasoned professional. The beginning archivist will find it a useful primer and good reference book for management fundamentals. The experienced archivist will find it valuable as a refresher. So, what is the value of the text to the archivist solely responsible for moving image collections? Although the text speaks generally and focuses on archivists responsible for mixed-media collections, it is certainly of value to archivists responsible for moving images. In the section on facilities management, a moving image archivist would need additional information on storage and equipment; however, the information relating to general facility requirements, construction, space planning and design are certainly pertinent. And what of the value to archivists outside of North America? Aside from the fact that all of the suggested readings are American, the management concepts at this level are universal.

In terms of the text's format, the dimensions of the publication are smaller (more manageable), but Kurtz essentially followed the design used by Wilsted and Nolte. Sample documents, photos, and charts are included in almost every chapter to illustrate points; the text is extremely user friendly and an easy read. The 255-page, soft-cover text contains thirteen chapters and is loaded with illustrations. Mr. Kurtz has worked at the National Archives and Records Administration in Washington, DC, for more than thirty years. He is currently Assistant Archivist for Records Services.

NOTE

1. In addition to this title, the series includes: Kathleen D. Roe, *Arranging and Describing Archives and Manuscripts* (2005); Frank Boles, *Selecting and Appraising Archives and Manuscripts* (2005); Mary Jo Pugh, *Providing Reference Services for Archives and Manuscripts* (2005); Mary Lynn Ritzenthaler, *Preserving Archives and Manuscripts* (forthcoming); James M. O'Toole and Richard Cox, *Understanding Archives and Manuscripts* (forthcoming); and Richard Pearce-Moses, *A Glossary of Archival and Records Terminology* (2005).

Coming Attractions: Reading American Movie Trailers
by Lisa Kernan
UNIVERSITY OF TEXAS PRESS, 2004

David Gibson

In a world where the line between promotional discourse and narrative form is increasingly blurred, movie trailers stand out as one of the purest distillations of both. Trailers exploit cinematic techniques to create a mini-narrative, which entertains the audience while promoting a film. Perhaps because of their entertainment value, movie trailers manage to skirt the criticism reserved for more blatant forms of advertising. In fact, the popularity of trailers has, in some ways, eclipsed that of the films they are paired with. Many believe that *Meet Joe Black,* released on November 15, 1998, by Universal Pictures, did better-than-expected business on its opening weekend because the film was released with the trailer for the upcoming *Star Wars* prequel, *The Phantom Menace:* a true testament to the power of the movie trailer in modern media culture. It is common knowledge of cinema and cultural studies that trailers are designed to speak directly to audience desire, although the true identity of this "audience," or the film studios' perception of the

"audience-as-consumer," has remained somewhat enigmatic throughout cinema's history. Lisa Kernan's new book, *Coming Attractions: Reading American Movie Trailers,* sets out to unmask both the audience itself and the studios' methods for enticing them to return to the theaters again and again.

In Kernan's view, trailers are not merely advertisements for the films they promote but a cinematic genre in and of itself, with its own set of features and conventions. Though the author acknowledges trailers' similarity to other forms of advertising, she points out that the main purpose of a movie trailer is to sell the desire for a unique cinematic experience rather than a specific physical object. The first chapter of the book includes an analysis of some of the generic features of movie trailers, such as montage, voice-over narration, and graphics, which work together to create a narrative that is at once separate from and tied to the film in question. Particular attention is paid to the fragmentary nature of trailers, which creates "a kind of pregnancy or underdeterminacy that allows audiences to create an imaginary (as-yet-unseen) film out of these fragments—[a] desire not [for] the real film but the film we want to see" (13). Kernan's exploration of audience expectations, and the studio's rhetorical appeals to these expectations, forms the basis of a compelling and convincing argument on the nature of American film advertising, and its evolution and transformation over the course of the last century.

Throughout the book, the author refers to the movie trailer genre as "a cinema of (coming) attractions" (2). Just as the concept of the "cinema of attractions" posits a view of a pre-narrative, spectacle-driven cinema in which an implicit awareness of the act of viewing exists within the audience, trailers resist narrative temporality in order to create audience desire. Kernan often alludes to trailers' two distinct temporal modes, which operate by "withholding the fullness of the cinema event, even as they display a unique sense of heightened presence" (24), a feature she argues is unique to the film trailer genre. The notion of a pure cinematic form that is alluded to through promotional discourse, but never attained, may be of most interest to the archival community, as it closely parallels the desire to preserve a cinematic experience that may be unattainable now. Kernan shows how the construction of the cinematic "event" through trailer rhetoric succeeds in promoting the film itself and the anticipation of the film, thus creating a commodified narrative while speaking to audience desire.

The vaudeville and circus traditions, which exerted a great influence on the birth of cinema in the United States, had a strong impact on the early development of movie trailer conventions as well, particularly in regard to audience address. The author relates vaudeville's "something for everyone" approach to movie trailers' attempts to appeal to "as broad an audience as possible ... by emphasizing the range of different aspects that might appeal to audiences within [a] specific genre" (19). Similarly, Kernan likens movie trailers to the rhetoric of the circus sideshow, an invitation to "'step right up' ... [and] to participate in the film's discourse in some way" (22). As much as these two modes of audience address relate to the idea of trailers as a cinema of coming attractions, they are also representative of the genre's historical development, an evolution that lies at the heart of the book's analysis. Literalizations of the vaudeville stage, of film actors addressing the audience firsthand before a curtained backdrop, were common during the beginning of what Kernan refers to as the classical era of movie trailers, but the practice soon faded like the vaudeville tradition itself. Even the last remnant of the circus mode, the announcement of a film "Coming Soon to a Theater Near You," endures simply based on its status as an iconic phrase, much like the term "coming attractions." In the modern era, when commerce through visual information has become such a large part of our daily lives, these modes have been eschewed in favor of quick cuts and reliance on flashy images rather than direct audience address.

With chapter 2 of the book, entitled "Trailer Rhetoric," Kernan outlines the various forms of rhetoric that trailer producers use to entice the assumed audience of a motion picture. The three central rhetorical appeals she focuses on, genre rhetoric, story rhetoric, and star rhetoric, each play on a different aspect of audience desire in order to achieve the same end, namely, to persuade the audience to return to the theater to see the next attraction. With emphasis on persuasion, Kernan justifies her use of Aristotelian rhetorical theory, principally the theory of the enthymeme, which she describes as "an implicit assumption within the logic of the remaining terms" of an abbreviated syllogism (40). Essentially, Kernan posits an image-based enthymeme in which the applied assumption on the part of the trailer producers in regard to the assumed audience may be "You're going to want to see these films!" (43). This is complicated territory, but Kernan succeeds in creating a clear and concise picture of the ways such rhetorical logic can be applied to the genre of trailers by stressing the audience's importance in the formation of such a persuasive text. The sole function of the trailer, to create in the audience the desire to see, hear, and "feel" a specific cinematic text, is moot without the participation of the audience itself.

Kernan concludes the first half of the book with an analysis of each of the three rhetorical appeals. Much has been written in history of film scholarship regarding cinematic genres, stories, and stars; however, this book treads new ground by exploring each facet in relation to movie trailers. By isolating the methods employed within each appeal toward the creation of audience desire, the author is able to reposition these familiar concepts in light of rhetorical analysis, while laying the foundation for the analyses that form the core of her study. Although, as the author herself admits, no one rhetorical appeal can be seen as mutually exclusive to any one trailer, Kernan succeeds in demonstrating how "in each era a dominant rhetorical appeal is discernable in most trailers" (42).

The bulk of the book is devoted to an in-depth rhetorical analysis of twenty-seven theatrical movie trailers, nine from each of the three defined historical periods. The examples are just a small sampling of the hundreds of trailers Kernan viewed for the project, a chronological list of which is included in the back of the book. Although the author does not spend much time expounding on the process by which she chose these particular trailers, it is implicit in the text that the examples included fell most closely within the bounds of the three rhetorical appeals. The majority of the trailers viewed, as the author points out, came from the collection of the UCLA Film and Television Archive. Kernan, herself an arts librarian at UCLA, is no stranger to the value of primary research, though she steps out on a limb at several points in her argument against modern historiography's tendency to favor the archival document about the text over the text itself. The author's formalist approach is certainly appropriate in this case, as the persuasive rhetoric that forms the basis of movie advertising exists as an unspoken enthymeme, hidden among the editorial decisions and self-conscious promotion of most movie trailers. At times, however, Kernan's formalist approach threatens to cloud the larger issues of rhetorical persuasion, particularly in regard to the shot-by-shot analyses of trailers from the modern era, where quick edits and visual overload are the order of the day. In these cases, words alone cannot do justice to the editorial rhythms and near subliminal imagery that form such a large part of the visual language of movie trailers. The illustrations, when included, do some work in resolving the disconnect between the text-based description of the trailer and the trailer itself. Perhaps the most successful aspect of this section of the book is the way the author shows how each of the rhetorical appeals evolves over time to correspond to the studios' changing ideas about their imagined "audience."

The three historical eras explored in the book Kernan identifies as the Classical Era, the Transitional Era and the Contemporary Era, and she argues that the three main rhetorical appeals conform to the studios' assumptions about the audience during each era. The Classical Era of movie trailers, which spans the 1930s and 1940s, is characterized in Kernan's investigation by a desire on the part of the studios to appeal to as wide an audience as possible, an extension of the aforementioned vaudeville and circus traditions. The Transitional Era, spanning the 1950s through the early 1970s, witnessed Hollywood's struggle to maintain and, at times, regain an audience that had begun to wane with the emergence of television after World War II. It was a time of experimentation and, as evidenced by the trailers made during this era, studios were unsure of the identity and desires of their potential audience.

Unlike earlier eras, the Contemporary Era finds the role of the movie trailer taking a subordinate position. With the proliferation of film advertising on television, the Internet, and the various home video formats that have come and gone, the theatrical venue has become just another platform through which the studios have been able to advertise their product. Nevertheless, the author shows how the language of promotional rhetoric is alive and well in today's cinematic global economy in the formation of a sense of desire and nostalgia for films yet to be seen by general audiences.

The notion of a trailer's ability to create a feeling of nostalgia for an unseen film raises interesting questions for the moving image archival community. The latest DVD collection to be released by the National Film Preservation Foundation, *More Treasures from American Film Archives,* includes a collection of early trailers for films that are believed to have been lost. Undoubtedly, this is just a small sampling of similar cases that reside in archives throughout the world. Without access to the films they were made to promote, such trailers take on even greater cultural and historical value, providing a glimpse, and thus creating an imaginary construct, of a film that can neither be confirmed nor denied. These trailers that outlive and transcend the films that they advertise confirm Kernan's view that trailers are a unique cinematic form. To view a trailer simply as a paratext of a given film does not allow for a full understanding of what the trailer can tell us about the film through closer textual and rhetorical analysis. Kernan's argument to consider trailers as both para- and metatexts is supported by the concept of the archival trailer as the missing link to lost films. This book may be a key to uncovering information about these films simply by placing emphasis on the ways that they were sold to an audience. If nothing else, the book will increase the historical research value of the countless trailers currently stored in the world's moving image archives.

Movie trailers have worked their way into almost all of the popular forms of moving image media, from television to the Internet and DVD. Kernan, however, is quick to establish her definition of a trailer in the context of the book as "a brief film text that usually displays images from a specific feature film while asserting its excellence, and that is created for the purpose of projecting in theaters to promote a film's theatrical release" (1). Although Kernan leaves the modern modes of film promotion out of her historical analysis (rightfully so, as theatrical trailers provide more than enough fodder for a book-length study), it is hoped that *Coming Attractions* may inspire further examination of the ways film promotion has evolved beyond traditional theatrical exhibition. Trailers on the Internet have become a particularly fascinating subject for study, as many trailers are "premiered" on-line and entire Web-based communities exist to scrutinize trailers on a shot-by-shot level in some effort to decode the mystery of films yet to be released. Although the book does not necessarily suffer from its omission of modern media trailers, it does open several avenues to be explored.

Coming Attractions: Reading American Movie Trailers takes a fresh look at an aspect of moving image visual culture that is almost as old as the cinema itself. Through close textual analysis of a small sampling of movie trailers, Kernan uncovers the ever-evolving ways the studio system uses the form to enhance audience desire for the films themselves, and the ideals represented by the films. The book raises important questions about what trailers can tell us about ourselves as filmgoers and what clues they can provide to fill gaps in film history. With the release of this book, archivists, scholars, and audiences may never again view trailers in quite the same way.

Shepperton Babylon: The Lost Worlds of British Cinema by Matthew Sweet

FABER AND FABER, 2005.

Aubry Anne D'Arminio

In the Q and A available at the Web site for the BBC Four documentary based on *Shepperton Babylon: The Lost Worlds of British Cinema,* Matthew Sweet explains how his idea for the book originated during an interview with the then-eighty-nine-year-old American expatriate Constance Cummings:

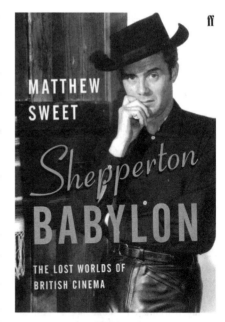

I wondered if there were other veterans who could talk about the experiences they had in the 1930s, perhaps even further back. Many of the silent actors didn't have careers into the sound period, and I wondered if any of them could still be alive. Could they be in a nursing home somewhere, telling a teenage care assistant that they used to be in pictures? Would it be possible to track them down and get them to tell me their stories?

Shepperton Babylon, Sweet affirms in the book's introduction, is the culmination of thousands of such conversations — "an attempt to pursue the story of our native cinema to the limits of living memory" (8). Yet the final product is not the oral history of the UK film industry that Sweet claims. Few of his "witnesses" actually speak for themselves. Their memories (culled from memoirs, biographies, fan magazines, trade papers, and archived collections, as well as Sweet's interviews and personal correspondence) are, for the most part, filtered through Sweet's own agenda and gift for storytelling. He exploits their personalities to create characters, and he recklessly fetishizes their behavior for effect. One can almost hear Sweet rejoice as he finds arthritic Joan Morgan sipping milky tea from a safety cup, jack-of-all-trades Ernest Dudley jogging well into his nineties, or former sex kitten Pamela Green eager to show him the contents of her underwear drawer.

The book's title is an allusion to Kenneth Anger's notorious account of filmland debauchery, *Hollywood Babylon*. But Sweet has loftier aims. He refers throughout to the vulnerability of celluloid and the careless treatment of early negatives in order to draw a correlation between lost films and forgotten movie stars, while emphasizing that the inaccessibility of their work contributed to their cultural abandonment in the first place. According to Sweet, British actors were particularly prone to this fate, for even British film critics and historians dismissed British cinema as being too conservative and boring for serious analysis, let alone preservation. Efforts to halt its destruction or inquire into the lives of its participants were openly discouraged: "Contempt for British cinema," writes Sweet, "was a badge of intellectual seriousness." His project is to overturn this misreading of British cinema by using the interview as a tool to reconstruct the history that lies hidden beneath these layers of myth, bad reputation, and poor archival practices.

Sweet is hardly the first to blaze this path of scholarship. But, whereas other historians of British cinema tend to either focus on industrial aspects, valorize certain auteurs, or engage in canon formation through textual analysis, Sweet calls attention to the role of production personnel who often fall through the cracks of such accounts. In doing so, he paints a picture of scandals and intrigue to offset any notion of the British industry as stodgy and uneventful, recounting enough self-immolations, homosexual love affairs, drug overdoses, and family feuds to make even Kenneth Anger blush. He resurrects dozens of neglected films, if not always successfully examining them himself, then at least enabling that kind of work to be done more extensively in the future. However, while claiming to rescue overlooked subjects and histories, Sweet's book paradoxically attends to some of the most visible and studied subjects in British film (such as Cecil M. Hepworth, Ivor Novello, Basil Dean, Michael Balcon, J. Arthur Rank, and Dirk Bogarde). This occurs partly because Sweet organizes the book around such monumental figures, and partly because his "oral histories" have more to say about those luminaries than their forgotten speakers. In other words, interviewees work less as living evidence than as talking heads in a story that at times narrowly concerns them. They serve as extras when Sweet would like to imagine them as protagonists—even if, on occasion, they add fresh insight to well-trod topics.

Shepperton Babylon consists of ten chapters, bracketed by an introduction and a conclusion, approaching its subject chronologically. Yet the book could just as well be sectioned into three distinct parts. Almost like watching the fashions change in a film that covers three decades, the attitudes of the characters in Sweet's narrative are neatly demarcated by period. Those who lived between the Hepworth Manufacturing Company's early experiments with editing and Basil Dean's resignation from the board of Associated Talking Pictures shortly before World War II were uniformly eccentric and adventurous, hopeful for what the new medium could bring them but ultimately either taken down by their excesses (Sweet repeatedly returns to the image of British cinema's acting pioneers snorting cocaine off a glass dance floor) or riddled with disappointment. Once ATP became Ealing Studios and Michael Balcon joined its board, British film workers were suddenly hardnosed pragmatists: "I was struck by their no-nonsense attitudes," Sweet writes about the actresses in Gainsborough's stock company, "their polite refusal to be intoxicated by the sentimental enthusiasms of others" (192). They also understood their limitations, saw filmmaking as a job like any other, and assumed responsibility for the end of their careers. As actor Richard Todd remarks to Sweet, "I never got terribly celluloid in my attitude about things" (253). When the late fifties signaled the end of the British studio system and the start of the most prolific two decades of British exploitation cinema, the actors, directors, and producers chronicled by Sweet became—according to his descriptions—daring, shrewd, and often very troubled. Well aware that their works were as popular as the Angry Young Man films being canonized at the time, they were desperate to have their contributions on record.

Given that Sweet weaves his tale around a staggering number of figures, at times dwelling on the most minute of details, I will not attempt to give a thorough, chapter-by-chapter summary of *Shepperton Babylon*. It might suffice to say, however, that most stories are in the tragic vein, like that of dancer Nita Foy: after being "picked up" by married actor Donald Calthrop—the blackmailer in Alfred Hitchcock's *Blackmail* (1929)—she accidentally set herself on fire in his dressing room. (It is worth noting that Sweet's brief section on Calthrop is actually one of the book's most compelling. While most film encyclopedias cite Foy's death as the end of his career, the actor made thirty films in the next five years. A member of Hitchcock's repertory company at British International Pictures, Calthrop has many surviving works, and Sweet gives ample evidence as to why they should be reevaluated.) Yet Sweet's chapter on the 1927 Cinematograph Films Act, "A Short Chapter about Quick Films," and his two chapters on British exploitation cinema, "No Future" and "The Oldest Living Sexploitation Star Tells All," are both troubling and insightful in ways that merit individual assessment.

The 1927 Cinematograph Films Act and the pictures made under it until its expiration in 1938 are without question the most maligned subjects in British film history. The Act aimed to promote British production by requiring distributors to obtain and exhibitors to show minimum percentages of British films. A measure to protect British filmmakers from the aggressive and unfair American export strategies that allowed U.S. films to dominate the British box office, the Act encouraged producers to flood the market with hastily made low-budget films that took advantage of the quota (hence their derogatory nickname "quota quickies"). In "A Short Chapter about Quick Films," Sweet nobly sets out to defend these films. However, it does not inspire a general sense of confidence in his argument that the definition he provides for the 1927 Act—that it "obliged [distributors] to fund the production of a rising percentage of British and Commonwealth movies before they would be allowed to continue to handle Holly-

wood films" (103)—is wrong, nor that his first few points draw on newspaper listings, release records, and audience surveys that he declines to footnote. Sweet also relies too heavily on the unsubstantiated claim that the poor quality of the quickies is a myth perpetuated by scholars who haven't bothered to watch them, aiming his attack (rather cowardly through footnoting) at Sarah Street's and Margaret Dickinson's *Cinema and State: The Film Industry and the British Government 1927–1984*. He is somewhat more convincing in his approach to the films themselves, asserting that the quota quickies have a vitality that more expensive prestige pictures lack. His analysis of Tod Slaughter's quickie films, which retained their vigor and popularity well into the 1940s and are currently available on DVD, supports this. He also points out that the quickies served the British industry well by providing a training ground for several British talents, including Robert Morley, Terrence Rattigan, David Lean, and Vivien Leigh (though she denied it to her death). To be sure, Sweet shows that a reassessment of the surviving quota quickies is necessary, but he fails to manage the task satisfactorily.

Sweet's two chapters on exploitation filmmaking are much more effective and offer the most new information to those interested in British cinema. In "No Future," he points to the conditions that led to the rise of British exploitation, namely the introduction of the "X" certificate, the installation of the Eady Levy that gave a percentage of box-office receipts back to producers to make more movies, the downsizing of studio operations in the United Kingdom, and the appointment of a more liberal, film-friendly censor. Sweet notes that there was little separation between the marketing and distribution of art films and exploitation films, and that most exploitation films reflected popular mores and anxieties. Although these observations are hardly groundbreaking, it's illuminating to see them discussed in the British context. Particularly striking is the way Sweet responds to the poor critical reputation of British exploitation filmmakers as compared to their foreign counterparts. After an initial discussion of the "low-brow" works of Richard Attenborough and Christopher Lee, Sweet focuses on interviewees: producer Tony Tenser (*Naked as Nature Intended* [1961], *Repulsion* [1965], *Witchfinder General* [1968]), director Pete Walker (*School for Sex* [1968], *The House of Whipcord* [1974], *Frightmare* [1975]), and their numerous films. Similarly, "The Oldest Living Sexploitation Star Tells All" recounts the careers of the aforementioned Pamela Green (*Peeping Tom* [1960], *Naked—As Nature Intended* [1961]) and producer/director John M. East (*Queen of the Blues* [1979], *Emmanuelle in Soho* [1980]), as well their friends and collaborators. The most notable of these is Mary Millington, whose suicide East turned into the exploitation "documentary" *Mary Millington: True Blue Confessions* in 1980. For Sweet, East brings *Shepperton Babylon* full circle, as he is the grandson of silent actor John Marlborough East, who is briefly mentioned at the book's beginning. The younger East was also a film historian himself, having written a book on his family and conducted several interviews with early filmmakers, many of which he eagerly passed on to Sweet before his death. However, as the self-proclaimed illegitimate son of actor Henry Edwards (who, together with his wife Chrissie White, was Britain's most celebrated acting couple), East also embodies the seedier side of the British film industry that Sweet is all too eager to depict at the expense of its undervalued and unconventional artistry.

Ultimately, what makes *Shepperton Babylon* so disappointing is its failure to make good on Sweet's promise to reverse British cinema's bland image. Rather than emphasizing the unique attributes of his subjects' works, Sweet hammers home the eccentricity of their lifestyles, producing less a work of historical inquiry than one of gossipy journalism. However, if one approaches the book for what it is and not what it professes to be, *Shepperton Babylon* provides not only a titillating read but a checklist of obscure films and filmmakers deserving of critical study.

A Culture of Light: Cinema and Technology in 1920s Germany by Frances Guerin

UNIVERSITY OF MINNESOTA PRESS, 2005

Michele L. Torre

A Culture of Light: Cinema and Technology in 1920s Germany is a compelling first book by Frances Guerin, a lecturer in film studies at Kent University, Canterbury. Guerin's book offers an engaging new analysis of the much-discussed topic of 1920s German cinema. What separates Guerin's book from previous scholarship is that she discusses an aspect of 1920s German cinema that has been for the most part ignored—light and lighting and the connection between technology and film meaning.

Guerin begins her book by stating rather obviously that "cinema is a medium of light" (xiii). Despite the transparency of the statement, that the cinematic image is manipulated in and of light is often ignored or downplayed by critics. As a new and emerging technology, cinema played a role similar to electrical lighting in modern Germany. Guerin sets out to investigate the relationship between 1920s German film and the various contemporaneous uses of light and lighting and their connection to the culture of German technological modernity.

This work by Guerin becomes especially important because, in addition to shedding some new light on old favorites like *Metropolis* (Fritz Lang, 1927) and *Die Straße* [*The Street*] (Karl Grüne, 1923), she also discusses some films that have been left out of existing histories, such as *Algol, Tragödie der Macht* [Algol, Tragedy of Power] (Hans Werkmesiter, 1920), *Der Stahlwerk der Poldihütte während des Weltkrieges* [The Poldihütte Steelworks during the World War] (1917), and *Der Golem: wie er in die Welt kam* [The Golem: How He Came in the World] (Paul Wegener, 1920). Avoiding a politically determinist analysis, Guerin instead places these films within a historical context, examining how various economic, social, and cultural crises are played out through new and innovative uses of film lighting. Rather than burdening the films with the responsibility of representing a national identity, Guerin points to the larger issue of Germany's embrace of technological modernity as being one kind of national cinema.

When discussing light, Guerin refers to the various ways it is manipulated, natural light, light as it interacts with the space and time of the real world, artificial light such as gas, and technologically mass-produced light such as electric light and neon light. The key to Guerin's argument about 1920s German cinema lies in a tripartite role of light and lighting in the films. Although this point is not initially clear in her opening arguments in the introduction, it becomes clear in her actual analysis of the films. The films Guerin has chosen to discuss stand out because (1) light and lighting play a central role in the frame composition, (2) light is a principle narrative structure; it provides the context for representational images and, (3) light is the language through which themes about technological innovation are communicated (79). According to Guerin, analysis of the use of light in these films offers a unique insight into representations of a new industrialized way of life in Germany, as well as providing a context for developing artistic and cultural activities.

Guerin astutely sets the stage for her analysis by accounting for the historical and artistic culture of light at a time when Germany was working hard to create a new, vibrant and strong self-image. She explores the developments in industrially produced light and how they altered all aspects of life, including conceptions of space, temporality, class distinction, the capitalist economy, and the entertainment industry, as well as the other arts within a larger landscape of Germany's progress toward technological modernity (7). In discussing the connection between light and German art forms like architecture, theater, and photography, Guerin also takes the opportunity to position her work within the theoretical arguments surrounding German cinema and modernity. Unlike Siegfried Kracuaer, Walter Benjamin, and Ernst Bloch, she suggests that the problematic portrayals of modernity in the films help them to conceive of a new concept of modernity.

Guerin then examines the use of light and lighting in two films from the teens, Fritz Bernhardt's *Und Das Light Erlosch* [And the Light Went Out] (1914) and *Der Stahlwerk der Poldihütte während des Weltkrieges*. By discussing these two films, Guerin points out that the tripartite uses of light and lighting seen in the 1920s were not isolated events. She even indicates the beginnings of preoccupations with such thematic issues as transformations of time and space and of familial and power relations (the social impact of modernity), and new forms of entertainment that were explored more in depth in the 1920s (xxxii). What separates these films from those made in the twenties, according to Guerin, is that "they did not always play out the possibilities of technical light to their full potential; that is, they did not necessarily use the new technology metonymically in conjunction with the cinema to represent the transformations of technological modernity" (52).

The bulk of the book, of course, is spent discussing eleven films from the 1920s, such as *Schatten* [Warning Shadows] (Arthur Robison, 1923), *Faust* (F. W. Murnau, 1926), *Der Golem: wie er in die Welt, Jenseits der Straße* [Beyond the Streets] (Leo Mittler, 1929), *Am Rande der Welt* [At the Edge of the World] (Karl Grüne, 1927), and *Sylvester* (Lupu Pick, 1923), among others. The films are grouped together and discussed according to their thematic concerns and their tripartite use of light and lighting. In chapter 3, Guerin discusses how light, the technology of the future, is self-consciously used to create a familiar mythical past. According to Guerin, the foregrounding of light and lighting in these films, in conjunction with their mythical themes and narratives, "establish a simultaneous continuity with and break between technological modernity and that which historically precedes it" (80).

In chapter 4, Guerin moves from mythology to magic, where she examines four films that not only rearticulate familiar myths but also use light and lighting in ways unique to cinema to foreground the themes of historicity and magical transformation, and questions of temporality. Guerin states, "the temporal distortions of film as magic lead to the films' discourses on the shape of history in the technologically developed world" (111). Guerin continues to explore the relationship between cinema and the reconfiguration of historical time in chapter 5, extending the exploration to the conjunction between cinema and historical or real space. The three films Guerin discusses in chapter 5 all "use light and lighting fragment, disconnect, and simultaneously extend space in order to represent the spatial and social reorganization of technological modernity" (156).

Again building on the work in previous chapters, Guerin's discussion of two final films in chapter 6 moves from the spectacle of the illuminated city streets to the social impact of the modern entertainment industry. Through a self-conscious use of light and lighting, the films discussed simultaneously contribute to and analyze the modern entertainment industry; they celebrate cinema as entertainment while also focusing on the devastating impact of such entertainment on society (194–96).

Guerin concludes her analysis of 1920s German cinema by briefly addressing the uses of light and film in the 1930s and '40s. Guerin does this to illustrate that the films she discusses in her book are not part of a separate isolated event but rather part of a continuum of themes that troubled and occupied the minds of Germans. Guerin successfully illustrates that "this group of films contributes to a culture of light that, in turn, was instrumental in the cultural definition of interwar Germany" (241) and in doing so has offered a wonderful piece of scholarship to academics and cinephiles alike.

Guerin's innovative analysis has also laid the groundwork for further study into the uses of light and lighting in silent cinema.

Soft Cinema: Navigating the Database by Lev Manovich and Andreas Kratky

MIT PRESS, 2005

Steve Anderson

Much has been written about the transformative impact of digital technology on contemporary cinema. But while digital imaging—from the large-scale visual effects spectacles of the studio blockbuster to low-end vector-based animation—may be comfortably positioned on a continuum with other "revolutionary" imaging technologies of the previous century (Technicolor, 3-D, high-definition video, and so on), the *Soft Cinema* media-processing engine created by media theorist Lev Manovich and designer Andreas Kratky proposes a somewhat more radical intervention into the evolution of cinema as a storytelling apparatus. Indeed, as Manovich notes in his introduction to the recently released DVD *Soft Cinema: Navigating the Database,* conventional cinema is anachronistically rooted in the logic of the industrial revolution and its assembly-line mentality for delivering sequential narratives. By contrast, *Soft Cinema* emerges more or less organically from the logic of the computer database and the revised patterns of production/consumption that characterize the digital age. Where *Soft Cinema* could previously be experienced only as a gallery installation, the DVD presents three short projects created using the *Soft Cinema* engine: two by Manovich *(Mission to Earth* and *Texas)* and one by Kratky *(Absences)*.

Although computational structures in film and video long pre-date the proliferation of digital technology, a computer-driven apparatus such as *Soft Cinema* allows artists and viewers to explore the intersection of database and narrative on a literal—rather than merely metaphorical—level. In his theoretical writings, Manovich has argued persuasively that, in our present historical moment, the logic of the computer has become the logic of culture at large, concluding that the database should be accorded the stature of a symbolic form on the order of cinema or the novel. For Manovich, there is something more at stake than narrative in creating database art. *Soft Cinema* attempts, with varying degrees of success, to question the ways computers and software-based art can be used to represent contemporary "distributed subjectivity," a project that Manovich likens to the literary modernist projects of Marcel Proust and James Joyce. With our "selves" continually scattered across multiple government and corporate databases and surveillance systems, Manovich looks to the networked computer as a more revealing metaphor for understanding contemporary identity than the linear, cinematic narrative.

A parallel effort may be found in the genre of the interactive database narrative, particularly the remarkable body of work created during the past decade by Marsha Kinder's Labyrinth project. Prior to designing and programming *Soft Cinema,* Kratky served as interface designer for two Labyrinth projects: Norman Klein's *Bleeding Through: Layers of Los Angeles 1920–1986* and *Three Winters in the Sun: Einstein in California.* Although Labyrinth has pursued by far the most sustained artistic and critical engagement with questions related to the intersection of cinematic narrative and

digital technology, its method is best understood in terms of the logic of the search engine rather than a pure computational structure. In interactive narratives, a user makes choices or expresses curiosities that result in (sometimes unexpected) variations in narrative combination. In contrast, *Soft Cinema* makes use of a mode of dynamic, real-time image assembly in which viewers offer no input beyond the initial selection of which piece to view. Once a project is launched, the *Soft Cinema* engine executes a series of choices, guided by carefully designed parameters and rules (algorithms), in order to deliver a narrative experience that varies each time it is played. The result is a kind of "ambient narrative" in which narrative meaning and aesthetic coherence must be discerned or constructed by the viewer.

Two particularly interesting effects are at work in *Soft Cinema.* First, the project involves the creation not only of a discrete artwork or series of artworks but a media processing engine that could, in theory, be applied to any existing media database. This merging of databases with interpretive tools for transforming their significance resonates widely across a variety of cultural practices, from Brian Eno's experiments with algorithmic music composition in the mid-1990s to Florian Thalhofer's interactive narrative engine known as the *Korsakow System.* Second, Manovich and Kratky have modeled a compositional mode in which the work of the "artist" is shifted from encoding desired meanings into a montage structure to establishing the rules and metadata by which the *Soft Cinema* engine will create its own combinations of media elements (video, text, sound, composition), the meaning of which will ultimately be produced through reception and interpretation by a viewer.

Experiments with this type of decentered authorship, from Marcel Duchamp's ready-mades to Andy Warhol's factory, have been characteristic of modern art since the early twentieth century. What is unique about the digital platform of *Soft Cinema* is the ability of the creator to invest a degree of agency in the computational power of the computer. However, the desire for an algorithmic structure in cinema pre-dates the digital age. Of particular relevance is the movement known as structural film in the 1960s and '70s that was exemplified by filmmakers such as Hollis Frampton, Michael Snow, and Ernie Gehr. Likewise, the mathematically structured optical printing and animation work by Zbig Rybczynski, Norman MacLaren, and the Whitney brothers suggest the rich history upon which *Soft Cinema* builds. More so than their digital counterparts, these early works fetishize the mathematical precision of cinema and the possibility of exploring questions of space, time, and consciousness through highly prescriptive formal structures. Because digital technology automates—even banalizes—many of the defining features of structural film (looping, temporal manipulation, the multiplication of frames and figures within the frame, and so on), it would seem incumbent upon digital media makers to lead the way in exploring new possibilities for narrative structure.

The original *Soft Cinema* installation debuted in the Future Cinema exhibition at Germany's ZKM in 2002. Although the *Soft Cinema* DVD presents only a simulation of the full dynamic apparatus (which requires a computer and database for playback), it actually improves on the original gallery installation in certain respects. While *Soft Cinema*'s original iteration (represented on the disk by *Texas*) relied on classifying and combining what appear to be home video images captured in cities around the world according to formal properties (such as color, brightness, composition, camera movement) and general content parameters (such as geography or the presence or absence of human figures), the DVD version of *Soft Cinema* introduces two new projects that suggest vibrant possibilities for work that originates with the computational platform in mind.

The first of these projects to be "born computational" is Manovich's *Mission to Earth,* a melancholy third-person account of an alien researcher who is neglected by her home planet during an extended assignment on Earth. In between filing weekly reports on human behavior, she meets a middle-aged artist who has immigrated from the former Soviet Union, and the two form an unlikely bond as outsiders in a conformist and solipsistic society. The strength of the piece lies in Manovich's insight into the predicament of immigrants who are faced with the tensions of assimilation versus alienation, a struggle that is underscored visually by the enigmatic performance of the Latvian artist Ilze Black. It is difficult not to read *Mission to Earth* as a thinly veiled allegory for Manovich's own experience, both as an immigrant and a theorist-practitioner in the rarefied field of new media art. In contrast with *Texas,* which presents a meandering concatenation of seemingly random content, *Mission to Earth* reveals the importance of addressing viewers' desires for conventional cinematic pleasures such as formal interest, character, and narrative evolution. And while resistance to these elements makes a statement about the formulaic nature of commercial cinema, this battle has already been fought and, depending on your perspective, either won or lost numerous times throughout the history of film and video.

The most tightly crafted of the three projects is Andreas Kratky's *Absences,* a subtle narrative about displacement and desire, accompanied by exquisitely processed, semi-abstract black-and-white imagery. In *Absences,* a series of seemingly routine first-person ruminations on the prospect of leaving a place where one was never entirely at home gives way to a story of unfulfilled longing. *Soft Cinema*'s potential for variation works at its best here, inviting viewers to unravel the story, delivered entirely through simple, scrolling texts, in conjunction with images that effectively create an atmosphere of loneliness and desolation. Of crucial importance in all three pieces is the effect of the algorithmic image assembly. Unlike related experiments with stochastic imaging, the sequences in *Soft Cinema* rarely appear entirely random. Some formal element seems always to resonate with another—the diagonal streaks of rain on a backlit window echo the shafts of light piercing a darkened alleyway, for example; or shadowy figures from one frame seem to reappear in the background of another. And while *Absences* could easily have been rendered as a single, linear narrative, the fascination that accrues through multiple viewings suggests the power of discovery that the computational form allows. Tensions between chaos and control play out with each viewing, while prescribed meanings compete with a sense of expansive possibilities.

The development of the original *Soft Cinema* engine emerged from a rare conjunction of interests: Manovich's exhaustive research and theorization of new media for his book *The Language of New Media* and the design possibilities enabled by Kratky's prodigious work as an artist and interface designer. In a field where art theory and practice often maintain strict boundaries, the collaboration of Manovich and Kratky suggests the extraordinary results that

may appear when the two are brought productively together. Although *Soft Cinema* may not exactly represent the future of narrative cinema, it at least offers a creative variant on digitally enabled storytelling and a thoughtful engagement with its most compelling problems and potentials.

Films

Courtesy of Milestone Film and Video

Hindle Wakes (1927), directed by Maurice Elvey

DVD FROM MILESTONE FILM AND VIDEO, 2005

James Kendrick

After an initial period of innovation that ended around World War I, the silent era of British cinema produced only a handful of memorable films and even fewer filmmakers who left a lasting mark on the cinematic landscape. In the teens and 1920s, while Hollywood was refining and perfecting the art of narrative, German filmmakers were forever changing the possibilities of expressive cinematography, and Soviet filmmaker-theorists were wringing new political significance out of editing, little emerged from the British cinema beyond the

early works of Alfred Hitchcock. Part of this was the fault of the British government's quota law of 1927, which required British movie theaters to play a certain number of "British-made films" and which, instead of encouraging quality output, resulted in a glut of "quota quickies" that invariably played as second features behind American films, thus calcifying the notion of English cinema's second-class status in the overwhelming shadow of Hollywood.

Yet, despite its less-then-stellar reputation, the British silent cinema did contribute some gems that are slowly being unearthed and presented on home video, some for the first time. Chief among these is Maurice Elvey's *Hindle Wakes*, recently released on DVD by Milestone Film and Video.

Hindle Wakes, which has been filmed five times from 1918 to 1976, is based on the 1912 four-act play by Stanley Houghton, which caused such a sensation in England that it was banned from being produced at Oxford. The 1927 film tells the story of Fanny Hawthorn (Estelle Brody), a young woman from the small Lancashire town of Hindle Vale, who works, like all the young women in town, in the local cotton mill. Her father (Humberston Wright) is the mill foreman, although at one time he could have been co-owner with his longtime friend Nathaniel Jeffcoat (Norman McKinnel), now the town's richest man, but shied away from the investment opportunity. Because of the missed opportunity, the Hawthorn family is working class, something Fanny's mother (Marie Ault) has never forgotten.

During "Wakes" week, the bank holiday celebrations when all businesses shut down, Fanny and her best friend Mary Hollins (Peggy Carlisle) head off for several days of fun at Blackpool, the English equivalent of Coney Island. There, Fanny meets up with Allan Jeffcoat (John Stuart), the pampered son of the mill owner. They leave Blackpool and spend the remaining days together at Llandudno, another resort in Wales. To cover up this impropriety, Fanny concocts a clever scheme in which she asks Mary to mail a postcard for her several days later, thus making it appear to her parents that she has remained with her friend at Blackpool. In an unfortunate, if somewhat hackneyed, turn of events, Mary accidentally drowns and Fanny's ruse is exposed.

Once it is discovered that Fanny and Allan spent several nights together (the sexual nature of the situation is made abundantly clear through subtext), a scandal threatens to erupt, especially since Allan is already engaged to the daughter of Hindle's mayor. The Hawthorn and Jeffcoat families decide it is best for Allan and Fanny to marry; the social/moral severity of the situation is epitomized by the fact that Mr. Jeffcoat and his son are both willing to sacrifice Allan's engagement and the clear economic and political rewards of uniting the town's most prominent families in order to "do the right thing."

Yet, throughout it all, no one brings Fanny into the discussions, much less asks her what she thinks or wants. She is expected to be a phantom presence in her own life, standing quietly by while others make decisions for her — something she resolutely refuses to do. She directly and unequivocally rejects the decision that has been made for her, thus going against one of the cornerstones of the patriarchal society in which she lives and works. Fanny's practical sensibilities — she doesn't reject marriage to Allan out of derision for the institution of marriage itself but rather because she does not love him and doesn't think that a few days of fun with him should be paid for with the rest of her life — mark her as a rare heroine of the silent era, one who is willing to stand up for herself to the bitter end, never caving in to social conventions or others' desires for her.

Fanny is thus a problematic central character, one whose worldview and moral outlook blurred the previously demarcated lines between masculinity and femininity. Her decision to reject marriage is a bold appropriation of a previously male-only prerogative (i.e., sex for fun), which is precisely what makes her so threatening to those around her. "I'm a woman, and I was your little fancy," she tells Allan. "You're a man and you were my little fancy. Don't you understand?"

Alas, he does not, and neither did many of the viewers who saw *Hindle Wakes* on stage or screen. One U.S. theatergoer in 1913 who saw the play was moved to write to the *Chicago Tribune* about the story's "disgusting and vulgar" theme: the "dangerous argument" for a "common standard of morality for [the] sexes." Thus, it is not so much conventional Edwardian morality that is subverted in *Hindle Wakes* but the socially structured inequality between men and women when it comes to certain forms of casual immorality. As anarchist Emma Goldman argued in a provocative essay reproduced in its entirety on the DVD, "The message of *Hindle Wakes* ... dispels the fog of silly sentimentalism and disgusting bombast that declares woman a thing apart from nature — one who neither does nor must crave the joys of life permissible to man."

Hindle Wakes was hardly the first play-turned-film to feature an unconventional heroine who subverts the convention of marriage. Both the U.S. and British film industry were awash in stories during the silent era about divorce, infidelity, and otherwise unhappily married people. For example, the heroine of *The High Road* (1915), based on a 1912 play by Edward Sheldon, refuses marriage and lives with an artist for three years before organizing a women workers' strike at a shirtwaist factory. *The Point of View* (1920), based on a play by Edith Ellis, is about a woman from a wealthy but endangered East Coast family who "sacrifices" herself by marrying a wealthy Westerner for his money.

However, the difference between these films and *Hindle Wakes* is that these earlier heroines eventually embrace marriage; they stray temporarily but are brought back into the fold. In *Hindle Wakes,* Fanny turns her back and walks out, making a profound statement about individuality and the cost of personal freedom. The story is closest in tone to Henrik Ibsen's frequently filmed play *A Doll's House* (1879), in which the heroine Nora leaves her husband after realizing the low esteem in which he holds her. Yet *Hindle Wakes* is even more socially subversive because, unlike Nora, Fanny walks out the door in advance of being disillusioned; it's a preemptive strike and one that costs her almost everything.

The 1927 film version of *Hindle Wakes* was actually the second time director Maurice Elvey had filmed the play, having made a five-reel version in 1918. Elvey was a prolific silent-era director, churning out numerous one-reelers in the early teens before turning to more ambitious, feature-length fare in the late teens and 1920s. Elvey's critical reputation is mixed, because his genuinely good films often get buried beneath all the forgettable biopics, bloodless literary adaptations, and quota quickies that make up much of his filmography.

Hindle Wakes, however, is a piece of genuine cinematic artistry whose visual merits enhance its social daring. The first half of the film is particularly cinematic in that it visualizes events that are merely referenced but do not appear in Houghton's play. Fanny's return from Blackpool, the point at which the stage play begins, doesn't occur until nearly forty-five minutes into the film. Screenwriter Victor Saville created an entire opening act that includes scenes at the cotton mill, in the streets of Hindle Vale, and, most crucially, at Blackpool, all of which allow Elvey to expand the film's visual scope and save it from the staginess that so often plagued silent-era film play adaptations. (The film's second half suffers somewhat in this respect but not terribly so.)

The opening shots of Hindle Vale's cobblestone streets are effectively expressionistic, and the scenes in the cotton mill have an almost documentary-like realism, which helps establish the story in a recognizable social context. There is a purposeful juxtaposition of the lives of the Hawthorns and the Jeffcoats that offers up both similarities (they go through similar morning rituals before work) and clear differences that stem from their divergent economic situations. Elvey uses frequent insert shots of clocks and whistles to suggest a sense of control in these early scenes; the structured nature of life in Hindle Vale is the dominant theme. He makes some unorthodox framing choices, particularly in the way he fragments the bodies of Hindle Vale's residents by using only their legs to convey the ritualized hustle and bustle of going to work in the morning or, most memorably, the excitement of the end of the day and the beginning of Wakes week as all the female mill works shed their work clogs in favor of more stylish footwear.

The scenes at Blackpool are justifiably cited as some of the film's best. They have an intensely subjective quality, allowing us to see the resort thought the eyes of workers for whom it is a genuine wonderland where they can escape their everyday lives. Elvey allows his camera a freedom that conveys the youthful allure of the fantasy-like amusement park and the Palais Ballroom—so different from the dreary world of cotton mills—without slipping into didactic moralism.

Elvey's camera goes with Fanny, Mary, and Allan onto the Big Dipper roller coaster, giving us exhilarating point-of-view moving shots as the car goes up and down the tracks, the camera lens sometimes thrown upward at the top of a tower so that all we see is an expanse of sky before suddenly descending again. It's an apt visual metaphor for the entire Blackpool experience. Later, at the Palais Ballroom, Elvey's camera takes in the sheer enormity of the dance floor and its dozens of spinning inhabitants, again emphasizing the sense of freedom in which Fanny indulges and which will later be the only thing she takes with her as she walks out on her previous life.

Milestone's DVD presents *Hindle Wakes* in a gorgeous new transfer taken from a print recently restored by the British Film Institute.

The transfer gives a sharp, well-detailed image that shows a surprising lack of damage given the film's age.

For the soundtrack, the viewer can choose between a traditional piano score composed and performed by Philip Carli or a modern electronic score commissioned by the Leeds International Film Festival and the BFI. The modern score was composed and performed by the British duo In the Nursery, whose "Optical Music" series includes recent scores for *The Cabinet of Dr. Caligari* (1919), *Man with a Movie Camera* (1929), and other silent movies. In the

Nursery's mix of subtle electronic beats and traditional arrangements coalesces well with the film's ahead-of-its-time social attitudes without feeling tacked on, as many updated scores do. It also adds understated audio effects, such as the sound of the gears and wheels turning in the roller-coaster sequence.

With either musical accompaniment, *Hindle Wakes* is a film that leaves an impression. This disc is a particularly welcome addition to the library of anyone interested in the socially progressive dimension of the silent era.

And Starring Pancho Villa as Himself, directed by Bruce Beresford

DVD FROM WARNER HOME VIDEO, 2003

Gregorio C. Rocha

Doroteo Arango was born in the state of Durango, Mexico in 1878. His childhood was marked by adversity, as if the world was at war against him. Defending his sister's honor (and his own), he shot a wealthy *hacendado* and ran for his life. In a country where justice was administered according to race and social position, Doroteo had no choice but to become an outlaw. Out of desperation, he declared war against the world and, more specifically, against

the wealthy class. In an intimate ritual, while hidden in the mountains, he changed his name to Pancho Villa, not knowing that the name was to become a legend not only in Mexico but throughout the world.

Why did Pancho Villa become part of American legend in particular? If you enter "Pancho Villa" into any Internet search engine, more than 300,000 entries pop up, most of U.S. origin. From motorcycle clubs to health spas, fan clubs to historical researchers, a wide range of interests maintain the Villa name in American popular culture. What is more fascinating is that during his own lifetime the real Pancho Villa served as raw material assimilated into the American imagination via the entertainment industry.

In 1914, at the peak of his military career, Villa became the protagonist of one of the first American biographical feature films, *The Life* of General Villa, a production as legendary as the subject himself. The movie, now presumed lost (except for some fragments), derived from a contract Villa signed with Mutual Film Corporation. But what we know about this incident has been filtered and tarnished by past film historians. Beginning with Terry Ramsaye and his account "Panchito Villa Sells a War" in the fanciful book A Million and One Nights (1926), almost every historian who has dealt with it has contributed to the confusion surrounding this odd event in motion picture history.[1]

It is possible to understand the misdemeanors of such interpretations, since film history has always been fueled by legend. And Pancho Villa has proven to be a complex and multilayered character, one who deftly evades the historian's microscope.[2] What is not understandable—or forgivable—today is to offer a strongly Eurocentric, pre-World War I perspective on Villa as historical character, as if nothing had changed in the field of historiography in the past ninety years. Yet that is what the latest screen incarnation of Mexico's celebrated revolutionary does.

On September 7, 2003, HBO premiered And Starring Pancho Villa as Himself, the network's most significant feature of the season. In a clumsy and expensive ($30 million) HDTV production, HBO attempted—for at least the fourth time in U.S. media history—to use Pancho Villa as an entertainment icon.[3]

This seemingly innocent TV production actually does little more than revive the negative stereotypes of the "greaser" genre that populated early American cinema, especially in the 1910s. Greaser films dominated early U.S. productions that featured Mexican characters. D. W. Griffith himself was an enthusiastic perpetrator, directing the prototype, Greaser's Gauntlet (1908). In this western subgenre, a Mexican character—a "greaser" or "half-breed"—appears as either the antagonist of or faithful companion to an Anglo protagonist. The contents of these films were so offensive that several Latin American countries raised diplomatic complaints, pressuring the American government to urge producers not to refer to specific countries or ethnicities in their scripts. "In 1922," Chon Noriega points out, "the newly constituted Mexican government instituted a ban on all films by any U.S. studio that re-

leased a derogatory film about Mexicans and Mexican Americans. Rather than reforming the portrayal of Latino characters, the entertainment industry simply stopped including them in films."[4]

Although this HBO production offers a storyline, a cast of characters, and a crew much different from the seminal 1914 Villa film, this new movie changes little of substance about the antiquated greaser formula. Into an otherwise fascinating story, writer Larry Gelbart and director Bruce Beresford insert a grayish gringo protagonist in the persona of Frank N. Thayer (Mutual Film Corporation's real-life executive at the time). Presumably to secure Anglo audiences, the filmmakers relegate the Villa of 2003 to a colorful and clownish secondary role, contrary even to the vision attributed to D. W. Griffith, who we see pitching a broad heroic sketch of Villa as movie hero.

Instead of the machoistic yet sympathetic interpretation of young Raoul Walsh in The Life of General Villa, HBO gives us the pretentious and sometimes pathetic presence of gachupín actor Antonio Banderas, a native of Spain.[5] Since leaving Pedro Almodovar's guidance, Banderas has been unable to differentiate any subtleties in the construction of his characters. In Mexico, critics of his casting saw Banderas as not only too short for the role but even too small for the hat he wears in the film! Replacing William Christy Cabanne, the American director who emanated from Griffith's stable in 1914, HBO hired Australian auteur Bruce Beresford. Despite a reported authorial skirmish with HBO, Beresford kept his name on the credits.

More important than these superficial changes between 1914 and 2003 is the new production's continued use of "filters." Instead of the literal lens filters developed by early cameramen to shoot the Mexican revolution battles (to increase image contrast), And Starring Pancho Villa as Himself applied other sorts of filters. A rosy "political correctness" filter is used to present Pancho Villa as a vaguely populist leader, avoiding the temptation in the American eye of 1914 to portray him as a merciless killer or simply a subject to be scorned. The same filter allowed HBO producers to call several renowned historians "advisors," as if they really cared about their opinions.

Then, to further give *And Starring Pancho Villa* a superficial makeover, they hired many Mexicans to work on the film, but only in secondary roles and as hundreds of extras. The producers hired an army of technicians, a couple of second-level historical advisors, and a few third-level production executives from Mexico, as if this would fill the void generated from a lack of a Mexican perspective on the subject.

A foggy filter called "action" is used to effectively stage several battles, but these hide an erratic script under the veil of fake gun smoke. This same filter was useful to avoid any deep engagement with the innermost motivations of any of the personalities on parade in the film. The "action" filter also serves to leave the audience with an ambiguous sensation about the film's assumed genre: is it a western? a failed comedy? Or, as it is pompously announced in promotional materials, a "docudrama"?

The "docudrama" filter is used with good intentions, I assume, but misleads the audience, presenting the piece as "based on actual events." But *And Starring Pancho Villa* is based more on commonplace film history clichés, which increase the cultural mélange that amuses an Anglo mentality but which fail to shed light on intercultural clashes so common in the Mexico-U.S. relations.

Another filter used is "nostalgia." Through it we see amazing recreations of early motion picture productions, carefully staged period representations, but we never see or hear any critical comment on the role played by the U.S. in the media circus that surrounded Villa. Even historical figures as problematic as Griffith and William Randolph Hearst appear only as mythic titans.

Perhaps the most effective filter used in this production is the one called "entertainment." A long-standing tradition in Hollywood, it has been used to transform most any crude, cruel, odd, exotic, or tragic event into simple spectacle. All of the standard "entertainment" ingredients are in the film: Love (Frank Thayer has a romance with a Mexican woman), violence (Villa shoots a woman in front of Charles Rosher's turning camera), sex (Villa beds dozens of young women), courage (Thayer is able to sign a second contract with Villa).[6] Add to this historicism, Hollywood style (Pancho Villa is compared not only to Napoleon but to George Washington, Robin Hood, and Billy the Kid!).

It seems as if the legendary "vengeance of Pancho Villa" fell hard on this project—not only when the Mexican technicians union went on strike in the middle of the shoot but from its very inception, and then permeating the whole process. Even though the whole 1914 production is lost, fragments survive, which neither Beresford nor the HBO executives cared to revive. Comparing the two, we can easily notice that the greaser-inflected flaws of the 1914 biopic extend to the one produced in 2003. History has taught us that we cannot expect a different outcome when we repeat the same actions.

To end this brief personal account of *And Starring Pancho Villa as Himself,* I humbly suggest a prayer: Dear Lord, let there be Rambos and/or Terminators, but please, never allow any more *gringo* and/or *gachupín* cinematic representations of Mexicans, ever again!

NOTES

1. In Kevin Brownlow's *The Parade's Gone By* (New York: Knopf, 1975), 226, cinematographer Charles Rosher narrated to the author his adventures with Villa. My further research demonstrates that Rosher actually appropriated the testimony of Charles Pryor, an independent cameraman who happened to be with Villa the same time as Rosher. Extant footage of the Battle of Ojinaga, for example, was actually shot by Pryor. In his memoir, *Each Man in His Time* (New York: Farrar, Strauss and Giroux, 1976), 91, Raoul Walsh spread a version of the tale in which Mutual commissioned him to write, direct, and act in a film with Villa.

2. Friedrich Katz, in his 900-page biography, *The Life and Times of Pancho Villa* (Stanford, CA: Stanford University Press, 1998), devotes only one page to Villa's relationship to the film industry. Although a rigorous social historian, Katz does not consider it an important issue—which is ironic, since he is listed as one of HBO's historical advisors.

3. The first American film on Pancho Villa was *The Life of General Villa* (1914), directed by William Christy Cabanne, supervised by D. W. Griffith, produced by Mutual Film Corporation, and played by Raoul Walsh, Teddy Samson, Mae Marsh, and Walter Long.

In 1933, Wallace Beery interpreted the general as a sympathetic drunkard in MGM's *Viva Villa,* based on a screenplay by Ben Hecht, directed by Jack Conway, and produced by David O. Selznick. The film was shot in Hacienda Tetlapayac, shortly after Sergei Eisenstein had used the same location for his aborted production *¡Que Viva México!*

Perhaps the most hilarious example of cultural misunderstanding is *Pancho Villa* (1972, UK/Spain), a "paella" western perpetrated by Spanish director

"Gene Martin" (Eugenio Martín), in which a lascivious, cynical, and cold-blooded Villa is played by Greek-American actor Telly Savalas. Another film on Villa, which may also be considered American, is *La Venganza de Pancho Villa* (ca. 1930), a rare compilation film by Texas-based exhibitors and producers Felix and Edmundo Padilla. See Rocha, "*The Vengeance of Pancho Villa*: A Lost and Found Border Film," *Journal of Film Preservation* 65 (December 2003): 24–31.

In Mexico, Pancho Villa has inspired many productions and a broad range of treatments. The most notable is *¡Vámonos con Pancho Villa!* (1936, C.L.A.S.A.), starring Domingo Soler, part of the famous Mexican revolution trilogy by director Fernando de Fuentes.

4. Chon Noriega, "Latinos in American Cinema: A Historical Essay," in *Missing in Action: Latinos In and Out of Hollywood*, ed. Harry P. Pachon et al. (Los Angeles: Tomás Rivera Policy Institute, 1999), 8.

5. *Gachupín* is a nonderogatory nickname used in Latin America to refer to Spaniards who settled on the continent. It is as friendly as when using *gringo* to refer to white, Anglo-Saxon Americans.

6. The copy of the Pancho Villa–Mutual Film contract, found by Friedrich Katz in Mexico during his research, is not signed. It never mentions battle re-enactments or the $25,000 advance payment. Neither contract suggests any possible influence of the cameramen in Villa's war strategies. The second contract, which supposedly existed but has not been found, is the one that ignited the fantasy of journalists and historians alike.

Los Rollos perdidos de Pancho Villa / The Lost Reels of Pancho Villa, directed by Gregorio Rocha

SubCine (www.subcine.com), 2003

Rita Gonzalez

Gregorio Rocha begins his film *The Lost Reels of Pancho Villa* (2003) by inviting archival materials to an impossible dialogue. To the mute photographic and filmic subjects, he plaintively demands, "Who are you standing there in front of the camera? Who took your picture? Where were you? What was going through your mind?" With this ruminative gesture, Rocha invokes a now well-circulated notion that the historical nuances of the archive are not located in the institutional documents and artifacts but can be glimpsed in the subjugated perspectives of those in the margins and in the backdrop.

The Lost Reels of Pancho Villa is a peripatetic video journey from the perspective of a displaced Mexican national looking for the displaced relics of a Mexican icon. This inventive metadocumentary (or *making of* the making of a documentary) can be read as a primer on what Joel Katz has dubbed *archiveology*. According to Katz, *archiveology* is a "metalevel of investigation [that] attempts to interrogate [the] archive on its many registers as historical record, mnemonic object, and emotive experience, [thus] making the material's historicity a central point of investigation."[1] Whereas experimental purveyors of archiveology (from Craig Baldwin to the duo of Angela Ricci Lucchi and Yervant Gianikian) foreground montage and its collision of historical meanings, Rocha uses *Lost Reels* as a forum to debate the grounds of archiveology.

Rocha departs from the anarchic impulse of Baldwin, Bruce Conner, and found-footage collagists to examine the fragility of the historical record and the interpenetration of the fictional and the actual in early cinema. We follow Rocha, the "amateur" (with a nod to Jan-Christopher Horak, a true "lover" of film) archivist traipsing around the world on planes, trains, and automobiles in search of his cinematic holy grail—the lost reels of a 1914 Mutual film entitled *The Life of General Villa*. The Mexican Revolution was one of the first historical events to be photographed by roving newsreel cinematographers. Cinema historian Aurelio de los Reyes notes that "between 1911 and 1920 over 80 cameramen [worked] either freelance or for various film companies" documenting the Revolution.[2] In 1914, Pancho Villa signed a contract presented to him by Frank Thayer of the Mutual Film Company. In this document, Villa apparently agreed to give Mutual "exclusive rights" to film the battle of Ojinaga in the state of Chihuahua. In return, Mutual would endow Villa with twenty percent of the film's revenue. Besides being an early biopic, *The Life of General Villa* was perhaps the first to feature a cameo by the historical figure whose life it attempted to depict—certainly a foreshadowing of the twentieth century's ensuing fusion of entertainment and actuality.

In an independently forged film career that now spans over two decades, Rocha has been exploring the uneven dynamics of Mexican and United States relations. He is part of a generation of documentary and experimental filmmakers that emerged from the *Centro Universitario de Estudios Cinematográficos* (University Center for Cinematographic Studies), a training ground for Mexican filmmakers that emerged in the early 1960s, largely due to the demands of student film clubs and a creative crisis that was plaguing the state-operated film industry at the time. Unlike others from his generation who have gone on to commercial production, Rocha's independent work (financed by teaching and grants) has evolved from cinema verité to an experimental forging of personal cinema with historical documentary. He has documented punks and street kids in Ciudad Nezahualcoyotl with his former partner Sarah Minter in *Sabado de Mierda* (1985–1987), a colony of North American utopians in northern Mexico in *Railroad to Utopia* (1995), his own journey to distinguish the myths and geopolitical realities of Aztlán in *The Arrow* (1996), and representations of Mexico in North American popular culture in *War and Images* (1996–1999).

The Lost Reels of Pancho Villa documents the pathos and solitude of archival research but also features the filmmaker's lively encounters with colleagues in the field. The highlight is Rocha's London appointment with the engaging and seemingly ageless Kevin Brownlow. Rocha marvels as Brownlow tells anecdotes and pulls treasures out of a musty cigar box given him by Charles Rosher, the pioneering cinematographer who purportedly shot battle sequences of Pancho Villa.

More than a mere case study for film preservationists, *Lost Reels* is a meditation on film's role in the field of history. The search for "lost reels" unsettles so much dust in the archive that other histories come to light. While the object of the hunt is foregrounded for the audience, it is the searcher himself whose peaks and disappointments provide an archival melodrama. Rocha turns the camera on himself to reveal the hours of travel and days spent in archive screening rooms. One critic has labeled Rocha's point of view self-indulgent, but rarely does one get a chance to witness a case study in action—with all the quirks and passions of the archivist dramatically chronicled. Rocha does play with reenactment in one apocryphal scene in which he receives a mysterious call from a nameless source steering him to the University of Texas at El Paso just before he is about to give up on his search for the missing reels.

For Rocha to connect his film to such a loaded genre as melodrama—especially since he comes from a national cinema that has been permeated by melodrama—is perhaps overblown. What he really achieves is akin to the chronicle. Long popular in Mexico, chronicles are fusions of journalism with elliptical, almost fictional flourishes. Rocha's video chronicle centers on the search for a lost cinematic treasure but also takes several thematic forays to consider the post-9/11 climate. We never get the sense of this study being dislocated from Rocha's sociopolitical context. Footage of the 1916 attack on Columbus, New Mexico, that was attributed to Villa's militia doubles in a split-screen with images of the fall of the World Trade Center.

While Rocha keeps us aware of the present tense of his search for the lost film, the inspiration for his journey turns out to be an unfulfilled project of Jay Leyda, who he quotes in the film's narration:

> Many years ago, when I became conscious of the importance to history of the Mexican Revolution, I planned an over-ambitious film to try to reflect its many facets. The center of the film was to be an attempt to bring together the newsreel footage of this world-shaking event, that had been filmed by cameramen sent there from every film-producing country of the world. I even dreamed of a fascinating world tour, digging in London and New York newsreel archives, finding Mexican footage in Copenhagen and Stockholm that had never been seen on the American continents. . . . [The] entire factual heart of the film was to be framed with nonfactual material to show less tangible things, attitudes, prejudices, inspirations.[3]

The visionary Leyda foresaw the archiveological impulse in contemporary experimental and documentary film and video. Rocha follows through on Leyda's "over-ambitious" scheme in a short montage that combines materials he has salvaged from his journey. In this tribute to Leyda's impossible film, prejudices and preoccupations about Mexico are phantasmatically released, rapid-fire. The sequence succinctly illustrates Mexican historian Enrique Florescano's statement that "the revolution is not just the series of historical acts that took place between 1910 and 1917, or between 1910 and 1920, or between 1910 and 1940; it is also the collection of projections, symbols, evocations, images, and myths that its participants, interpreters, and heirs forged and continue to construct around this event."[4]

Rocha sets out to unravel the enigma surrounding the cinematic career of General Villa. Ultimately, he finds the conversation he was looking for, not with the tragic-heroic figure of Villa but with two unknown players in the film histories of the United States and Mexico—Edmundo and Felix Padilla of El Paso, Texas. Although Rocha has set out to find the presumably defunct footage of one of history's most charismatic figures, he ends up discovering a border history so fascinating that it merits its own full-length treatment—a "to be continued" at which Rocha hints during the final words of *Lost Reels*. (In fact, he is now editing a documentary about the Padillas and has written a screenplay for feature version of their life story.)

After the dramatized mystery call, Rocha ends up at the University of Texas at El Paso, where he finds a cache of 35mm nitrate prints.[5] He tracks down some surviving members of the Padilla family. With the assistance of an oral history conducted by Padilla's grandniece, Rocha fills in the gray areas surrounding the mysterious reels labeled *La Venganza de Pancho Villa* (The Vengeance of Pancho Villa). Rocha has stumbled upon the holdings of itinerant movie exhibitors on the U.S./Mexico border and what may be the first U.S./Mexican border film. The father and son duo of Edmundo and Felix traveled throughout El Paso and the northern Mexican state Chihuahua showing *La Venganza*. Rocha unearths detailed editing logs and journals that prove that the Padillas purchased outdated silent prints (including *The Life of General Villa*) and edited together their own revisionist version of Villa's contributions to Mexican history. They often changed the compilation reel, even adding their own reenactment of the 1923 assassination of Villa.

Rocha declares the Padilla concoction an ingenious act of "cultural resistance" that foreshadows the work of future Mexican-American and Chicano films. Similarly, Rocha has taken his cues from Leyda and the Padillas in creating his own "dreamy mixture" of chronicle, compilation film, and diary from the lost and found reels of the archive.

NOTES

1. Joel Katz, "From Archive to Archiveology," *Cinematograph* 4 (1991): 100.

2. Aurelio de los Reyes, "Francisco Villa: The Use and Abuse of Colonialist Cinema," *Journal of Film Preservation* 63 (2001): 36. See also Gregorio C. Rocha, "*The Vengeance of Pancho Villa:* A Lost and Found Border Film," *Journal of Film Preservation* 65 (2002): 24–29. Emily Cohen places Rocha's film within a "growing apocalyptic cultural movement of film preservationists," in "The Orphanista Manifesto: Orphan Films and the Politics of Reproduction," *American Anthropologist* 106, no. 4 (2004): 719–31, which also includes an interview with the filmmaker.

3. Jay Leyda, *Films Beget Films* (London: Allen and Unwin, 1964), 113.

4. Quoted in John Mraz, "How Real is Reel?" in *Framing Latin American Cinema: Contemporary Critical Perspectives,* ed. Anne Marie Stock (Minneapolis: University of Minnesota Press, 1997), 93.

5. Mexican Revolution Photograph Collection, C. L. Sonnichson Special Collections Department, University of Texas at El Paso Library. The library catalog describes the holdings: "[Series VI] includes seven reels (800 ft.) of 35mm nitrate film. The reels were originally housed in a metal container titled 'Edmundo Padilla Collection: La Venganza de Pancho Villa.' The films contain newsreel and motion picture footage.... A few copy prints show movie posters about Pancho

Villa. Titles of these movies include *Pancho Villa, La Venganza del Guerrillero!!, Pancho Villa en Columbus, El Reino del Terror* and *La Venganza de Pancho Villa* starring Doroteo Arango—Pancho Villa himself. In conjunction to the stills, the nitrate films, once restored and copied, will bring to light an important part of the history of the Revolution as seen through cinematography.

"The movie stills, poster copies, and motion picture films were donated by Magdalena Arias and were originally called the Edmundo Padilla Collection. Magdalena Arias is the daughter of Edmundo Padilla who was an El Paso film producer and distributor."

Courtesy of Milestone Film and Video

Mary Pickford Films on DVD

HEART O' THE HILLS (1919), *M'LISS* (1918), *SUDS* (1920), *THROUGH THE BACK DOOR* (1922), AND *CINDERELLA* (1914)

Christel Schmidt

In the early 1990s, it was nearly impossible to view the films of Mary Pickford outside a motion picture archive. Public screenings were rare, and local video stores and libraries rarely stocked the handful of Pickford titles released by Kino, Grapevine, and Blackhawk. Today, much has changed, due to the growing DVD

market, revived public interest, and the efforts of Milestone Film and Video.

In 1999, riding on the success of its theatrical tour of Pickford films, Milestone (in collaboration with the Mary Pickford Institute and Timeline Films) released the first of eleven Pickford DVDs to date. Fifteen features, four shorts, and several clips of actuality footage are now easily accessible. The latest of these include *Heart O' the Hills* (1919), *Suds* (1920), and *Through the Back Door* (1922).

Heart O' the Hills, the best of the three new DVD releases, is perfectly paired with *M'liss* (1918), a bonus feature. In many ways the films overlap: each takes place in a poor rural area, and each involves a murder of a parent, a trial, and mountain justice. Tensions unfold between rich and poor, and between the learned and the untaught. Each features a rough-and-tumble teenage girl who rides horses, knows how to handle weapons, and enjoys terrorizing townsfolk. And though Pickford's two protagonists have little knowledge of proper social behavior, they are morally respectable.

Pickford made her career portraying young women on the verge of adulthood who were often unruly, willful, even violent. This signature had already surfaced in films such as *Tess of the Storm Country* (1914/1922), *Fanchon the Cricket* and *Rags* (both 1915), as well as Biographs such as *Wilful Peggy* (1910) and *Lena and the Geese* (1912). Remarkably, Pickford had even played M'liss before. *The School Teacher and the Waif* (1912), a D. W. Griffith one-reeler, is based, like the 1918 feature, on Bret Harte's 1863 novelette *M'liss*. It's a shame Milestone did not include the one-reeler as an extra on the DVD, as it is not currently available.

In *Heart O' the Hills*, Pickford plays Mavis Hawn, a poor Kentucky mountain girl who lives with her abusive mother in a rundown shack. An unknown assailant has recently murdered her father, and Mavis swears to avenge his death. After a number of scenes highlighting her skill with a rifle, the viewer has no doubt that she is up to the task. In the interim, Mavis has been busy threatening city folks who have come to the mountains with plans to con locals out of their land. Two men from the city, one a southerner the other a northerner, have teamed up with local bad guy, Steve Honeycutt, to inspect the soon-to-be spoils. Mavis verbally confronts the intruders, then uses her gun to let them know they're not welcome. It is remarkable that the five-foot tall Pickford had the ability, with or without a rifle, to appear genuinely intimidating.

The situation reaches a boiling point when Mavis's mother, played by Claire McDowell, marries Steve and lets him sell the family's land. Mavis incites the local men to rise up and scare off the poachers. In one of the most striking scenes in the film, she dons a white sheet and hood and joins a group of nightriders to intimidate the northern city slicker. The man is killed and Mavis is put on trial for his murder, only to be set free due to a lack of evidence. The scene, filmed as a comic moment, seems disturbing today, as jurors, many of whom are Mavis's fellow nightriders, stand up one by one taking credit for the murder. Years later, justice finally prevails when the man who murdered her father is killed. Mavis, now grown up and educated, throws over a wealthy suitor (John Gilbert) for a life in the hills with a childhood beau.

M'liss Smith, the very "limb of satan" we are told, makes Mavis Hawn seem almost tame. She lives in a dilapidated cabin in a California mining town where she takes care of her alcoholic father. While the old man trades chicken eggs for whiskey, his daughter plays at stagecoach robbery. The movie centers on the impish antics of the girl and her growing relationship with the new schoolmaster (Thomas Meighan). Screenwriter Frances Marion fills the screen with hilarious scenes and intertitles. She creates a particularly funny exchange when the schoolmaster tells M'liss she must curb her swearing, which is "worse than [that of her] poor drunken father." M'liss, hands on her hips, responds: "It's a damn lie! I don't swear! An' he ain't a drunkard—he's haunted."

Though *M'liss* is a comedy, there are some dramatic turns. While fighting the town bully, M'liss shatters the head of her porcelain doll. She grieves for the loss of the doll, her last connection with girlhood, holding a funeral and leaving an epitaph: "In this yere grave lies the little gal dreams of Melissa Smith." The dreams of the girl are quickly replaced by those of a woman when M'liss, who previously avoided the schoolhouse, enrolls to be closer to the schoolmaster. I can hardly think of another film that captures the transition from girlhood to womanhood so poignantly. The story takes a melodramatic twist when M'liss's father inherits money from his brother. Rivals for the fortune murder him and the schoolmaster is arrested for the crime. Pickford reacts with an uncanny balance of shock, grief, and pain, providing a rare opportunity to see M'liss's vulnerability. As in *Heart O' the Hills,* there is vigilantism and a trial in which justice is not served, but all ends happily as the young woman gets the money and her man.

Both films are notable for beautiful location shots in the gorgeous San Bernardino Mountains *(Heart O' the Hills)* and in Northern California *(M'liss)*. *Heart O' the Hills* is well served by the exceptional quality of the material used for the DVD, transferred from 35mm material in the Pickford Foundation Collection. I do not believe a better source can be found. Unfortunately, *M'liss* is not of the same quality, with scratches and contrast problems that could have been improved. In a few scenes, facial features are almost completely washed out, and beautiful outdoor shots are blandly grey. On a positive note, Donald Sosin's piano music for *M'liss* complements the film. *Heart O' the Hills* fares less well. Maria Newman's score, though excellent in parts, is ultimately ruined by unnecessary sound effects and an annoying slide whistle.

After the formation of United Artists, Pickford was under pressure to release a film that would guarantee financial success for the new corporation. She reluctantly chose *Pollyanna* (1920), a story and character she despised but one that became a box office smash. With this mission accomplished, Pickford went to work on *Suds,* a funny but dark tale whose main character was very different from the Glad Girl.

Suds was adapted from a one-act play called "'Op o' Me Thumb" (1905) starring Maude Adams, a famous stage actress with whom Pickford had often been compared. Its main character, Amanda Afflick, is a graceless and homely young woman who works in a laundry in the London slums. Her active fantasy life keeps the other laundresses in stitches and helps her survive the harsh realities of daily existence. The tall tales she constructs revolve around Horace Greensmith (Albert Austin), a customer who left a shirt for cleaning. Amanda fantasizes a future of romance and wealth when "'Orace" returns and removes her from the laundry grind. But dreams and reality collide when Horace does return and rejects her. Wretched and alone, Amanda collapses on the laundry steps and weeps.

Screenwriter Waldemar Young brought a much-needed levity to the original story with the addition of slapstick sequences. He also gave Amanda, who is devastatingly alone in the play, friends, including Ben (Harold Goodwin), a kind delivery boy, and Lavender, a scrawny horse the laundress saves from the glue factory. Young also made a slight change to the heartbreaking finale. The film ends as the play does, with Amanda grieving on the laundry steps, but now Ben, who has watched the scene between Horace and Amanda, sadly stands outside the laundry with a romantic bouquet he brought for her. Happiness with Ben may lie in Amanda's future, but at the fade out, Amanda cannot see it or him. This is how *Suds* ended—until after its New York premiere. Then there were second thoughts.

Suds received mixed reviews. Several critics disliked the ambiguous ending and predicted that audiences would too. Pickford must have worried that this would happen, because UA offered exhibitors a final reel with a clearly happy ending almost immediately after the premiere. According to trade journals, a scene was added (after the original fade out) showing Amanda and Ben sharing a playful day in the country with Lavender. This ending appears on the *Suds* bonus feature and on a 16mm print at George Eastman House. But unlike her experience with *Pollyanna,* Pickford was not prepared to totally sacrifice her creative desires. Exhibitors were offered both endings and they decided which version to showcase based on their box office needs. Evidence suggests that both versions received screen time in the United States.

The same was true of the European distribution of *Suds.* When the movie opened a year later in Britain, the *Kinematograph Weekly* review noted a happy ending, the same screened domestically. A Russian release print of the film found in Prague has the original ambiguous ending. It is likely, then, that the overseas market, like in the United States, had access to both resolutions. More research must be done before anyone can say which version of *Suds* played where, but we do know that there is no single definitive version of the film.

The history of *Suds* seems to have been unknown to Milestone or the Pickford Institute, and they have confused matters by releasing a DVD that offers a third ending found on a 16mm print at the Library of Congress (LC). In this version, Amanda has been hired to work in service on a British estate; Horace, who has just rejected Amanda in the previous scene, is a groom who tends to Lavender. The couple flirts as the film fades out. This, the least plausible of the resolutions, feels hasty and tacked on. The ending, found at LC on material in Pickford's personal collection, may simply be an ending she considered using and then rejected before the film premiered. Although the DVD identifies this version as a domestic release, no evidence has been found that this denouement was ever shown anywhere.

This leads me to the major flaw in Milestone's presentation: the selection of questionable material from a substandard source for the main feature. The DVD includes two versions of *Suds,* one identified as the American release (the main feature) and the other (a bonus feature) as foreign. This is pure speculation; there is no definitive evidence as to which version was made for which market. Making this assertion will lead to confusion for historians and archivists who might assume that the statement is authoritative.

This classification of one print as the American version (believed by some to be inherently better) seems to be the decisive factor in the selection of an inferior print, a visually poor 16mm copy from the Library of Congress's Pickford Collection, for the DVD. Its inadequacy is only highlighted when compared against the bonus feature, which comes from a 35mm source. Viewers may ask if the choice adequately serves Mary Pickford, her film, and their own enjoyment. Certainly, no one should accept the statement on the cover box that *Suds* has been "restored by the Mary Pickford Institute and Timeline Films." Neither version of *Suds* on the DVD has been restored, nor have any print of *Suds* anywhere.

Nevertheless, *Suds* is an entertaining film and one of Pickford's better features. And despite the fame of *Stella Maris* (1918), in which she played both a beauty and a drudge, her slavey roles are not well known. Biograph's *An Arcadian Maid* and *Simply Charity* (both 1910), and the feature *Johanna Enlists* (1917) are perfect for watching her evolving work in this mode; their inclusion on the DVD would have been welcome. *Suds* is also unusual for its slapstick. Although humor was es-

sential to her films, Pickford attempted this level of physical comedy only a few times before. She would wait until *Kiki,* eleven years later, to try it again.

The score on the featured version, performed by the Mont Alto Orchestra, doesn't help her. It often overwhelms the comedy sequences, which require a light touch. It is particularly glaring when Amanda spins a tale about being thrown out of her palatial home and separated from Horace by her rich father. The scene, a wonderful spoof of silent costume dramas, is played straight but with intertitles that read with a Cockney accent. The music seems unaware of the parody. The visually superior bonus version fares only marginally better, with a dated score by Gaylord Carter, who, in a sadly kitsch introduction, is also shown taking bows and sitting at the organ.

Through the Back Door (1922), the third of these recent Pickford DVD releases, is the least noteworthy. The ninety-minute production, filmed after she played a dramatic adult role in *The Love Light* (1921), begins with Pickford in her widely known guise as a little girl. Silent cinema audiences were captivated by her skill in recreating childhood on screen. Pickford's small size helped achieve the mannerisms and movement of youth, but it was her acting ability that was essential in capturing a child's inner being.

Pickford's desire to escape these roles is well documented, but as co-owner of United Artists she had financial responsibilities that outweighed her artistic wishes. So in *Through the Back Door* she took the role of Jeanne, a lively ten-year-old whose widowed mother has remarried and abandoned her. The child ends up living on a farm in Belgium with her former nurse, who she calls Mamma Maria. Jeanne engages in the childish antics that many Pickford fans found endearing. She fishes in a deep puddle with a dog twice her size, has a battle of the wills with a donkey, uses a wood chess board to protect her backside from a paddling, and after leaving footprints all over a house floor, cleans up the mess by putting scrub brushes on her feet and skating around the floor. The latter is one of Pickford's most famous comic sequences, but like most of the movie, it goes on too long.

After thirty minutes, Jeanne is shown as a fifteen year old. Unfortunately, the teenager is even less interesting than the girl, and though nearly all of the basic elements of the Pickford feature are present, they never pull together. The film suffers from a predictable storyline, remote characters, and a star who is performing on autopilot.

The strength and weakness of Pickford's films is that they are always character driven. Audiences wanted to see the actress in films that showcased her performance but in roles that they had grown to love. The character of Jeanne lacks both the fire of a Mavis Hawn and the humor and vulnerability of an Amanda Af- flick. These contradictions—sweet but angry, shy but fierce, fragile but self-possessed—are key to the success of every Pickford character. But Jeanne, who is modest, good-natured, and passive, doesn't seem to have engaged Pick- ford's head or her heart.

Still, the actress looks absolutely radiant, and the film has excellent production values. The print used for the DVD is flawed but satis- factory, although it has not been restored. Robert Israel's score is uninspired but ade- quately complements the material.

The bonus title, *Cinderella* (1915), is a lackluster early feature that Pickford made with director James Kirkwood and husband/costar Owen Moore. The film's trick photography and beautiful location shots cannot overcome the slow pace and dull performances. Pickford and Moore's chemistry, so evident in their Biograph and IMP shorts and in the feature *Mistress Nell* (1915), is absent here. The picture may be of interest to those who have a special taste for fairy tales, but viewers will find *Snow White* (1916), found on the *Treasures From American Film Archives* DVD and starring Pickford's on- screen rival Marguerite Clark, a better bet.

The material used for the *Cinderella* DVD is from a restoration completed by the Library of Congress from a tinted nitrate print that Pickford herself had a hand in procuring from a Dutch collector. After erroneously promoting the other DVD features as restored, it is ironic that Milestone fails to mention the Library of Congress's work. In fact, the Library isn't cred- ited anywhere on the packaging. But in the end it may be for the best, as the heavy handed

score, composed and performed by Donald Sosin (with a dreadful song by Joanna Seaton), overwhelms any charm the visuals offer.

Though I applaud Milestone and the Mary Pickford Institute for their efforts to make the films of Mary Pickford available to the public, I cannot overlook the often misleading manner in which it is done. Video and DVD distributors are generally careless about information pro- vided to the consumer on packaging and in promotion materials. Words like "preserva- tion" and "restoration" are used with little concern for their meaning. These terms sug- gest that viewers are buying the best version, and that an archive or a studio has recently completed sophisticated maintenance on the film material.

The word "restoration" can also imply that those involved in producing the DVD are active participants in the effort to save the film. Those who work in the field know that is rarely the case and that the public is not get- ting what is advertised. Associating a DVD with film restoration helps sales, especially with buyers frustrated by the poor quality of most vintage films offered on video.

When the Pickford Institute and Timeline Films claim to have restored *Suds,* they encour- age the perception that they are actively involved in restoring Pickford film material. They are not. They do provide archives and re- searchers with information and material for Pickford projects, and are generous in making her films available. But, though they carry on her name, the Institute and Timeline have no specific mission or mandate to preserve Mary Pickford's films.

In 1990, the Mary Pickford Company, then headed by Matty Kemp, released six Pickford features and four Biograph shorts on laser disc. Nearly a decade later, the Pickford Institute offers the same films and more on DVD and VHS. These materials are valuable access tools, but the longevity of the Pickford films relies on preservation and restoration. Without it, the work of Mary Pickford will not be available for future generations. If you do not believe that, then I have some laser discs I'd like to sell you.

The Blot (1921), directed by Lois Weber; restoration by Photoplay Productions, with a new score by Jim Parker

DVD FROM MILESTONE FILM AND VIDEO, 2004

Drake Stutesman

The Milestone Collection has released, on DVD, Lois Weber's 1921 *The Blot,* with an articulate commentary by Shelly Stamp, creating a welcome opportunity for cinephiles to examine Weber's work. The film is ostensibly about lovers from separate classes and stars a gangly Louis Calhern (still known for his role in John Huston's 1950 *The Asphalt Jungle*) as wealthy college boy Phil West, and a haunted Claire Windsor as poor local librarian Amelia Griggs. Her father is West's professor at the town's university, her mother a middle-class woman exhausted by the poverty in which she and her family must live, and her would-be suitor, the impoverished, artistic young minister, Reverend Gates. However, *The Blot*'s true theme is money. The film explicitly argues the need to pay, and pay well, for education and spiritual guidance. Instead, money serves only commerce and consumption—represented by the Griggs family's neighbors, the well-to-do, uneducated Olsens, immigrants who have flourished through the father's shoemaking skills. Phil West also represents wealth's privilege. If the Olsens love and flaunt what they have, he simply takes his status for granted. The "blot" is society's dishonor in underappreciating teachers and clergy and keeping them poor.

Weber, wanting to raise social consciousness, guarantees that the audience recognizes her theme immediately. The first intertitle states that Griggs makes "less than bare living wage," and another recognizes that the family "lacked even the bare necessities of life." She goes to great lengths in a potentially tired boy-meets-girl story to ensure, both visually and structurally, that the "blot" is not abstracted and makes us see that "money" translates to a better life and that its lack causes humiliation and crime. Weber uses three means to get her points across: the polemic of intertitles, sharp visual details, and an accomplished use of contrasts and framing.

Lois Weber can only be described as a political director. *The Blot* was her most successful film in a long line of social realist dramas. Some of her films were attacked on legal and religious grounds and even closed by police, but these uproars only made Weber more famous. Driven to show how people suffered without social reform, she regarded cinema as a force or, in her words, a "powerful means of putting out a creed,"[1] because she had "faith in the picture which carries with it an idea and affords a basis for the argument of questions concerned with the real life of people who go to see it."[2] While her contemporaries D. W. Griffith and Cecil B. de Mille filmed well-known literary or Biblical texts, Weber wrote her own stories. She dramatized hot subjects untouched or untouchable by most directors: abortion, contraceptive rights, social inequality, spiritual and political corruption, the minimum wage, capital punishment, prostitution, education reform, anti-Semitism, drug addiction, and

poverty. Preceding *The Blot,* her strongest social films were *The Hypocrites* (1915), which, as
Moving Picture World described it, "aimed to
unmask the mean hypocrisies of modern society";[3] *Scandal* (1915), which underscored gos-
sip's destructiveness; *Hop, the Devil's Brew*
(1916), about opium addiction in the middle
class and the U.S. Customs Service; *Where
Are My Children?* (1916), about abortion's
perils; *The Hand That Rocks the Cradle* (1917),
which pressed for contraception's legalization;
and *The People vs. John Doe* (1916), which argued against capital punishment by dramatiz-
ing the real-life case of Charles Stielow, who
had been wrongfully convicted and sentenced
to death.

Her approach to these topics was head
on: she had serious opinions and she stated
them, not only in interviews but in the intertitles of her motion pictures. Despite this courage, Weber's focus has made it difficult, until
recently, to set her comfortably in film history.
Scholarship ignored her groundbreaking work
for decades as just that of a "woman director,"
but when her films began to be screened again
through the women's movement of the 1970s,
her work still wasn't easily appreciated. Although Weber focused on women in her films,
and gave them a sympathetic naturalism, her
attitude, especially on marriage, wasn't necessarily feminist. She believed that a wife should
favor her husband's needs but also felt that
any marriage was profoundly complex. What
seems to modern audiences ambivalence about
women's rights was a reflection of Weber's era
as much as her personal choice. She was anti-
abortion but procontraception, both topics of
raging debate in the teens, as legislation tried
to defame the latter as "pornographic" (i.e., an
unseemly topic) or even unpatriotic (that is,
boys should be born to serve the nation) while
pioneers like Dr. Margaret Sanger fought these
dangerous ideas in the courts. Despite the
emergence of the New Woman suffragette of
the 1900s, it was hard for a working woman,
especially one at Weber's level of creativity
and success, to shed entirely the mores of her
time—a situation that repeats itself even now.

As a teenager, Lois Weber had been a
small-circuit, touring concert pianist but left
that potential career to perform in an evangel-

istic missionary group that particularly helped
prostitutes. To make money after her father
died, she took stage work as a light-comedy
actress, but by 1908 was writing and directing
at Gaumount Talking Pictures in Fort Lee, New
Jersey. She then worked in partnership with
her husband Phillips Smalley at Edwin Porter's
company Rex, which became a Universal subsidiary. (For many decades, Smalley took far
greater credit for their films than he deserved.
His role was primarily advisory, though his
name often appeared in the titles either as
director or, at least, above hers.) After a move
to Bosworth Inc., she returned to Universal in
1915 and rose to be a top director-writer, lauded
by studio head Carl Laemmle as a hard worker
who delivered on time, on budget, and with
substantial profit.

The fervor and social consciousness so
apparent in her teenage years infused her filmmaking. By 1916, her accessible but controver-
sial films had made Weber probably the highest paid director, female or male, in Hollywood.
She earned $5,000 a week at Universal and
was regarded as among the best in the industry, named as such by the press alongside D. W.
Griffith and Thomas Ince.[4] She made 134 films
(not including many shorts) between 1911 and
1934 (though it's possible that she worked on
as many as four hundred), usually as writer, director, actor, editor, producer, and publicist.
These abilities, for historian Anthony Slide,
place her alongside Griffith as American cinema's first auteur and one of its very few
auteurs of any era.[5]

In 1917, she left Universal to form her own
studio in New Jersey, Lois Weber Productions,
where this auteurism flourished. Often using
the same acting troupe, Weber orchestrated all
aspects of production, writing the scenario (typically from her original story), arranging lighting, constructing titles, processing film stock,
and editing. She also handled publicity, marketing, distribution, and financing.

The Blot is considered her masterwork. A
true synthesis of Weber's goal for "the picture," it argues, raises questions, and depicts
real life—all through a visual tale. Her characters, as she thought her audience should do,
come to see the world around them as if for the
first time. Appreciating cinema as a medium

for the populace, Weber builds the film as a parable, never talking down, and grounds her politics in simple everyday details. Weber wants us to *see* what she means, though she also walks the line between polemicist and story-teller, using the intertitles to state facts, for example, that Olsen makes a hundred dollars a week (a shop clerk would make five).

Weber's direction employs three devices to convey the narrative: an early version of deep focus, framing, and contrasts. A typical Weber deep focus shot, where foreground and background action are simultaneously vital, has a bulky shape almost occluding the frame and a tiny but active scene beyond. This is memorably achieved in the episode where the rich girl, Juanita, who loves Phil, watches as he picks up Amelia at work. Juanita's parked car, where she sits, looms in three quarters of the shot's foreground. To the left, far in the distance, we see Phil and Amelia run out of the library in the rain and get into his car. Although Juanita's sadness is apparent as she sits alone in her large, safe automobile, the two lovers are equally important. Although they appear small, running (toward shelter), and unprotected, they are, obviously, with each other. The scene's composition echoes its theme: Phil has entered Amelia's space (exposure to hardship, symbolized by the rain) but they are together moving toward the shelter that money (symbolized by the car) provides. The tables have turned. Juanita's secure car suddenly is only an immobile object and her loss as crushingly static as anything the Griggses have felt. This reversal is typical of *The Blot,* where one character feels or even inhabits another's state. That is the film's message.

Weber often sets one frame within another to heighten a sense of psychic claustrophobia. Enhancing this symbolic framing, the *The Blot* uses numerous visual parallels, between body types (thin versus fat) and car types (Ford versus Packard), between car versus shoe, plush versus bare, light versus dark, interior versus exterior—all to show the divisions between rich and poor. The gaunt, penurious Griggs parents are introduced in dark tones and interior settings. The worn father is seen in the lecture hall and the mother, with a troubled, exhausted face in her first close-up,

appears in a striped dress within a black doorway. By contrast, the wealthy, plump Olsens are introduced outside, the women dressed in white, busily clustered around a car in front of their home. They have plenty, mobility, and space. Unlike the Griggs family, they are not trapped within their circumstances.

Another motif involves Amelia's mother, who is commonly shot within verticals, such as fence slats, doorways, or pinstriped clothes. When her daughter falls ill, she is tempted to steal the Olsens' chicken dinner. Weber renders this painful scene with stark polarities. The Olsen window, where Mrs. Griggs sees the food, is a plain, large, white square flanked by two clean, white, voluptuous curtains tied to form sweeping curves. The window takes up the entire screen. Mrs. Olsen is within, her large body and working hands part of this abundance. The raw chicken, in a light pan, sits centrally on the windowsill. Mrs. Griggs, in her dark striped dress, stands beside the grey slatted fence that separates her world from the Olsens' and looks with crazed envy at this food. In contrast to the wide Olsen window, Amelia's tiny upstairs window frames her as she watches her mother steal the chicken (although she does not see her return it immediately). She then goes to Mrs. Olsen, exhausted and mortified, to try to explain, whereupon Mrs. Olsen finally recognizes Amelia as an anguished person and not a middle-class snob.

Weber weaves the film with these observations and awakenings. *The Blot* opens with Griggs lecturing to a group of bored, rich students, uninterested in what he has to say. The film closes with these same students coming into a new consciousness about what Professor Griggs, and teachers in general, have to offer. They are led by Phil West, who insists that his father, the university's wealthiest trustee, raise teacher salaries. Phil shows him a newspaper editorial that demands the same. (Characteristically, Weber uses an actual newspaper clipping of the time.) West recognizes that the Griggses are living without the "bare necessities of life," and the film follows his growing awareness. When he visits Amelia at her home, he meets her other suitor, Reverend Gates, who is his own age but vibrant, talented, and

conscientious. Phil feels a sense of "inferi-
ority," a sensation he's never felt before.
Through his eyes, we see what "the blot" actually creates. He sees the holes in the Griggs's
carpets and in Amelia's gloves and shoes; he
sees their lack of decent food in contrast to the
indulgent platters of delicacies he eats at his
country club.

Other characters come to consciousness
by noticing what they never saw before.
Mr. Olsen sees that Mrs. Griggs can't afford to
feed her cat and must take food scraps, surrep-
titiously, from the Olsens' garbage; Mrs. Olsen,
who had condemned the Griggs as haughty,
sees that Amelia is just a young woman trying
to do the right thing; Juanita sees that Phil
wants Amelia and not her. The audience sees
through the characters' eyes. It's a conversation of sightlines, each group finally noticing
what the other has or doesn't have. The haves
begin to understand the have-nots and the
have-nots begin to communicate with the
haves.

Weber ends on a note of reconciliation
between child and parent as well as love between the two lovers (although Gates, in the
last scene, is alone on a dark walkway, suggesting that spirituality is its own solitary difficult path). This is followed by an intertitle
editorial on service, honor, and a thriving
livelihood, deftly blending diatribe and life
story, which is *The Blot*'s greatest asset. Weber makes an emotional drama into an enlight-
enment fable that urges communal action, as
Phil's insistence to Amelia underscores when
he tells her that her father's inadequate salary
is not just her family's concern but is "everyone's business."

NOTES
1. *Overland Monthly,* September 1916, quoted in Anthony Slide, *Lois Weber: The Director Who Lost Her
Way in History* (Westport, CT: Greenwood, 1996), 82.
2. *New York Dramatic Mirror,* June 23, 1917, quoted in
Slide, 66.
3. *Motion Picture World,* June 19, 1915, quoted in
Slide, 75.
4. *New York Dramatic Mirror,* July 15, 1916, quoted in
Slide, 101.
5. Slide, 6.

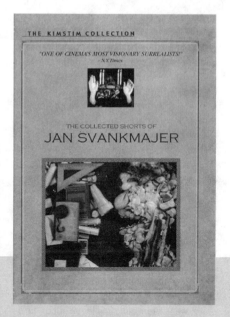

The Collected Shorts of Jan Svankmajer, produced by Kimstim Films

DVD FROM KINO INTERNATIONAL, 2005

Maureen Furniss

Some reviews are harder to write than others.
This is not one of them. Being asked to comment on the collected short films of Czech surrealist Jan Svankmajer is like being asked to
assess the impact of John Ford on the western
or the artistic validity of Federico Fellini. Svankmajer is such a major figure in cinema that it is
difficult to be anything but grateful that his
short works are being offered in a DVD set.
Thankfully, the collection is quite good in that
it not only offers a wide range of films but also
a documentary, images of Svankmajer's work
in various visual art media, examples of his
poetry, and a brief biography.

Actually, this double set is a rerelease of
two earlier DVDs that sold separately. The present set contains fourteen short films made over
the course of three decades: *A Game with
Stones* (1965), *Punch and Judy* (1966), *Et Cetera*
(1966), *Picnic with Weissmann* (1969), *The Flat*
(1969), *A Quiet Week in the House* (1969), *The*

Fall of the House of Usher (1980), *Dimensions of Dialogue* (1982), *Down to the Cellar* (1982), *The Pendulum, the Pit, and Hope* (1983), *Meat Love* (1989), *Flora* (1989), *The Death of Stalinism in Bohemia* (1990), and *Food* (1992). Also included is *The Animator of Prague,* a nearly half-hour BBC documentary directed by James Marsh and released in 1990.

Svankmajer's work is critically acclaimed for several good reasons. He is recognized as a leading figure in avant-garde cinema, producing provocative works reflecting the influence of surrealism and mannerism, and he is somewhat unique in his ability to parlay his success as an experimental filmmaker into several feature-length films. Svankmajer's artistic statements are all the more interesting because he has accomplished his work within the changing political contexts of Czech history during the past four decades. He has been censored heavily (to the point of not being able to make films at all) but has found the means for continuing to speak out; his already multilayered work is made all the more complex when it is considered as a statement of resistance. As if all this were not enough, Svankmajer has yet another accomplishment of note: he bridges the gap between live-action and animation, proving without a doubt that the two practices are not at all separate entities but merely variations within the larger realm of motion picture production.

Several factors have profoundly influenced Svankmajer's art practices. Among them are his early association with puppetry and theater, including his education at the Institute of Applied Arts in the early 1950s and his work at the Theatre of Masks, the Black Theatre, and the Lanterna Magika Puppet Theatre. Aesthetically, Svankmajer's work is generally discussed within the parameters of mannerism and surrealism; he has been a member of the Prague surrealist group since the early 1970s. Then, of course, there are the several political contexts in which he has worked. Peter Hames observes in the introduction to his edited collection *Dark Alchemy: The Films of Jan Svankmajer* (Praeger, 1995) that "Svankmajer was born in 1934, which means he has undergone the unusual experience of six different political regimes and their attendant ideologies" (2).

Svankmajer was banned from cinema production for some years and subject to close scrutiny when he was allowed to work, but during his time out of cinema he channeled his artistic energy into other projects. He explains, "I never made it out to be a tragedy whenever they banned one of my films. I got on with other things. I devoted my time above all to tactile experiments. I made collages, graphics, and various sculptures and objects" (*Dark Alchemy,* 100). Examples of some of these works appear on the DVD. They include ceramics, collages, "image lexicon" drawings, and puppets, as well as his "natural history cabinets," which depict an alternative view of fish, birds, and other entities of the natural world filtered through Svankmajer's eerie lens. Many of these extras are from the early 1970s, at the beginning of the filmmaker's enforced silence, though there are also examples from more recent decades up to the present.

One of Svankmajer's primary concerns is "inner life," which can be discussed in terms of dream states and suppressed impulses related to sexuality, violence, and fear. However, this focus extends beyond human psychology into the world of inanimate objects; in fact, they make up the greater subject of interest. He consistently depicts objects that have come to life, whether they are model figures (that is, puppets) that move about as though they were alive or found objects that tend to be bizarre. He is also known for creating Frankenstein-esque figures out of unrelated objects amassed together. The acknowledged influence of the mannerist artist Giuseppe Archimboldo is apparent in much of Svankmajer's work—perhaps most notably in *Dimensions of Dialogue.* The film is divided into three parts, one of which features Archimboldo-type heads (formed from a wide range of materials) charging together, one of them ultimately eating the other. For Svankmajer, the act of eating can be highly communicative: violent, aggressive, sexual, visceral, and grotesque. His use of raw meat, animal innards, chopped and churned food items, and oozing liquids is a means of connecting with the viewer on sensory levels not usually associated with cinema, evoking a sort of tactile experience and taste along with the more standard use of visual and aural stimuli.

Clearly, Svankmajer is an intriguing, provocative filmmaker, which is part of the reason he has been so widely acclaimed; still, in the big picture of cinema studies, he has not been widely discussed in scholarly writing. It has been ten years since the publication of *Dark Alchemy*, which contains discussion of links between surrealism and mannerism, aesthetic analysis of Svankmajer's work, and an interview with the filmmaker touching on influences and objectives, along with a filmography and bibliography. It is a useful book, but hardly the last word on the subject. Svankmajer gets at least cursory mention in some cinema history books but not the level of attention he deserves. Michael Brooke's well-constructed Web site, "Jan Svankmajer: Alchemist of the Surreal" (http://www.illumin.co.uk/svank) is perhaps the most useful resource available. It lists the small number of videos and DVDs that have made some of his films available for viewing. A look at the mission statement of Kimstim Films, producer of *The Collected Shorts of Jan Svankmajer*, comes to the point: "Founded by Ian Stimler and Mika Kimoto in 1999, Kimstim's mission is to release overlooked, underappreciated master works of world cinema to home video and theaters" (www.kimstim.com). According to Stimler, one of the DVD's producers, the challenge of accessing the work made in various contexts within Czechoslovakia was a major hurdle and contributed to the problems of access to Svankmajer films. Thankfully, Svankmajer's features have been available on DVD for some time: *Alice* (1988), *Faust* (1995), *Conspirators of Pleasure* (1997), and *Little Otik* (2000).

Svankmajer finds himself in a no-man's land of sorts because his subject matter and his actual practice elide borders of live-action and animated cinema, the animate and inanimate, the real and unreal, narrative and non-narrative, Eastern and Western, and past and eternal. His relatively invisible status within critical studies is due in part to the fact that he's not an American filmmaker, not in the commercial mainstream, and not using new technologies; in other words, he is marginal. He's not alone of course. Look at the great experimental animator Norman McLaren, who spent many years at the National Film Board of Canada creating groundbreaking work but has not rated a level of discussion even close to worthy of his accomplishments (although the NFB soon will release a "complete set" of McLaren's work, including supplements). In Svankmajer's case, language barriers and a somewhat reclusive nature also contribute to what one might call the overdetermined nature of his absence from scholarship. This position is ironic, given the many years when Svankmajer was silenced in the Czech film industry by government oppression and censorship of his work; certainly, absence occurs in various contexts.

Stimler and Kimoto were inspired to add Svankmajer to their collection of DVDs after they saw a screening of his work at New York's Film Forum in July 2001. According to Stimler, the collection of prints brought together for the screenings helped with the logistics of creating the Svankmajer DVD. However, there were still some hurdles in gaining permissions for films from four different rights holders. The producers actually had very little interaction with Svankmajer himself, securing the rights to images of his visual art and poetry only through correspondence with the filmmaker. No restoration work was done on the films, but fortunately the quality of the prints is fairly good.

This Kino release combines two DVD compilations previously issued through Image Films in 2002 (*The Collected Shorts of Jan Svankmajer: Volume 1, The Early Years* and *Volume 2, The Later Years*). Stimler says he and Kimoto made the switch because Kino's catalog is more in line with their own interests as producers. He acknowledges that the popular following for Svankmajer's work is small, which is ironic considering that some of the individuals he has greatly influenced—the Brothers Quay, Tim Burton, and Terry Gilliam—are quite popular. Nonetheless, Svankmajer's appeal is broad enough that his work has secured sponsorship with such organizations as the BBC in England and MTV in America.

The range of productions included on Kimstim's collection is good, and the supplements provide the kind of breadth necessary for understanding the range of Svankmajer's practice. It would have been nice to have more contextual information included in the form of a commentary track, but the included documentary helps in that regard. It should be noted that the DVD insert contains some errors related to content: *The Fall of the House of Usher* is left off the film list, *The Coffin House* is given as an alternate title to *Punch and Judy*, and some release dates are incorrect. Also, the navigation between films is somewhat awkward on these disks. Even with these relatively minor problems, the set is noteworthy—and more than welcome. It is highly recommended, and should be considered a vital addition to any cinema library.

Now that this collection is available, perhaps Svankmajer will be more widely discussed within cinema studies. In terms of accessibility, at least viewers now have a convenient means of seeing a range of his short films. Of course, when it comes to viewer comprehension, Svankmajer remains challenging. Exploring the bizarre, fantastic, intangible realms of life is his specialty.

The Olive Thomas Collection: The Flapper (1920), directed by Alan Crosland, and *Olive Thomas: Everybody's Sweetheart* (2004), directed by Andi Hicks

DVD FROM MILESTONE FILM AND VIDEO THROUGH IMAGE ENTERTAINMENT, 2005

Michael Baskett

Over the past two decades there has been a gradual but noticeable shift in the tastes of silent film audiences. Due in part to the rapid growth and high penetration rates of inexpensive home video formats and a growing body of research on early cinema, audiences now have greater exposure and access to films, filmmakers, and national cinemas that had once been excluded from traditional narratives about the development of cinema.[1] This has reinvigorated the study of silent film and led to

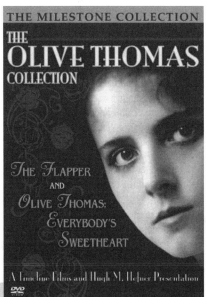

THE MILESTONE COLLECTION

THE OLIVE THOMAS COLLECTION

The Flapper AND *Olive Thomas: Everybody's Sweetheart*

A Timeline Films and Hugh M. Hefner Presentation

a reevaluation of its canons. Recently indications of this shift include the release of DVD box sets of early films by African American, Native American, and Asian American directors, collections of gay-themed silents, early women directors, and avant-garde films, as well as retrospectives of Chinese, Japanese, and Indian silents at festivals from Italy to San Francisco. Clearly mainstream interest in traditionally underrepresented areas has never been higher.[2]

Milestone Film and Video, cofounded in 1990 by Dennis Doros and Amy Heller, has been a key contributor to the popular and academic promotion of silent-era film. As part of its mission to "discover and distribute films of enduring artistry," Milestone has made great efforts to release a variety of mainstream and neglected films that range from the canonical *Phantom of the Opera* (1925) to such legendary "lost" titles as *Beyond the Rocks* (1922). *The Olive Thomas Collection* is the latest in a series of documentaries on silent performers released as part of the Milestone Collection. According to the brief essay on the disk's jacket, Olive Thomas was "one of the first onscreen flappers" and this DVD contains *The Flapper* (1920), one of her last screen appearances before her untimely death. The disk also includes a made-for-television documentary on her life and career entitled *Olive Thomas: Everybody's Sweetheart* (Andi Hicks, 2004), which was produced by Timeline Films. Included as an extra, *The Flapper* is the real centerpiece of the collection and is complemented by the documentary. Taken together the films produce an effect greater than the sum of their parts.

Written by renowned screenwriter Frances Marion (the subject of *Without Lying Down* [2000], another fine documentary distributed by Milestone), *The Flapper* tells the story of sixteen-year-old Genevieve "Ginger" King, a young girl who is sent to live in a New York boarding school by Senator King, her authoritarian father. Ginger wants desperately to be treated as an adult and will do anything in search of experience and adventure. Energetic and impetuous, Ginger is an extension of the cross-dressing, upperclass girl-heroes first popularized in the teens and embodied by the likes of Gloria Swanson in *Danger Girl* (1917) or Pearl White in her serials. In contrast to boy-heroes like Charles Ray or (pre–costume film) Douglas Fairbanks, Ginger does not seek adventure in order to escape from the responsibilities of adult society. Instead, she actively and at times awkwardly seeks out those responsibilities from which she is excluded. Eventually, she finds more adventure than she can handle and winds up assuming a phony identity in order to teach her parents a lesson and "vamp" an older man with whom she is infatuated. She narrowly escapes being framed by jewel thieves before the film winds its way to its inevitable happy ending.

Throughout, Thomas effectively communicates Ginger's sense of adolescent awe for the "dangerous" double lives she is certain all adults lead. There is a relaxed confidence to her performance that resembles that of her real life sister-in-law, Mary Pickford. Like Pickford, Thomas (who was twenty-five at the time) is called upon to play the role of a girl nearly ten years her junior. She ably conveys an almost palpable sense of awkward immaturity, both physical and emotional.

The Flapper was the second of three films in which Thomas was directed by journeyman Alan Crosland, who went on to make *Don Juan* (1926), *The Jazz Singer* (1927), and dozens of other studio features. In *The Flapper,* he clearly focuses the film around his star's unique character. As the disk's supplemental materials suggest, Thomas's appeal was a combination of childlike innocence and tomboyish mischievousness, which makes it difficult for contemporary audiences to associate her with the stereotypical image of the brassy, independent, and sexually liberated flapper.

Pudgy, with long curly hair, Thomas looks more like a baby Gibson girl than a Colleen Moore (usually credited as being the first film flapper). Even when she dresses up as a woman of the world, she lacks the smoldering aura of adult sexuality that was popularized by other vamp icons such as Theda Bara. Of course her character is meant to be an innocent but feisty young girl, but that image itself runs counter to the expectations that the word *flapper* invariably conjures. Granted, these observations are being made in an entirely different context than that within which the film was produced, but it might be that in 1920 flappers had not yet learned how to look and act like flappers. Moreover, given the general absence of the term from the film's narrative and the comparatively frequent use of the term "vamp," the movie's title may have been an afterthought, added to make it more topical. Even contemporary reviewers found nothing new about the plot or its characters. *Variety* called it "the fluffiest sort of fluff."[3] The only hint of any possible social disruption that *The Flapper* might have caused can be found in a single quote by a distributor who warned in 1920 that "the picture contains scenes which, though not offensive to those who go to a theater to be entertained, make it unsuitable for schools."[4] The defiant image of the flapper would would clearly take several more years to fully codify.

Released for the first time on home video, *The Flapper* offers contemporary viewers the chance to see Thomas at the height of her brief four-year career in a beautifully preserved print provided by the George Eastman House. It also gives us a glimpse of one of the few surviving Selznick silents. Print damage is minimal throughout and the intertitles are original (including some very charmingly illustrated scene titles that bear the Selznick Pictures trademark). Unfortunately, the film's original opening titles appear to have been lost, so Milestone has recreated them with unobtrusive period-style fonts. Milestone has also added a new tinting scheme for this DVD release. Robert Israel composed a pleasing original music score for *The Flapper,* which he also accompanies on the piano.

The next film on the disk is *Olive Thomas: Everybody's Sweetheart,* an uneven but at times engaging documentary on the brief and troubled life of Olive Thomas. It was made by part of the same creative team responsible for several important documentaries on women in silent cinema that include ones on Mary Pickford, Clara Bow, and others.[5] Although nowhere near as famous as these other actresses, Thomas's fascinating life does contain all the components of a compelling story: a childhood in a dirt-poor Pennsylvania coalmining town, an early failed marriage, rise to fame as a New York model, Ziegfeld girl, and movie star; marriage to Jack Pickford (brother of Mary); and finally a death shrouded in controversy. Much of the documentary is given over to a discussion of Olive's relationship with Jack and the Pickford family. Olive and Jack are presented as a volatile couple who loved and fought each other with a self-destructive intensity. Their relationship was further complicated, according to the documentary, by the meddling of Mary Pickford and Mary's mother Charlotte, who disapproved of Thomas's growing celebrity and/or her influence over Jack. By focusing on the excesses of Thomas's life—particularly her relationships with abusive men and her decadent lifestyle with Jack—Thomas is established as the spiritual mother of the flapper movement.

The Flapper may be hailed as the first on-screen appearance of a flapper, but we get a somewhat clearer sense of why Thomas's image might have inspired a generation of embryonic flappers from the documentary's discussion of her Triangle pictures. In *Love's Prisoner* (1919), for example, she plays a Robin Hood–like jewel thief, while in *Toton* (1919) she is a cross-dressing, streetwise pickpocket. However, the documentary neglects to mention that during the same period she also played a pampered spendthrift (*Heiress for a Day,* 1918), a gold digger (*Limousine Life,* 1919) and a showgirl (*Follies Girl,* 1919). The film, therefore, can only partly buttress its central claim, that Thomas "may seem tame compared to flappers of the late 1920s," but "she was in fact the anti-Lillian Gish, the anti-Mary Pickford." This is not only an obvious oversimplification of both Pickford and Gish, but it ignores

the unmistakable crossover between Thomas's on-screen persona and Pickford's. Thanks to the inclusion of *The Flapper* on the Milestone disk, it is possible for viewers to judge for themselves.

Everybody's Sweetheart is not without other flaws. While Thomas's life needs no dramatic embellishment, the documentary appears strangely obsessed with enhancing certain elements of her story in a tone that borders on exploitation. The framing of the documentary itself reveals some of these obsessions. For example, the film begins by stating that Thomas's ghost "haunts" the New Amsterdam Theater (home to the Ziegfeld Follies in Olive's day), a claim that the filmmakers appear to take literally. This claim links to the epilogue that rather obviously attempts to influence viewers to read Thomas's death as murder by husband Jack Pickford. The Pickfords in general come in for a rigorous drubbing as a conspiratorial, paranoid, jealous clan who wield almost absolute power over everyone from the Secretary of the Navy to the French police. Claims like these only raise questions about the reliability of some of the documentary's talking heads. Quite a few are distant relatives with no direct memories of Thomas who offer third- or fourth-hand hearsay as fact: "My dad talks about his father discussing with his wife the Pickfords," says cousin Patricia Erhardt. Similarly, the level of their insight is questionable, as when great-niece Nora Erhardt offers: "I'm so lucky that my grandfather remembers [Olive]. I mean he tells me about how he remembers her visiting the house of Mary Pickford 'cause I guess they did eventually become close. And I'm just like, that is just so cool!" That said, when it elaborates on the verifiable details of Thomas's life, *Everybody's Sweetheart* is quite engaging. We learn, for instance, that Norma Shearer not only debuted in *The Flapper* but also met Irving Thalberg at that time. Similarly, it was an impressive piece of research that turned up an original copy of Thomas's death certificate in France seventy years after the fact.

In addition to the two films, the disk includes four bonus features. The first two are reenactments of anecdotes about Thomas from longtime D. W. Griffith cinematographer Billy Bitzer and screenwriter Lenore Coffee. Shot in a mock silent film style and starring Thomas's great-niece, these dramatized sequences are a strange choice for inclusion on the disk. Not crude enough to be charming or clever enough to be homage, the overall effect distances viewers from the material. The next supplement is a dramatization of a 1931 interview with Olive's first husband, Bernard Krug Thomas. Whereas the documentary presents Thomas's divorce as bitter, Bernard describes it in relatively amicable terms. Rounding out the supplements are audio performances of two songs written for Thomas and a gallery of stills from *The Flapper*. (One suggestion I would make for this and other Milestone releases is the inclusion of English captions for the hearing impaired.)

Milestone's decision to release their documentaries with representative feature films is a welcome trend that not only adds value for average consumers but also makes the disks attractive to academics and libraries that need to justify acquisitions of audiovisual materials based on their scholarly relevance.

NOTES

1. See, for example, Jennifer Bean and Diane Negra, eds., *A Feminist Reader in Early Cinema* (Durham, NC: Duke University Press, 2002); Pearl Bowser, Jane Gaines, and Charles Musser, eds., *Oscar Micheaux and His Circle: African-American Filmmaking and Race Cinema of the Silent Era* (Bloomington: Indiana University Press, 2001); Hillel Tryster, *Israel before Israel: Silent Cinema in the Holy Land* (London: BFI, 1996); Suresh Chabria, ed., *Light of Asia: Indian Silent Cinema, 1912–1934* (New Delhi: National Film Archive of India, 1994); Suyuan and Hu Jubin, *Chinese Silent Film History* (Beijing: China Film Press, 1997); and so on.

2. *Treasures from American Film Archives: 50 Preserved Films* (National Film Preservation Foundation; distributed on DVD by Image Entertainment, 2000/ encore edition, 2005); *More Treasures from American Film Archives, 1894–1931* (NFPF/Image, 2004). Kino International's DVD series "Gay-themed Films of the German Silent Era" consists of *Different from the Others/Anders als die Anderen* (Richard Oswald, 1919), *Michael* (Carl Theodor Dreyer, 1924) and *Sex in Chains/ Geschlecht in Fesseln: Die Sexualnot der Gefangenen* (William Dieterle, 1928). On VHS, Kino distributes *First Ladies: Early Women Filmmakers*, which includes *Hypocrites* (Lois Weber, 1915), *Eleanor's Catch* (Cleo Madison, 1916), *Ocean Waif* (Alice Guy-Blaché, 1916), *49–17* (Ruth Ann Baldwin, 1917), and *The Red Kimona* (Dorothy Davenport Reid, 1925). For experimental films on DVD see *Avant-garde: Experimental Cinema of the 1920s and 1930s* (Kino, 2005) and the seven-disk set *Unseen Cinema: Early American Avant-garde Film 1894–1941* (Image Entertainment, 2005).

3. "The Flapper," *Variety*, May 21, 1920.

4. "'The Flapper' with Olive Thomas," *Harrison's Reports*, May 22, 1920, 3.

5. Hugh Munro Neely has directed three documentaries with Hugh Hefner as executive producer: *Mary Pickford: A Life on Film* (1997), written by Rita Mae Brown; *Clara Bow: Discovering the "It" Girl* (1999), produced and written by Elaina Archer, John J. Flynn, and Munro Neely; *Captured on Film: The True Story of Marion Davies* (2001), also produced and written by Elaina Archer, John J. Flynn, and Munro Neely. He also directed the Timeline films *Louise Brooks: Looking for Lulu* (Turner Classic Movies, 1998), *Star Power: The Creation of United Artists* (1996), and *Buddy Rogers: Anytime's the Time to Fall in Love* (1996). Elaina Archer directed *In Mary's Shadow: The Story of Jack Pickford* (2000).

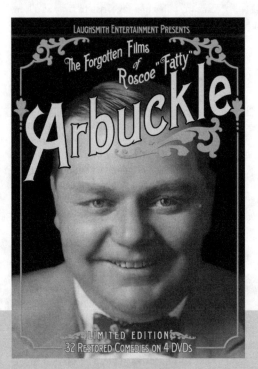

The Forgotten Films of Roscoe "Fatty" Arbuckle

DVD FROM LAUGHSMITH ENTERTAINMENT AND MACKINAC MEDIA, 2005

Richard Ward

This is a golden age for fans of silent film comedy legend Roscoe "Fatty" Arbuckle. Both Kino on Video and Image Entertainment offer DVD collections of Arbuckle's best short comedy work from the late 1910s with Buster Keaton, and a third DVD contribution from Milestone, *The Cook and Other Treasures,* serves up a previously lost Arbuckle-Keaton collaboration, *The Cook* (1918), and the Arbuckle solo effort *A Reckless Romeo* (1917).

Now comes *The Forgotten Films of Roscoe "Fatty" Arbuckle* from Laughsmith Entertainment and Mackinac Media, a breathtaking four-disk set containing thirty-two films that covers Arbuckle's career from the beginning (or as close as possible, given the dismal survival rate of early cinema) to the end (or as close as possible, given the difficulties of negotiating with a media titan for the use of copyrighted material). Wisely, Laughsmith has mostly avoided duplicating films available on the other DVD sets (with the exception of a couple that are mandatory for any Arbuckle set). Hence, this collection beautifully complements, rather than competes against, the earlier Arbuckle collections. The films have been transferred into the digital domain and given new musical scores by people with a real passion for Arbuckle and his work. The love and care put into this volume are evident in the finished product.

Roscoe Arbuckle was born in 1887. An extremely difficult childhood forced him to fend for himself at an early age. A good singing voice and a talent for physical comedy, despite his great heft, led him into vaudeville and then the movies. His earliest film work for Selig Polyscope in 1909 and 1910 is believed lost. After this initial foray into the movies, Arbuckle returned to the stage. He re-entered films in early 1913, working briefly at Selig and Nestor, before landing at Mack Sennett's Keystone studio. Of his 1913 films, only a handful of the Keystones are known to survive. Arbuckle's imposing figure combined with amazing physical grace and agility to make an immediate impression, and he quickly became an audience favorite. By March 1914, Arbuckle was directing his own films, albeit under Sennett's watchful eye.

Disk 1 contains a single Keystone from 1913, *Fatty Joins the Force,* four films from 1914, and four films from 1915. Of the films from 1914, two feature Charlie Chaplin, who arrived at Keystone some nine months after Arbuckle. One of these Arbuckle-Chaplin pairings, *The Rounders,* has been widely available in other collections, most notably Kino's *Slapstick Encyclopedia,* but the remarkable chemistry between the two comics makes its inclusion here mandatory. *The Knockout* is a less well-known Arbuckle film in which Chaplin does an extended supporting bit as the referee of a boxing match.

A far more significant teaming for Arbuckle at Keystone was his partnership with Mabel Normand. In total, this collection presents eight of the Normand-Arbuckle films scattered through disks 1, 2, and 3. Some of these films present them as a courting couple and others have them married to domineering or shiftless spouses and having a relatively innocent fling, but perhaps the most interesting of the group are those dark and cynical efforts in which Fatty and Mabel are married. Perhaps the most striking of these are *That Little Band of Gold* (1915), found on disk 2, and *He Did and He Didn't* (1916) on disk 3. *That Little Band of Gold* begins where many comedies of the period ended: Roscoe proposes to Mabel and she accepts. A marriage ceremony is followed by an iris out and the title card "And now she waits for him." A drunken Roscoe arrives home to a less-than-hospitable reception from Mabel and her mother. The situation deteriorates, and by the end of the film Roscoe and Mabel are in divorce court. An obligatory last-minute happy ending in which the couple is reconciled does little to undermine the film's surprisingly pessimistic view of married life.

More striking is *He Did and He Didn't,* one of Arbuckle's last Keystone films. The bulk of Arbuckle's work for Keystone was at the company's studio in Edendale, California, where he worked under the personal supervision and control of Mack Sennett. Arbuckle's last Keystone comedies were done after the merger into Triangle, and they were produced at Triangle's studio in Fort Lee, New Jersey. It has been argued that, with a continent between Arbuckle and the opinionated Mr. Sennett, Arbuckle enjoyed a degree of creative freedom not possible in Edendale. *He Did and He Didn't* would seem to support this theory, as it demonstrates a level of photographic and directorial sophistication that was rare for comedies of the period. However, one film not included in this set (and, arguably, it should have been) somewhat complicates the tidy formula that Arbuckle minus Sennett equaled better movies. *Fatty and Mabel Adrift* (1916, available in Kino's *Slapstick Encyclopedia*) was the last of Arbuckle's Keystone films made on the West Coast, and it demonstrates many of the technical advances touted in *He Did and He Didn't*. The two films are almost mirror images of the same story, and they could virtually be cut together to form Keystone's version of *Scenes from a Marriage*. In *Fatty and Mabel Adrift*, Arbuckle and Normand are a young couple, courting in the beginning and then newly married. In *He Did and He Didn't*, they are a bickering married couple (although their socioeconomic status has improved considerably, from rural folk to a city doctor and his wife). Mabel's childhood sweetheart arrives, and Arbuckle becomes jealous and rather menacing. The film progresses to homicide, one of the few Keystone films in which the bullets don't bounce off the intended victim. Although the end reveals that the murder was just a nightmare brought on by a heavy dinner, the viewer is left with the distinct impression that the next series entry will be *Fatty and Mabel in Marriage on the Rocks*. Beyond the dark theme, *He Did and He Didn't* is dark visually, a virtual Keystone film noir. Perhaps inspired (as many were) by the photography in Cecil B. DeMille's *The Cheat* from the previous year, Arbuckle and his cinematographer made the most of light and shadow in the film's many interior scenes, and it stands as one of the most visually striking films from any comedian of the period, including Chaplin.

Possibly because the look of *He Did and He Didn't* is so important, it appears on disk 3 in two different versions. One is black and white, except for exterior nighttime shots, which were shot in broad daylight and tinted blue. The other version is largely tinted except for a very few straight black-and-white shots. Much can be said for each version: the light and shadow play of the cinematography is best served by the black-and-white version, but the tinted version is well done and features one scene that is tinted and toned, with the dark areas toned sepia and the light areas, supposedly illuminated by a fireplace, tinted yellow. Still, it seems that the producers of the DVD set should have picked one version.

This isn't the only unexplained quirk in the process of selection and presentation in this set. The very first film, *Fatty Joins the Force*, features two different musical scores, done in much the same style but by different people. The last item on disk 1 is a "slide show" of Arbuckle caricatures done by an ILM animator: cute, but pointless. Seven of the films feature secondary commentary tracks, but there is little clue as to why most of these films, and not others, were selected for this treatment. Six of the commentaries are done by Paul Gierucki (the president of Laughsmith Entertainment and this project's restoration producer and director), Bruce Lawton (the project's producer) and Steve Massa (a research consultant). The trio comes off as mostly engaging but occasionally annoying. At their best they share important insights and little-known facts, at their worst they seem the type of obsessive fans to be avoided at a film screening, especially when they speak aloud what the characters are mouthing onscreen and speculate whether a fight Arbuckle and real-life wife Minta Durfee are having onscreen resembled those they had at home. As with most on-the-fly group commentaries in vogue these days, they occasionally speak on top of one another. A bit of rehearsal and planning might have made the audio track of greater value. The seventh commentary is by Richard Roberts for a curious film entitled *Character Studies*. Roberts outlines the interesting detective work that led him to conclude when and why the film was made.

By far the most inexplicable editorial choice, however, is to be found on disk 2, which consists entirely of Arbuckle's Keystone films from 1915. Between the nine films on this disk, four on disk 1 and one on disk 3, the year 1915 is represented by a grand total of fourteen films, nearly half of the films in this thirty-two-film set. Although this was a productive year for Arbuckle, and the films were enormously popular with audiences of the period, a modern audience is likely to be struck by the mind-numbing sameness of these "primitive" efforts (as the audio commentary for *Leap Year* labels them), many made within weeks of one another. The producers of the set obviously admire Arbuckle and would love to see him assume his "rightful place" in the pantheon of silent film comedians, but this isn't likely to happen on the basis of the 1915 films, which are stuck in the Keystone mode of outrageously broad pantomime with the actors playing excessively to the camera. Even acknowledging the soundness of largely ignoring Arbuckle's 1917–1920 work with Buster Keaton that has been released on DVD by others, more balance and sense of progression would have been achieved by including more of the existing films from 1913 and 1914, and more of Arbuckle's post-1920 work. As it is, the producers give no insight into their process of selecting films for this set.

The collection gets back on track with disk 3 (after one last 1915 film, *Fatty's Tintype Tangle*). The remarkable *He Did and He Didn't* is followed by the slapstick ballet of Arbuckle's Keystone finale, *The Waiter's Ball*. Arbuckle left Keystone to work for Joe Schenck in a series of independently produced shorts, the Comique Comedies, released through Paramount. Most featured Buster Keaton and have already been released on DVD. However, the producers of this set were understandably unable to ignore this pivotal phase of Arbuckle's career, so they included *Coney Island* (1917). The disk concludes with one of the real jewels of the collection, *Love* (1919). Assembled from source material found in Italy and Denmark and released in the United States for the first time in decades, *Love* presents Arbuckle in his prime without Buster Keaton, who was serving in the Army at the time. The film is significant because, as one of the commentary tracks suggests, there has been a tendency to credit Keaton for practically anything innovative or clever in the Comique films. *Love,* however, is as good as any of Arbuckle's collaborations with Keaton and proves Arbuckle entirely capable of producing a beautifully timed and staged comedy with Keaton nowhere in sight.

In 1920, Arbuckle moved from short comedies to feature-length pictures, beating Chaplin into features by more than a year, as the producers of this set like to point out. He completed nine features in less than two years before he had the misfortune of going to San Francisco for a Labor Day weekend party in 1921. He was implicated in the death of a young woman at the party, and, despite his ultimate acquittal on manslaughter charges, the lurid press coverage did irreparable damage to his career. He was effectively banned from appearing on screen for more than a decade, during which time he worked mainly as a short-comedy director using the pseudonym William Goodrich, his abusive father's first and middle names.

Disk 4 opens with *Leap Year* (1921), a film completed before the scandal but because of it never released in the United States (although it and another completed but unreleased Arbuckle feature, *Freight Prepaid,* did make the theatrical rounds in Europe). Like all of Arbuckle's features, *Leap Year* was directed by someone else (James Cruze, in this case), and it presents a more subdued Arbuckle with less heavy slapstick comedy and more attention to character and story. Although not unique at the time, the film engages the audience's understanding of the mechanics of filmmaking from the very beginning with introductory titles, which say, "The opening scene of the trouble is a long shot of Piper Hall, with a doctor approaching the house." After showing this action, the next title reads, "Cutting inside we find the patient. . . ." For the final title card, Arbuckle and his romantic interest agree to "have a fade-out without the usual clinch." And they do, shaking hands instead of embracing.

While a second of Arbuckle's features might have been preferable to the glut of 1915 Keystone shorts (at least two other Arbuckle features are known to survive), *Leap Year* is the only entry in its class. Disk 4 continues with an odd little film called *Character Studies,* in which an actor named Carter DeHaven "impersonates" Buster Keaton, Roscoe Arbuckle, Harold Lloyd, Douglas Fairbanks, Rudolph Valentino, and Jackie Coogan. The joke is that the actors are actually all present, playing themselves, being edited in at a strategic moment when DeHaven ducks behind his makeup kit. Richard Roberts states in his commentary track that this film was produced in 1925 by Douglas Fairbanks and Mary Pickford to be shown at a party they were giving Chaplin to celebrate the release of *The Gold Rush*. The glimpses of all of these actors in a heretofore unknown film are fascinating, particularly the bit with Arbuckle, since this was during his banishment from the screen.

The remainder of disk 4 consists largely of four silent short comedies and a single talkie comedy directed by Arbuckle as William Goodrich. All of these films reinforce the notion that Arbuckle was a first-class comedy director. Three return to Arbuckle's penchant for parodying the movies. The first, perhaps the best, is a 1925 short called *Curses* featuring Arbuckle's nephew (and frequent supporting comic from both the Keystone and Comique films) Al St. John. *Curses* is a surprisingly fresh and vibrant spoof of western serials. *The Movies* (1925) features another forgotten comic from the 1920s, Lloyd Hamilton, in yet another self-referential work. Hamilton plays a country boy who heads to the city and finds work in movies as a double for . . . Lloyd Hamilton! A climactic chase ends when the main character runs into the one place that highly paid movie stars and directors dared not follow, the local IRS office. The remaining Arbuckle-directed films on the disk are *My Stars* (1926) with Johnny Arthur, *Fool's Luck* (1926) with Lupino Lane, and the talkie, *Bridge Wives* (1932) with Al St. John. The disk concludes with a "music video" called *The Arbuckle Shuffle*. This actually serves as a nice introduction to Arbuckle's work, with clips showing some of his best physical bits of business set to a pleasant piano jazz piece.

By 1932, with the scandal more than a decade in the past, Warner Bros.' Vitaphone short subjects unit signed Arbuckle to do a series of two-reel comedies, to be produced at the company's Brooklyn facility. Although pale, low-budget semblances of Arbuckle's work from his glory days, the films were well received, spurring speculation of a comeback. However, on June 28, 1933, Arbuckle finished the final take on the sixth film in the Vitaphone series, returned to his hotel room for the night, and suffered a fatal heart attack. He was forty-six years old. None of Arbuckle's Vitaphone shorts is included in this collection, presumably because the films are still under copyright to Time Warner. Their omission is unfortunate, if understandable.

In addition to its four disks, *The Forgotten Films of Roscoe "Fatty" Arbuckle* comes with a handsome thirty-five-page booklet containing an eclectic collection of essays about Arbuckle's career. Maddening in its absence is a thorough discussion of the source material for this collection. The restoration of *Love* from 35mm European sources is described, as are the difficulties involved in transferring to video severely shrunken 16mm prints (presumably of Kodascope origin) of *The Movies* and *Fool's Luck*. The audio commentaries indicate that *Wished on Mabel* (1915) came from "one of those very nice paper prints," and *Bridge Wives* is from a "battered" 16mm release print. There is no other indication of the origins or format of the source material. The visual quality ranges from stunning (especially for *Love*) to fair, but it is generally the best one will find on this material, especially with regard to the Keystones. One curious quirk on fourteen of the Keystones is that they were transferred with a 1.33:1 matte surrounding the image, and on many (but not all) of the fourteen, the image sharpness on the left side of the screen is a bit soft. As a final note (quite literally), the musical scores are very good and come from several silent film accompanists, including Donald Sosin and Rodney Sauer and the Mont Alto Motion Picture Orchestra.

Taken as a whole, this DVD set is essential for silent film media libraries. Although a more balanced approach to Arbuckle's work was certainly possible, this collection provides a vital first step in the rediscovery of a film artist better known today for controversy than for his work. A second Laughsmith volume would be a welcome sequel.

Filmmuseum Biennale

NEDERLANDS FILMMUSEUM, AMSTERDAM,
APRIL 5–10, 2005

Andreas Busche

It's possible that in the future, the Filmmuseum Biennale, organized by the Nederlands Filmmuseum, will be recognized alongside the Cinema Ritrovata in Bologna and the Le Giornate del Cinema Muto in Pordenone, Italy, as one of the leading archive film festivals in Europe. The second edition took place April 5–10, 2005, and left a great impression on the public, fulfilling the Filmmuseum's ambition to make a case for the preservation of our collective film heritage. Taking place in the mundane Vondelpark Pavillon and in the Filmmuseum's second movie theater "Cinerama," both in the heart of Amsterdam, the festival could not have asked for a more prominent location. The open, relaxed atmosphere, undoubtedly indebted to the smooth, professional production by the engaging and friendly Filmmuseum staff, made the five days in Amsterdam a highly pleasant experience.

For more than twenty years now, the Nederlands Filmmuseum has been one of the most active outposts in the European archival community. A cofounder of the Cinema Ritrovata festival, the Filmmuseum pulled out of that festival a couple of years ago in order to focus more on its own activities. The Biennale, as a complement to the biannual Amsterdam Workshops, was initially launched as a showcase for the Filmmuseum's own restoration work. However, this year's program was as diverse and colorful as one could wish, including two "world premieres" (not necessarily a dubious term for an archive festival), the presentation of several lost-and-found features from France, Denmark, and America, a whole day dedicated to recent restorations of the Danish Film Institute (including a Danish breakfast), and a variety of, as Martin Körber rightly put it in his introduction to the newly scored version of *Menschen am Sonntag* (People on Sunday; Robert Siodmak, 1929), sometimes "bizarre" musical endeavors.

The festival started with a big bang. The opening gala in the historic Pathé Tuschinski movie palace was highlighted by the "second world premiere" of Sam Wood's *Beyond the Rocks* (1922), the only feature starring Rudolph Valentino and Gloria Swanson. Presumed lost forever, a partly deteriorated copy that had miraculously reappeared in a private collection was donated to the Nederlands Filmmuseum a couple of years ago. A virtual guest of the glamorous opening gala (archivists are rarely seen in suits and black ties, which was the dress code for the evening) was Martin Scorsese, who thanked the Filmmuseum for its continuous preservation efforts via a tape-recorded message. Considered one of the most spectacular archival finds in recent years, *Beyond the Rocks* turned out to be disappointingly mediocre, more a case for the history books and die-hard Valentino aficionados. Still, the accompanying restoration panel gave cause for speculation. Even though *Beyond the Rocks* had legally entered into the public domain, why did Paramount let go the DVD rights for the U.S. market? The film has now been released by Milestone. Considering the international buzz over the rediscovery of *Beyond the Rocks,* the film has easily the potential for an "archival blockbuster." Does Paramount believe that it cannot present a DVD in such an allegedly poor condition (with severe deterioration, scratches, missing frames)? Barry Allen, Paramount's head of preservation, who had joined the festival, remained vague during the Q and A.

We might still have a long way to go before the outside world truly recognizes the wealth of our audiovisual heritage and understands that what is left, in whatever condition it might be, is still valuable and should be appreciated for what it is. The digital restoration (2K), conducted by Giovanna Fossati from a tinted 35mm print with Dutch intertitles, is an important statement in that respect. Her scrupulous reconstruction of the image information demonstrates that digital restoration hardly means "anything goes"; there are ethical limits to the practical possibilities. Digital restoration by no means implies that "old films," no matter how historically (or economically) significant they are, have to look "new" again. *Beyond the Rocks* is a great example in that respect.

Announced by the Filmmuseum not as a restoration or reconstruction but as a "2005 production," *Beyond the Rocks* in other respects left many people in a state of sheer confusion. The new soundtrack by Henny Vrienten, who had previously scored the Filmmuseum's restoration of "Zeemansvrouwen" (Henk Kleinmann, 1930), did not add much to the film—apart from an at times painfully cartoonish tone. But, granted, here we are entering the old aesthetical discussion between purists and artistic entrepreneurs.

Presentation (and the aesthetic experience that comes with it) being a pivotal concern of the Filmmuseum's preservation work, it is no surprise that the Biennale is partly seen as a creative outlet for musical experiments. Curator Mark-Paul Meyer's effort to present silent films with modern scores as means of reinterpretation was one of the strong currents in this year's program. The splendid restoration of Germaine Dulac's surrealist masterpiece *La coquille et le clergyman* (The Seashell and the Clergyman, 1928) got an edgy New Music treatment by the Dutch composer Iris ter Schiphorst that would have worked superbly on its own but unfortunately failed to harmonize with Dulac's hauntingly dreamy images.

Julien Duvivier's *Le mystère de la Tour Eiffel* (Mystery of the Eiffel Tower, 1927) was a completely different case, though. Struck from the only surviving film print, this rather neglected early work of the well-known French director is a delightful adventure/mystery serial with a touch of slapstick comedy. The strong Parisian flair corresponds perfectly with the film's absurdist imagery (Ku Klux Klan–style conspirators and a shadow play in which klansmen torture the main character with gigantic pliers). The film's inconsistencies are forgivable: the extensive car chase through the winding roads of the picturesque south of France and the spectacular showdown on the second platform of the Eiffel Tower with a gang of klansmen (I was not the only one who wondered how they brought the cameras up there) are only two examples of Duvivier's excellent direction. Although it is not a lost masterpiece, it certainly is a film that has to be taken into consideration for future assessments of the director's career. Fay Lovsky's new score, performed by a four-piece ensemble, emphasized the Parisian flavor of the film with a pastiche of folkloresque and humorous motifs.

The most admirable aspect of the Filmmuseum's preservation work was hidden in the Friday night slot of the Biennale program. For more than a decade now, the Filmmuseum has been dedicated to preserving fragments from their collection: surviving elements, sometimes no longer than forty or fifty seconds, of no apparent historical value except a certain peculiarity that aroused the curiosity of the Filmmuseum's curatorial staff. The criteria are highly subjective: in one case it might be the content, in another a magnificent stencil coloring. Compiled in fifteen-minute programs called "Bits & Pieces," these fragments are among the most beautiful films I've ever seen; it is a visual pleasure in its own right. Accompanied by a trippy live set by DJ Aardvarck, the "Bits & Pieces" clips were more than just tapestry in the cozily dimmed theater; it was an intriguing rush through some of the most obscure and compelling images from the Filmmuseum collection.

In contrast to the archive festivals in Bologna and Sacile/Pordenone, the Biennale is less structured according to themes, although some loose motifs meandered throughout the program: apart from obvious blocks such as the retrospective of the Dutch experimental filmmaker Henri Plaat, the aforementioned Danish day, and the experiments with musical scores, there was an affinity for silent film divas, most notably Asta Nielsen and Mary Miles Minter. Nielsen's debut *Afgrunden* (The Abyss; Sven Gad, 1910), presented in Amsterdam in a new digital restoration done by the Danish Film Institute, is curious for several reasons. It made her an overnight star, not least thanks to an erotic "mating dance" scene that was surprisingly explicit even by today's standards. The scene was cut by the Danish censors before its initial release in 1910 and reappeared only recently in impeccable condition (in contrast to the rest of the film that had suffered wear and tear). Seeing *Afgrunden* for the first time as it was meant to be seen, with a beautifully scored live soundtrack, was one of the memorable moments of the Biennale. The re-integrated dance scene put Nielsen's character in a new light that foreshadowed her reputation as a femme fatale.

Im Lebenswirbel (In the Storm of Life; Heinz Schall, 1916), made in her German period and one of eight films produced for her own company, Neutral Film, is rather a footnote in Nielsen's career but struck me as a film that revealed the tomboyish nature of her well-known diva image. Nielsen's cheekiness in the first half of the film is almost irresistible, lifting this otherwise generic melodrama to above average. As with *Le mystère de la Tour Eiffel,* this tinted and newly scored version was restored from the only surviving element, held by the Nederland's Filmmuseum.

Innocence of Lizette and *A Dream of Two,* both directed by James Kirkwood in 1916, are two of the eight surviving films from the short career of Mary Miles Minter, which came to an abrupt end in the mid-1920 after a scandal surrounding the murder of producer William Desmond Taylor. The Biennale offered a rare opportunity to rediscover Minter, here at the age of fourteen, as one of the rising stars of her era. Often compared with the young Mary Pickford, *Innocence of Lizette* in particular revealed Minter's fascinating, innocent camera presence that was equaled by few of her contemporaries. It is hard to imagine how she would be perceived by film historians and silent film fans today if she would not have "retired" at the age of 22.

The festival's second world premiere—and another link to the overarching film music theme—was the resynchronized sound version of Joris Ivens's "cinépoème" *Regen* (Rain, 1929) with the original score "Vierzehn Arten den Regen zu beschreiben" (Fourteen Ways to Describe Rain) by Hanns Eisler. The history of *Regen* is nearly as complex as the history of *Metropolis* (Fritz Lang, 1927). Throughout the last seventy years, several attempts had been made to restore the Ivens/Eisler version, but a lack of documentation had resulted in only half-baked results. Therefore, the recent discoveries of two original sets of 78rpm discs of "Vierzehn Arten den Regen zu beschreiben," conducted by Rudolf Kolisch particularly for two *Regen* screenings in America in 1941, and a cropped composite sound print with the original Eisler/Kolisch score were perceived as a small sensation. In Amsterdam, the silent version by Ivens from 1929, the first commissioned sound version from 1929, composed by Lou Lichtveld (1932), and the resynchronized Eisler version, reconstructed by Eisler scholar Johannes Gall and Mark-Paul Meyer, could be seen together for the first time ever. Considering the significance of Ivens's film, this triple screening was a truly historical moment, and many of us had wished that *Regen* would only last longer than its eleven magical minutes.

Those who could find some time between screenings also had the opportunity to attend the "Archives and Education" panel, a showcase for the MA program "Preservation and Presentation" that had been launched only two years ago by the University of Amsterdam in cooperation with the Nederlands Filmmuseum. The four presentations gave an overview of the variety of subjects the Amsterdam program offers to its students. Particularly interesting was the digital restoration of a Baby Pathé 9.5mm educational film and the development of an interactive research CD-ROM on Italian silent film comedians. Unfortunately, almost ten years after the groundbreaking Archimedia project, such close collaborations between archives and universities are still—unlike in the United States—a rarity in Europe.

Five days, with three screening slots per day, turned out to be quite exhausting for a noncompetitive festival attendee. Those who once in a while considered taking advantage of the social gatherings instead of being locked up in a dark theater for nine hours necessarily missed out on some program highlights. I had to pass on the recently restored version of the British music film *The Robber Symphony* (Friedrich Fehèr, 1936), the Dutch expressionistic silent *Evangeliemandens liv* (Holger-Madsen, 1915), the Olive Thomas star vehicle *Out Yonder* (Ralph Ince, 1919), and Billy Wilder's *Sunset Boulevard*. However, I was lucky enough to catch a film that was widely overlooked: the Dutch adventure, *Dakota* (Wim Verstappen, 1974). Shot in Techniscope by Jan de Bont, this film, about a pilot who smuggles goods in his one-engine plane between the Netherlands and the Caribbean, was quite an ambitious production for the small Dutch film industry of the seventies, and a great genre film that did not bother too much about genre conventions. Also, it was nice for a change to hear some human voices pouring out the speakers, even though my Dutch is not exactly great. I have another year to improve on that.

Contributors

Steve Anderson is assistant professor of interactive media at the University of Southern California School of Cinema-Television and associate editor of *Vectors Journal of Culture and Technology in a Dynamic Vernacular*.

Michael Baskett is assistant professor of film studies in the Department of Theatre and Film at the University of Kansas, where he specializes in Japanese and Asian film and early world cinema.

Andreas Busche is a 2005 MA graduate in film archiving from the University of East Anglia. His thesis is on restoration ethics.

Aubry Anne D'Arminio is a master's student in film studies at Emory University and a researcher for Turner Classic Movies. Her thesis focuses on Hugh Grant and the British production company Working Title.

Maree Delofski is a filmmaker and senior lecturer teaching screen production in the department of media at Macquarie University in Sydney. Her award-winning documentaries have screened on television and at local and international festivals. They include *Philippines my Philippines* (1989), *A Calcutta Christmas* (1998), and *The Trouble with Merle* (2002).

Maureen Furniss is the founding editor of *Animation Journal* and member of *The Moving Image* editorial board. She is on the faculty of the California Institute of the Arts and is the author of *Art in Motion: Animation Aesthetics* (1998) and a forth-coming book on experimental animation production, as well as numerous articles on animation.

David Gibson received a master's degree in moving image archive studies from UCLA in 2004. He is currently the Web master for the Dorothy and Lillian Gish Film Theater and Gallery at Bowling Green State University and a volunteer at the Library of Congress's Motion Picture Conservation Center in Dayton, Ohio.

Rita Gonzalez is a videomaker, independent curator, and writer living in Los Angeles. Her co-curated collaboration, Mexperimental Cinema, was the first survey of experimental and avant-garde work from Mexico. She is the coordinator of arts projects for the Chicano Studies Research Center at UCLA and is also working on her doctoral dissertation, "Incidents of Travel: Translocated Identities in Contemporary Mexican and Latino Media."

Judi Hetrick teaches journalism at Miami University in Oxford, Ohio. She earned a PhD in folklore at Indiana University in 1999 and is completing a book manuscript, "Grassroots News, Grassroots Video."

Jan-Christopher Horak is curator of the Hollywood Entertainment Museum, adjunct professor in critical studies at UCLA and founding vice president of AMIA. Horak is author of numerous books and articles, including *Making Images Move: Photographers and Avant-Garde Cinema, Lovers of Cinema: The First American Film Avant-Garde,* and *The Dream Merchants: Making and Selling Films in Hollywood's Golden Age.*

James Kendrick is assistant professor of communication studies at Baylor University. He holds a PhD in communication and culture from Indiana University. His research interests include film history, violence in the media, horror films, and cinema and new technologies. His work has appeared in *The Journal of Popular Film and Television, The Journal of Film and Video,* and *The Velvet Light Trap.* He is also the film and DVD critic for the Web site QNetwork.com.

Andrea Leigh received her MLIS from the department of information studies at UCLA and is a founding member of UCLA's AMIA student chapter. She is metadata librarian at the UCLA Film & Television Archive and is actively involved in the Library of Congress–Association of Moving Image Archivists collaboration Moving Image Collections (MIC).

Gabriel M. Paletz earned the first PhD in critical studies with a minor in film production from the University of Southern California. He has followed a dual path into directing a documentary on the transformation of a small Nevada town and writing a book that offers a new perspective on the career of Orson Welles. He has also published on restorations of the paper print collection as well as on the films of Alfred Hitchcock and Max Ophuls. He is currently on the faculty of the PCFE Film School in Prague.

Gregorio C. Rocha was born in Mexico City in 1957. He attended film school and has developed a career as a documentarist specializing in subjects related to the U.S.-Mexico vicinity. He has been a visiting professor at New York University and Pitzer College. He is currently teaching at Centro de Capacitación Cinematografica in Mexico City and is advising a film restoration project with the American Film Institute.

Christel Schmidt is a public services assistant at the Library of Congress Motion Picture, Broadcasting, and Recorded Sound Division. She is the curator of *Pickford Restored,* a tour of Mary Pickford film restorations currently traveling the United States, Europe, and Canada. The National Endowment for the Humanities awarded her grants in 2000 and 2004 for research into Pickford holdings in FIAF archives in the United States and Europe. Her project findings are on the Web at www.pickfordfilmlegacy.com.

Janice Simpson graduated from the School of Library, Archival, and Information Studies at the University of British Columbia with a Master of Archival Studies (MAS) degree. With more than fifteen years work and volunteer experience in the archival community, she is currently Director of Global Preservation Programs for Ascent Media Group based in Los Angeles and president of AMIA.

Emily Staresina is a graduate of the Moving Image Archive Studies program at UCLA. While penning this article, she worked in Vancouver at the Canadian Broadcasting Corporation as a media archivist and content manager. She now resides in Sydney, Australia.

Drake Stutesman is the editor of *Framework: The Journal of Cinema and Media* and a freelance writer. She is on the selection committee of the Women's Film Preservation Fund, which provided a 2001 grant to the Library of Congress for its own restoration of *The Blot* (separate from the one reviewed here). She is currently writing a biography of milliner-couturier Mr. John.

Michele L. Torre is a doctoral candidate in the critical studies department at the University of Southern California, where she is finishing her dissertation on Pre-Revolutionary Russian Cinema. She has lectured at USC, at The Institute of Modern Russian Culture, and at the University of California–Irvine. She has published in the journal *American Cinematographer,* and her article "Perceptions of Decadent Sexuality in Evgenii Baueris Films" was recently published in *Screen Culture: History and Textuality,* edited by John Fullerton.

Arianna Turci graduated in 2002 the University of Turin's Humanity, Arts, and Philosophy Department with a degree in cinema. In 2003, she attended the University of Paris program "Valorisation des Patrimoines Cinématographiques et Audiovisuels." She has interned at Arte-television. In 2004 she received an MA in Preservation and Presentation of Moving Images from the University of Amsterdam. Her most recent work has been at the Laboratoires Éclair–Paris, where she was involved in digital restoration.

Richard Ward is author of *A History of the Hal Roach Studios.* He is associate professor in the communication department at the University of South Alabama.